Little Green Men

Putin's Wars since 2014
The Inside Story of Russia's New Military Power

By

Tim Ripley

This edition published by Telic-Herrick Publications in 2021

Telic-Herrick Publications, 5 St Andrews Close, Lancaster, LA1 3RL, United Kingdom
www.timripley.co.uk

ISBN978-0-9929458-3-1
Cover Design: Graham Baines, John Freeman, Pete Sandeman

Little Green Men
Putin's Wars Since 2014
The Inside Story of Russia's New Military Power

Russia's operation to seize the Crimea in 2014 caught the world by surprise. Since then Russian troops have fought wars in the Eastern Ukraine and Syria. A new Russia operation is now underway in Libya.
This book looks at how these Russian military operations unfolded, and examines their implications.
Drawing on a wide array of sources - including hundreds of satellite images of Russian bases in Russia, Syria, Ukraine and Libya - Little Green Men gives an unprecedented insight into the most important Russian military campaigns since the Soviet intervention in Afghanistan in the 1980s.

About the Author

Since 2014 Tim Ripley has reported on the Russian interventions in Crimea, Eastern Ukraine and Syria for The Sunday Times, The Scotsman, Jane's Defence Weekly and Jane's Intelligence Review. He has reported extensively on the Russian military for more than 25 years. His book, *Operation Aleppo: Russia's War in Syria*, was published in 2018

Little Green Men

In February and March 2014 Russian troops - with their rank badges and unit insignia removed - began to seize control of Crimea. They blockaded Ukrainian personnel in the peninsula inside their bases. At first, the Kremlin denied its military was involved. When journalists phoned up government spokesmen in Moscow or the Black Sea Fleet headquarters in Sevastopol to ask if the troops were Russian, they were met with point blank denials. "They are more likely to be little green men from outer space than Russian soldiers" was one of more flippant the responses. Few people believed the Kremlin spin but the ironic reference to "little green men" entered media folklore and took on a life of its own. By early March 2014 the phrase was in widespread use in news reports from Crimea and on the internet but I have not been able to identify the first occasion of its use.

The phrase "little green men" became forever linked to the idea that Russia waged a sneaky, devious and underhand campaign to capture Crimea. Subsequently, whenever Russian troops were involved in foreign military operations they were referred to by the world's media as "little green men".

Russian President Vladimir Putin eventually owned up to the fact that his troops had carried out the operation, not local self-defence volunteers as his government had initially claimed. In Russia, the troops and their commanders became heroes for pulling off a daring and successful operation by outwitting their opponents to win a great victory, without firing a shot They were soon dubbed "the polite men" by the Russian media.

Table of Contents

Preface		7
Sources and Methods - Hiding in Plain Sight		9
1	Operation Crimea Spring	13
2	Putin and His Generals	24
3	Hybrid Warfare - Dial Moscow for Subversion	29
4	The Russian Army Rolls	44
5	Frozen War - Battle of Debaltsevo	57
6	War Against Ukraine Assessed	65
7	The Syria Express	67
8	Air War Russian Style	75
9	Finding a Winning Strategy?	89
10	Mediterranean Squadron	99
11	A2AD and Douma Crisis	105
12	America's Great Escape	112
13	Battle of Idlib – Drone Battles with Turkey	119
14	Russia in Libya	133
15	Russia's War in Syria Assessed	138
16	Understanding Putin's Military	140
17	Russia's Warriors	147
18	Russia's Land Power	156
19	Russia's Surface Fleet	166
20	Submarines of the Northern Fleet	180
21	Russia's Air Power	197
22	Russia's Defence Industrial Complex	209
23	Putin's Wonder Weapons	215
Conclusion – What has Putin Got for His Money?		222
Sources and References		226
Bibliography		233
Glossary		235
Index		236

With Thanks

Several individuals have helped in my research during the writing of Little Green Men but any errors and omissions are mine alone.

My colleagues at Jane's Information Group - Peter Felstead, Nick de Larrinaga, Richard Scott, Kate Tringham, Jimmy Nicholls and Rob Monks - have been a great support over the years and have encouraged me to research and write about Russia's military. A big thank you to Jeremy Binnie of Jane's Defence Weekly magazine for assistance in mastering the "black arts" of geo-location and imagery analysis. Jamie Hunter of Combat Aircraft magazine and Thomas Newdick of Air Forces Monthly magazine provided important information about the Russian air force. Johnny Crook provided many insights into modern Russia and its love of the internet. Graham Edmonds was very generous with his advice about all things nautical. A special mention has to go to Bruce Jones for allowing me to access to his encyclopaedic knowledge of the Soviet and Russian military. A final thank you goes to Igor Sutyagin of RUSI for his invaluable advice over the years and for sparking my interest in President Putin's military.

A number of individuals helped with the physical production of this book. Angus Batey did sterling work proof-reading. John Freeman and his colleague Graham Baines, assisted by Pete Sandeman, put together the book jacket.

Language and Names

Russia has a diverse and ancient cultural, ethnic and linguistic history. This has created a great deal of confusion over the names of cities, towns, rivers and regions of the country. Specific locations often have different Russian, Ukrainian, Arabic, Turkish and other names through history. These in turn are often translated into English, Russian, Ukrainian and other languages, adding layers of confusion.

As in many wars, language has become central to the Syrian and Ukrainian conflicts and many sides weaponise how they assign names to locations.

For the purposes of this book, I have deferred to using the most widespread English version of names. This is solely for ease of understanding, rather than signifying any political judgement on the status of the location.

Photographs

The author has attempted to trace and credit all the photographs used in this book to their originators. If any updates or corrections to these credits are needed they will be incorporated in future editions.

Preface

One March morning in 2014 I was approached by senior executive at a major British newspaper. Only days before Russian troops had blockaded scores of Ukrainian military bases across the Crimea peninsula and fears were swirling that Russian President Vladimir Putin might launch other foreign adventures.

The executive said his paper wanted to run a double-page spread on the Russian threat to the Baltic States – Estonia, Latvia and Lithuania - and how Putin's troops could roll through their defences in a matter of hours. He wanted a rundown on Russian bases close to the Baltic states, the data on Russian troop numbers along their borders and an assessment of NATO's weaknesses. They wanted to run a large graphic showing how Putin's troops would invade the Baltic States, complete with pictures of Russian tanks and fighter jets. This was the full tabloid treatment.

That all seemed like it would be very straightforward. I fired up my laptop, opened up my Russia folder and within a few hours had emailed off several megabites of information to the paper, complete with maps and graphs. Everyone on the paper's news desk seemed happy with my maps of troop deployments, listings of weapons and assessment of likely Russian invasion routes. The newspaper's art department did a nice job on the graphic and the news desk team soon reported "job done".

With a few hours to go before deadline, I received a panicked phone call from the executive. It seems the paper's editor was not happy. The top man had looked over the graphic and was surprised that it showed NATO actually had more troops, tanks, ships and planes in Eastern Europe than the Russian military. This was not what he wanted. How could the Russians pose a threat if they were outnumbered by NATO? The Soviet military had massive supremacy over NATO during the Cold War so how come the things were now so different? A major re-shuffle was needed. Just in time for the print deadline the graphic was re-jigged to narrow the map of troop deployment to a small section of Estonia's eastern border where Russian troops did have a tactical advantage over the Baltic state's small and poorly equipped army.

It is never pleasant for journalists to be on the receiving end of an editor's concern about the veracity of their copy but the incident highlighted many aspects of how the British media covered the Crimea crisis and the subsequent escalating confrontation with Putin's Russia. It was clear that many of the current generation of British newspaper editors and journalists have little understanding of events in Eastern Europe in the 21st Century, the state of the Russian military or even the geography of Europe to the east of Berlin. It was so much easier to revert to Cold War stereotypes.

In Britain and other Western countries, the ignorance and prejudices of newspapers are often reflected across the political sphere, with government ministers and many other politicians often making up policy on the fly or opting to go along with conventional wisdom.

This book aims to address some of those misperceptions and look at the real state of Russia's armed forces in the 21st Century. How did they actually capture Crimea and achieve successes in the Donbass region and Syria? What kind of threat do Putin's armed forces really pose to the West today and in the future? The story of Russia's military adventures over the past seven years is remarkable one - even without the spin and hype that normally surround modern military campaigns. I hope this book helps readers gain a deeper understanding of the modern Russian armed forces so they appreciate the world as it is, not how some people wish it to be.

Tim Ripley
November 2021

Sources and Methods - Hiding in Plain Sight?

Like good spymasters, good journalists don't normally reveal their top secret sources. They all want to protect them from discovery and retribution. Just as importantly, they want to keep precious information flowing.

Journalism and espionage share many attributes - they are both aimed at revealing information that others might not want to be made public.

When I first started investigating Russia's armed forces in the wake of the Crimea crisis in 2014 and Moscow's intervention in Syria the following year, the size of the task seemed monumental. Although Russia's armed forces were a shadow of the Soviet war machine that cast during the Cold War, they were still numerically the world's fifth largest military, coming behind China, India, North Korea and the USA in terms of personnel in uniform and most types of equipment holdings.

Much of Russia's military hardware has its origins in Soviet times and when I first started making internet searches for information about current Russian tanks, ships and planes, some intriguing declassified US Central Intelligence Agency (CIA) documents appeared. The famous US spy agency has a historical project to declassify many of its Cold War-era documents.

One of these is a study of the efforts to track down and identify the Alfa class nuclear attack submarine. (1) It tells the story of how two generations of Soviet analysts at the CIA tried to confirm if the world's first titanium-hulled submarine really existed. Using a combination of first-generation satellite imagery, underwater surveillance reports from allied submarines patrolling the Barents Sea, and old-fashioned human spies, the CIA team eventually refuted claims by some of America's most prestigious scientists and the cream of country's metallurgists that it was impossible to build a submarine's hull from titanium. This read like the plot of a Tom Clancy novel.

Fast forward to December 2017 and I was trying to find out some information about the Russian Navy's newest attack submarine, the Kazan. The top search result on Google was a YouTube clip posted by the Russian Ministry of Defence's Zvezda television network showing the submarine's launch at the Sevmash yard in the northern city of Severodvinsk. I immediately dug out the CIA report into the Alfa submarine project and it was clear this was the same yard that had built one of the first titanium submarines. If any of the long-retired CIA analysts had been able to view the 38-minute-long YouTube clip they would have been able to find the answers to many of their questions about the mysterious Sevmash yard. It is now Russia's only nuclear submarine building yard. Throughout the Cold War it was one of US intelligence's top targets but now the inside of its submarine assembly halls were on full view on the internet. If the YouTube exposé was not enough, a visit to the satellite imagery website Google Earth quickly revealed that it had been posting 1 metre resolution imagery of the Sevmash yard for several years. The Google Earth archive facility allowed imagery from four or five times per year over the past two decades to be accessed and compared. These are full colour images in a digital format, that can be enlarged and manipulated at the click of a computer mouse. Helpfully, Google Earth has a measuring tool to allow the length and width of submarines in the yard to be recorded.

According to the old CIA documents, the 1960s and 1970s submarine analysts had none of this. They had to make do with grainy black-and-white prints. Often they resorted to using old-fashioned rulers to measure items of interest and had to compare them to the size of known objects, such cars and trucks. The work of these analysts had to remain top secret for decades as the US was locked in a game of cat and mouse with the Soviets. This was to prevent the capabilities of US satellites being revealed or agents inside the Soviet Union being compromised.

This transformation from the closed world of Cold War intelligence gathering to 21st Century open-source intelligence, or OSINT, techniques is at the heart of this study. It is now possible for people outside the closed world of intelligence agencies to find out things about Russia's military that were impossible during the Cold War.

It must be remembered that Russia is not the Soviet Union. Unlike in the Cold War when the Soviet Union was a closed society, 21st Century Russia is in love with the internet. The country has seen some of the world's highest growth in internet usage, with most rating tables putting it in the top 10 nations for internet use. According to some accounts, in 2000 only some three million Russians were internet users. In 2016 this had surged to 102 million users out of a total population of 143 million. (2)

The young men who serve in Russian armed forces are some of the most prolific users of the internet and social-media platforms. This makes Russia a top target for OSINT analysis. Those Russian servicemen just can't resist putting up pictures of themselves sitting on tanks, visiting foreign ports or loading missiles on fighter planes.

Moscow's Ministry of Defence has also embraced the internet as a recruiting tool and it is keen to portray Russia's armed forces as a good place to work, to attract young men and women into the ranks as professional or contract soldiers. There is a daily data dump online of pictures, videos and news reports showing the bases, exercises and operations of Russia's military.

Russia's defence industry is also trying to compete on the international market so it is keen to advertise its wares online and show off its production facilities to potential customers.

Over the past seven years I been collecting and analysing this torrent of information and pulling it together in a series of Powerpoint briefings that were used to support articles for Jane's Intelligence Review, Jane's Defence Weekly and Jane's Navy International magazines. I combined commercial satellite imagery, screen grabs from video clips, still imagery from the Russian Ministry of Defence website, news imagery and social-media posts. The result of fusing together these multiple sources was a "ground truth" that could be treated with a high degree of confidence. These briefings have become the core references for this book and have been posted on my website, www.timripley.co.uk.

This work can also be validated via a series of online communities that collect and analyse similar information. A retired Russian naval officer who lives in Sevastopol, for example, has a Twitter feed that features a daily upload of images from Russia's main Black Sea naval base. Aircraft and ship spotters track the movement of Russian planes and ships via their transponder and radio traffic. There is a group of missile spotters who have pinpointed every air defence base around the world and produced a Google Earth data layer that can be overlaid on the mapping website. This can be used to find every Russia surface-to-air missile site in a matter of minutes.

The Ukrainian and Syrian conflicts have also thrown up online communities that "fight" these wars in the virtual domain. They are akin to sports supporters who use the online world to post information to denigrate or undermine the narratives of their opponents. In the process they produce some of the best information about the participants in these conflicts, but they need a "health warning" to remind users that they rarely post information that shows their own side in a bad light. Ukrainian online activists have produced a wealth of important information on Russian intervention in the Donbass conflict in 2014 but they also reflect the divisions in Ukrainian society with some groups being blindly anti-Russian and others concentrate on exposing the failings of their own high command, which they say led to the defeat of Kiev's troops.

A similar online environment has grown up around the Syria conflict, with rival communities backing their side in the war. One Russian online activist has even been accused of using OSINT techniques to identify rebel targets that were subsequently bombed by Russian aircraft.

Although there is much in common between traditional intelligence gathering and OSINT techniques, it is perhaps going too far to say that OSINT has all the answers. OSINT provides a window on Russia that is far better than anything that possible during the Cold War. It is very good at building a detailed order of battle of the Russian armed forces. Ports, air bases and army barracks are very easy to spot on satellite imagery and can be compared with ground level imagery. Tanks, ships, submarines, missile launchers and planes can all be counted with considerable accuracy on satellite imagery. Ultimately, the Google Street View application allows the location of most Russian military bases to be inspected at close quarters. This, for example, even allows you to read the signs on the front door to the Russian Southern Military District headquarters building in the centre of Rostov-on-Don.

It is also very difficult to hide the movement of naval vessels and aircraft outside of Russian ports and airspace because of online tracking technology. Russian citizens are also prolific users of dashboard cameras and they routinely post videos of troop trains and military truck convoys online, which make it difficult to conceal the movement of large formations of ground troops by train or road around the country. Aircraft and ship tracking websites display their positions live around the world and Russian jets and warships can be routinely picked up on these sites.

Most OSINT operatives, however, are aware of limitations to their work. They do not have the scale of resources available to government or military intelligence organisations to monitor multiple locations in real-time. Even in the 1960s and 1970s, CIA analysts had far more satellite pictures to work from than are routinely posted on Google Earth and eventually they were able to photograph locations in Russia on a weekly and sometimes daily or even hourly basis. Secret signals intelligence or underwater surveillance data is also not available outside military organisations or intelligence agencies.

Cold War intelligence documents provide an interesting insight into the competing utility of secret intelligence versus OSINT techniques. During the 1970s, a US Navy funded think tank, the Centre for Naval Analysis, began reporting that Soviet naval war strategy was not focused on swarming submarines into the Atlantic to sink allied shipping carrying reinforcements to central Europe. (3) The analysts who studied Soviet military publications and news media reports of naval activity concluded that Moscow's navy would, in fact, concentrate on defending its nuclear missile firing submarines in so-called "coastal bastions" in waters such as the Barents Sea.

It took almost a decade for the leadership of the US Navy to admit it had got it wrong and its change of mind only occurred after a high-level defector provided inside secret information of Soviet naval plans. Senior American naval officers refused to believe their OSINT analysts and rubbished their ideas, stating that the Soviets would never announce their strategy in public. Professional intelligence organisations may be well resourced but the saga of Soviet naval plans illustrates that secret intelligence agencies have their own institutional biases, to reinforce established policies or views. The concept of "group think" makes them unwilling to confront inconvenient truths or go against established opinion. Senior US Navy officers were all taught to think and act aggressively, so in the 1970s they could not understand why their potential foe would not behave in the same way by adopting a defensive strategy.

This book first looks at the Russian campaigns in Ukraine and Syria, before profiling the Russian armed forces in 2020. It is not an academic thesis about Russian military doctrine or a technical assessment of every one of the country's weapon systems. I aim to look at how the Russian military fights today and how President Vladimir Putin uses his armed forces for political effect. This is often very different from how the leadership of the Russian military would like to operate, but as with everything involving Putin, political context is all, rather than esoteric military doctrine. He is pumping a considerable chunk of the revenue from Russia's state budget into his military and the leaders of its armed forces do what he wants.

Hopefully readers of this book will appreciate that all types of intelligence – both open and secret - have their limitations and caveats.

Chapter 1
Operation Crimea Spring

During the afternoon of 26th February 2014 officers of the Russian Aerospace Force's (RuAF) 334th Berlin Red Banner Military Transport Aviation Regiment at Pskov air base received orders to launch the first of ten Ilyushin Il-76MD transport aircraft. Hundreds of paratroopers from the 76th Guards Air Assault Division were on trucks heading to the air base from their nearby garrison. The paratroopers are the Kremlin's strategic rapid-reaction force and are kept on a few hours' notice to move for missions of the highest national importance. Within two hours the airlifters touched down at the Russian Black Sea Fleet-controlled Gvardeyskoye air base on Crimea and the paratrooper headed into the region's capital, Simferopol, to spearhead an assault on its parliament building.

Three days later grainy CCTV camera images from the building's security systems appeared on news broadcasts around the world showing the paratroopers bashing open the parliament's front doors and then fanning out around the building. (1) It was fitting that the opening moves of the Russian operation were captured on video and then shared on social-media, as this would soon become a familiar way that key events in the conflict between Russia and Ukraine would become public. This would soon be a fully fledged social-media war.

It is still not clear how the video got from the Crimean parliament's security systems onto the internet and this illustrates how both sides in the conflict would eventually use social-media and other forms of propaganda to make their case. Both sides had a motive for getting the video of the Russian assault out. Moscow would have been keen to show it was now in full control of Crimea, while Ukrainians would have wanted to use images to prove that their country was being invaded. It is most likely that the original imagery was put out by a local citizen with no links to the Russian or Ukrainian authorities who was just keen to tell his friends or family what has happening. The video clip then took on a life of its own.

The video footage of the assault shows a group of around 10 heavily armed soldiers throwing stun grenades through the building's main front doors and moving inside. Other sections of the film showed more troops entering through other doors around the building. All the soldiers were loaded with rucksacks and sleeping mats, indicating they were expecting a long stay. They also sported a mix of impressive weaponry including rocket-propelled grenade launchers, silenced sniper rifles and what appeared to be a satellite radio system. Their uniforms and equipment unmistakeably identified them as members of the elite Russian Airborne Forces or the VDV.

Each soldier had a strip of white cloth wrapped around their arm, which was an identification device so they would be able to differentiate friends from foes in the heat of battle. Time and again over the coming months, these arm bands would be seen repeatedly in imagery of Russian troops operating inside the

Ukraine. Mixed in among the Russian paratroopers were several armed men who did not appear to be wearing military uniforms. These were most likely locally based operatives of the famous Russian General Staff's intelligence organisation, or as it is known by its Russian abbreviation, the GRU.

Several Kremlin insiders have since given their accounts of the Crimea operation and President Vladimir Putin has featured in a two-hour-long Russian television documentary, entitled "Crimea - Way Back Home", describing in some detail his role in the crisis. (2) Putin and other senior Russian leaders are proud of their role and happy boast about what they achieved. These accounts laid out the Russian narrative for the takeover of Crimea and it is possible to corroborate many of the details from other sources to confirm important aspects. Most importantly, it is now possible to build up a detailed timeline of Russian decision-making and military actions.

When news teams arrived outside the Crimea parliament later on 27th February and started to film the Russian troops - who had by then removed their unit and rank insignia from their uniforms - the soldiers politely refused to answer any questions. These soldiers were soon dubbed "little green men" and they came to epitomise the shadowy undeclared war between Russia and Ukraine that unfolded over the next year. This conflict eventually escalated into an all-out shooting war between the two country's armed forces, although to this day the Kremlin refuses to acknowledge the role played by their regular military in the fighting in eastern Ukraine.

Events in the centre of the Ukrainian capital Kiev in February 2014 captivated the world. Thousands of pro-European and pro-democracy demonstrators took to the streets in an escalating confrontation with government security forces. The crisis turned violent with police snipers opening fire on the demonstrators. It looked like the crackdown by Ukrainian President Viktor Yanukovych was on the verge of success. In a series of events that have never really been satisfactorily explained, on the night of 21st February the police and special forces withdrew from the high-rise buildings overlooking the Maidan Square or Euromaidan demonstration. Yanukovych had lost his nerve and he fled Kiev, abandoning his opulent country estate, known as the Mezhyhirya Residence, to the protestors. He first travelled to the eastern city of Kharkov, where he hoped to rally his demoralised supporters. Few in the city were up for a fight and within hours he was driving south to Crimea, where eventually President Putin organised a helicopter to pick up Yanukovych and fly him to a Russian warship of the Black Sea Fleet. (3)

For the next week Western television anchors flooded to Kiev to broadcast live from the Maidan Square protest site. They interviewed a stream of buoyant demonstrators who now seemed to transform themselves into Ukraine's new government. International journalists were led into Yanukovych's ransacked office to pick over the remains of his secret correspondence. Their next port of call was the Mezhyhirya Residence to view his private zoo and opulent bedroom. This was a bizarre experience as one of my acquaintances only a few days before had recounted how he had supplied the bathroom fittings and mirrors, in an order measured in several hundred thousand dollars. Yanukovych was one of his best customers after the Gulf Arab monarchs. "This is very bad for business," said the disgruntled bathroom supplier.

It all seemed too good to be true. After the Western journalists came a posse of European and US politicians and diplomats, who hailed the success of what was now being called the "Euromaidan Revolution".

Amid all this euphoria at the triumph of democracy little attention was paid to events in Moscow by Western governments or the media. In the years since the demise of Yanukovych's government a lot of information has entered the public domain about decision-making in the Kremlin. This paints an intriguing picture of a crisis among senior decision-makers in Moscow as Putin tried to figure out what to do. Yanukovych was "Putin's guy" in Kiev and the Kremlin saw his presence as a guarantee that its interests in Ukraine would be protected. Top Russian priorities were protecting the interests in Ukraine of several important Russian businessmen, who are popularly known as oligarchs, and the position of the Black Sea Fleet's bases in Crimea.

To help him face down the Euromaidan protestors, Putin dispatched his trusted fixer Vladislav Surkov to Kiev with a posse of intelligence operatives. The youthful-looking Surkov has been dubbed the "Grey Cardinal of the Kremlin" because of his alleged power and influence over Putin. He typifies a new brand of Russian political operative, who speaks fluent English and is fully at home in the social-media age. As well as being the author of a gangsta fiction novel, the 49-year-old is seen as the architect of Putin's nationalist philosophy and his successful election campaigns. More importantly, his proximity and access to Putin meant he radiated power where ever he went.

Working from the Russian Embassy in Kiev, Surkov was in constant touch with the Kremlin, keeping it abreast of developments. His other task was to corral support from pro-Russian elements across Ukraine, particularly key oligarchs. According to Kremlin insiders, Putin was dismayed that Surkov could not work his magic on Yanukovych. All of the Kremlin's plans were turning to dust and Surkov had to return to Moscow with his tail between his legs. (4)

The key day of decision was 23rd February as Putin gathered his key advisors in the president's Novo-Orgaryovo residence outside Moscow. With Yanukovych and his security forces driven from Kiev, there seemed little prospect of returning the Ukrainian president to office. Attention turned to protecting the Russian bases on Crimea. A plan was needed to translate Putin's intentions into action. Russia's defence minister, Sergei Shoigu, was ordered to make the necessary preparations.

Shoigu is one of Putin's oldest political allies and he had played a key role in building up the president's tough-guy image, including organising the famous television footage of Putin hunting bare-chested in a Siberian forest. Putin considered Shoigu to be one of his most efficient ministers so it was not a surprise that he entrusted the high-risk adventure in Crimea to him.

Later on 23rd February, Shoigu dispatched his own fixer, Oleg Belaventsev, to Crimea to come up with ideas on how to protect Russia's interests. (5) He toured Simferopol meeting pro-Russian politicians, looking for someone to formally ask Moscow "for protection". Belaventsev was a retired Soviet rear admiral and intelligence operative who was expelled from the UK in 1985 as a suspected spy. As an alumni of Sevastopol's Pavel Nakhimov Naval Academy he knew Crimea well. His presence in Crimea, as well as Surkov's presence in Kiev a few weeks earlier, demonstrated the weakness of the Ukrainian government. It showed that Kiev could do little to stop senior Russian officials interfering in their affairs and the degree to which Kremlin leaders regarded Ukraine as their backyard.

The situation was extremely tense and fluid with rival political groups staging demonstrations in Simferopol and Sevastopol. On 26th February there was a major incident outside the Autonomous Republic of Crimea parliament in Simferopol between pro-Moscow and pro-Ukrainian groups. Two people died and several were injured when the incident degenerated into a street drawl. (6)

Things looked touch and go. As Belaventsev was at work, the Russian military were working up their own plans. Prior to the fall of Yanukovych, there had been no contingency plans for this eventuality. Up to this point Shoigu, had been cautious and warned that any military operation would be high-risk. No one knew how the Ukrainians would react. The prospect that the Euromaidan revolution could spread to Crimea had to be headed off. So during the evening of 26th February Shoigu ordered the 76th Guards Air Assault Division to dispatch troops to Simferopol to seize the parliament. Events moved so fast that the paratroopers did not know where they were heading when their Il-76s took off from Pskov air base. (7)

After landing at the Russian-controlled air base at Gvardeyskoye, some 20 kilometres north of Simferopol, the first paratroopers met up with operatives from the GRU and headed into the centre of the city in a convoy of trucks and mini buses. The assault started at just after 4am and was unopposed. By dawn the 100 or so paratroopers had secured and barricaded the building. When a group of journalists approached the building's front doors to investigate, a stun grenade was thrown out to persuade them to keep their distance. For the rest of the day journalists and Ukrainian police kept their distance from the building. A posse of pro-Russian "self-protection" operatives, including several members of the city's Berkut riot unit which had been disbanded by the new government in Kiev a few days before, arrived to patrol outside the parliament building, liaising with the Russian soldiers and several politicians inside the building.

Later that afternoon, pro-Russian representatives arrived in the parliament under the protection of the paratroopers and in a matter of minutes voted to accept the "resignation" of the regional prime minister. When the leader of the local branch of Putin's Russian Unity Party, Sergey Aksyonov, was proposed as the new prime minister, he was elected by 42 votes out of 53 representatives present.

With political top cover secured, it was now time for the Russian Black Sea Fleet to swing in to action to prevent any Ukrainian intervention to reverse the change of regime in Crimea. The fleet's commander, Admiral Aleksandr Vitko, was also a graduate of Sevastopol's Pavel Nakhimov Naval Academy and so was a former comrade-in-arms of many of the senior Ukrainian navy officers based in the city.

The Black Sea Fleet is one of the most historic Russian military units and can trace its history back to the days of Catherine the Great in the 18th Century. By 2014 it was a shadow of its former glory, with just five major warships, seven landing ships, one submarine, five corvettes, 10 minesweepers and 10 missile boats. Although the treaty between Russia and Ukraine in theory allowed the Black Sea Fleet to have some 25,000 personnel on Crimea, by 2014 there was probably only half that number based on the peninsula. These included probably no more than 2,000 Naval Infantrymen or marines of the 810th Brigade. These were well-equipped professional or contract soldiers, who would play a key role in the upcoming operation. They had benefited from President Putin's defence reform programme and sported new uniforms, had new and modern vehicles and were some of the most competent soldiers in the Russian military. The challenge for Admiral Vitko was that there were not very many Naval Infantrymen available to head off counter-action by the Ukrainian military on Crimea or any reinforcements sent from Kiev. Some 16,000 sailors and airmen formed Kiev's garrison on Crimea, including a battalion of 500 marines. They were backed up by 4,000 paramilitary border guards and coast guards. (8)

The first Black Sea Fleet units and ships were put on alert during 23rd February but Operation Crimea Spring was not fully activated until 26th February with the dispatch of the 76th Division's paratroopers. Admiral Vitko had to scramble to move his troops to protect them. (9) It seems that the Black Sea Fleet command did not receive any earlier warning of the crisis as there is no sign of its moving reinforcements to bolster the 810th Brigade before then. The first reinforcements arrived just before 9pm on 27th February when the amphibious assault ship Azov docked at Pivdenna Bay in the heart of Sevastopol harbour and unloaded 300 troops and 15 Kamaz trucks from the 382nd Separate Naval Infantry Battalion, which was based on the Russian mainland side of the Kerch Straits. It had taken the Azov 10 hours or so to make the crossing from its home port at Novorossiysk. These troop movements were reported by pro- Euromaidan activists, who passed on sightings to the young officials in Ukrainian Border Guards headquarters in Simferopol. They then posted them on a rolling internet blog over the next month, creating one of the most important records of the Russian operation. (10)

Later that night the first units of the 810th Brigade began to start moving to secure key points across Crimea. Their first objectives were to secure the main airport and air bases to prevent Ukrainian reinforcements flying in. One contingent of 150 troops headed up to the Ukrainian naval air station at Novofedorivka. Another group of a similar size headed out to Simferopol civilian airport to seize its control tower and secure its terminal building.

A group of 300 Naval Infantry, backed by two BTR armoured personnel carriers, also moved to take control of Sevastopol's civil airport at Balbek. The airport shared a runway with the Ukrainian air force's only fighter unit on Crimea. To stop it putting its MiG-29 fighters in the air the Russians drove three trucks onto the main runway. Russian officers telephoned the Ukrainian air force commander to warn him that if any of his jets tried to take off they would be fired upon. By midday on 28th February, air links between Crimea and Kiev had been cut. (11) A column of the 810th Brigade also headed up to the narrow isthmus that connected Crimea to mainland Ukraine to block the road and rail routes on to the Peninsula.

Another column of Naval Infantry had also been able to get through to the parliament in the centre of Simferopol to set up a wider security cordon around the building, where the 76th Division paratroopers were still barricaded inside. International news media crews soon started filming the newly arrived Naval Infantrymen who did not sport any unit insignia or ranks badges. They politely declined to engage in conversations with the journalists and the Russian military command on Crimea and in Moscow denied they were their soldiers. Soon the Russian media dubbed them the "polite men" on account of their friendly behaviour towards local people, while the Ukrainian and international media started to call them "little green men" for reasons explained at the start of this book.

During 28th February, the pace of activity stepped up with more Naval Infantry moving to blockade Ukrainian naval bases and border guard posts around Sevastopol city. Russian navy warships started to position themselves to stop Ukrainian vessels being able to pull away from their berths. A flotilla of five Russian warships, led by the cruiser Moskova, set sail from Sevastopol to blockade the naval anchorage at Lake Donuzlav and trap seven Ukrainian warships and 10 support vessels inside. To complete the neutralisation of the Ukrainian air defence capability on Crimea, detachments of Naval Infantry were sent to blockade surface-to-air-missile units at Yevpatoriy, to the north of Sevastopol, and Cape Fiolent on the southern outskirts of the city.

A major operation was now activated by the Russian Southern Military District headquarters in Rostov-on Don to reinforce the Black Sea Fleet. During 28th February, 11 Russian Mil Mi-24 gunships and Mi-8 troop transport helicopters of the 55th Helicopter Regiment were filmed by passengers on the Kerch ferry flying towards Crimea. (12) They took up residence at Gvardeyskoye air base which was rapidly becoming the main hub for Russian airborne and ground force units arriving from the mainland. A steady stream of Il-76s were now arriving every 15 minutes or so to deliver more paratroopers and vehicles from the 76th Division.

Amid this deployment a group of a couple of hundred armed Russian men arrived on Crimea who did not appear to be regular military or security service personnel. They have been variously linked to the military agency the GRU, the

FSB intelligence service, the Wagner private security company, Afghan veterans groups and extreme Russian nationalist political parties. During their time in Crimea these groups were involved in several public ceremonies to mark the formation of local self-defence militia units. It was not clear who these men answered to but they clearly had top-level political support from the Kremlin.

Across southern Russia, troops began to be mobilised to move to Crimea by sea or air. Commercial satellite imagery showed large convoys of vehicles backed up waiting to board the ferry across the Kerch Straits. These included BTR armoured vehicles of the 18th Motor Rifle Brigade, the 108th Guards Air Assault Regiment and the 943rd Rocket Artillery Regiment, along with GRU special forces troops from the two Spetsnaz brigades assigned to the Southern Military District. (13)

With more troops arriving, Admiral Vitko started to expand the scope of the operation to eventually blockade all of the 190 or so Ukrainian military bases across the Crimea. As the Russian paratroopers moved into the parliament building in the early hours of 27th February, its security staff can be clearly seen on the video co-operating with them. This illustrated the divided loyalties of Crimea's population, as well as Ukrainian security and military units based on the peninsula. Crimea's connections to Russia stretch back to the 18th Century when it was seized from the Ottoman Turks by the Romanov Empire. In Communist times, Crimea was eventually placed under the administrative control of the Ukrainian Soviet Socialist Republic. So by accident of history when the Soviet Union collapsed and Ukraine declared its independence in August 1991 Crimea found itself no longer part of Russia.

Russian influence, however, remained strong. Moscow and Kiev divided the Soviet Black Sea Fleet and the Russian-controlled elements were allowed to remain on their bases on Crimea. More than half of Crimea's 2.2 million population spoke Russian as their first language and professed to have the Orthodox Christian faith. The families of the Russian Black Sea Fleet sailors continued to live on the peninsula and thousands of civilians worked for the Russian military. The Ukrainian Navy officers had served alongside their Russian counterparts in the Soviet Navy. Many of the Russian and Ukrainian units shared bases around Sevastopol harbour. This intertwining of the Russian and Ukrainian navies on Crimea meant it was almost impossible for Kiev's forces to organise effective resistance.

The Russian blockade strategy played on these military, social and even family links within Crimea. Over the next month the isolated Ukrainian airmen, soldiers and sailors were bombarded with offers of better-paid jobs in the Russian military, or gruesome threats. The Russians cut their phone links to the Ukrainian high command in Kiev and switched off power and water to make life as uncomfortable as possible. The fact that the families of Ukrainian personnel lived nearby, often on the same streets as their Russian counterparts, made them even more vulnerable to Moscow's campaign of psychological warfare. The Russians offered free passage to any Ukrainian personnel who wanted to leave for Kiev but this would have meant taking their families to live as refugees in a country in turmoil. Russia's Crimea seemed a bastion of stability compared to Ukraine. In Kiev, the new government was still pressing its military men to hold out but Western governments were urging the Ukrainians not to provoke the Russians. US President Barack Obama met his top advisors hours after the first reports of the Russian moves on Crimea started to emerge. He quickly concluded that there was little the US could do to stop the Russian operation without sparking a war between NATO and Russia. That was not on the cards, so the word came from Washington that there would be no US intervention, no arms supplies for the Ukrainians and a peaceful solution was the way forward. Not surprisingly, the Ukrainian troops soon worked out no-one was coming to rescue them. As March ground on, one by one the Ukrainian bases surrendered as Kiev's strategy looked increasing futile. Those bases that held out saw a steady trickle of men opting to leave Crimea or to sign up to serve in the Russian military.

Senior Russian officers toured Ukrainian bases trying to persuade officers and soldiers to defect. Lieutenant General Igor Nikolaevich Turcheniuk, the deputy commander of Russia's Southern Military District, arrived at the Ukrainian Marines base in Feodosia on 3rd March and was recorded by the RBC news agency describing why he and his troops were in Crimea. Western journalists also witnessed the encounter, with the General telling the Ukrainians "with the agreement of your legally elected president [Viktor Yanukovych], [Russian President Vladimir] Putin has given the directive that control of all military organisations in Crimea is transferred to me, under the leadership of the prime minister of the Crimea [Sergey Aksyonov] until 25th [May]. Putin's request is to render assistance to the Crimean government in line with the request [of the government of Crimea]..." (14)

These sieges or blockades generally passed off peacefully, expect for one incident in downtown Simferopol when a locally recruited pro-Russian self-defence force militia clashed with Kiev's troops leaving one Ukrainian soldier dead.

The Russian government adopted a very unusual media strategy during this phase of the crisis. International and even Ukrainian journalists were allowed to freely visit Crimea and there were few restrictions on what they did. The "little green men" continued to politely refuse to talk to the media but no-one was arrested or shot for speaking or photographing them. Some of the so-called self-defence units got aggressive with foreign journalists but in general the Kremlin wanted the world to see Russia's troops being welcomed by the population. This was very different from how the Russian military behaved in Chechnya in the 1990s and Georgia in 2008. Crucially no attempt was made by the Kremlin to close down the internet on Crimea so local people were able to upload a torrent of social-media posts and imagery showing the progress of the Russian operation. The era of the Russian military being able to operate totally in secret had passed.

The fate of the most senior Ukrainian naval officer in Crimea, Rear Admiral Denis Berezovsky, epitomised the dismal resistance offered by Kiev's men. In a bid to stiffen morale, on 1st March Berezovsky was appointed as commander of the Ukrainian Navy by the Kiev government. Yet the following day Admiral Vitko went to visit Berezovsky in his blockaded headquarters and persuaded him to defect. The Ukrainian admiral called on his former comrades to join him and within the month he was appointed deputy commander of the Russian Black Sea Fleet. (15)

By 24th March the last Ukrainian base on Crimea surrendered and a day later the last navy ship struck their colours at Lake Donuzlav. According to the Ukrainian military, out of the 20,315 of its personnel on Crimea at the end of February 2014 some 6,010 chose to be repatriated to Kiev. The rest choose to stay behind and were reported as deserters by the Ukrainian authorities, including 9,500 Ukrainian army soldiers and navy sailors, 1,386 interior ministry paramilitary police, 1,350 border guards and 1,372 SBU intelligence agency staff. (16)

Amid this dismal record the aviators of the 62nd Fighter Regiment at Balbek air base achieved worldwide respect when they marched unarmed to protest to Russian troops about their imprisonment. Ukrainian naval aviators of the 10th Saki Naval Aviation Brigade, at Novofedorivka air base, were able to organise the escape of several of their aircraft and helicopters to safety in Odessa on 5th March from under the noses of their Russian besiegers. These included one Kamov Ka-29, three Mil Mi-14s, two Antonov An-26s and one Beriev Be-12. (17)

As the operation to secure Crimea unfolded during March 2014, the Kremlin began mobilising its assets across southern Russia to establish a strong defence network around the peninsula.

A Russian Ground Force armoured battalion arrived in Crimea equipped with the first main battle tanks at the end of March. The unit, which included more than 30 T-72 tanks, was shown off to the international media being unloaded at a railway cargo yard near the large Russian air and logistic base at Gvardeyskoye on 31st March (18)

Two troop trains delivered the tanks to the base in central Crimea after they were transported to the peninsula from the Russian mainland via the roll-on roll-off rail ferry terminal at Kerch. The Russian military had been using this route as its main transhipment point for vehicles and cargos since the start of its operation on Crimea on 27th February.

Up to this deployment, the Russian military had relied on wheeled armoured vehicles during its operation on Crimea. The units deployed up to then had been predominately equipped with wheeled BTR-80 armoured personnel carriers, backed by 122mm and 152mm towed artillery.

Social-media imagery also emerged showing a Russian S-300 surface-to-air missile battery protecting Gvardeyskoye air base on 30th March. (19) The imagery, which included a number of distinctive geographic features specific to the base, showed eight S-300PMU launcher erector vehicles, positioned on the northern edge of the airfield, supported by a number of command vehicles, as well as 30N6E1 Tomb Stone and 5N63S Flap Lid B radars. Several of the vehicles were shielded by camouflage netting. The radars were positioned to scan in a northerly direction to detect a possible Ukrainian air attack on the air base. Also pictured at the air base were two Pantsir-S1 point gun/missile combined air defence systems, suggesting a layered air defence had been put in place to protect it. Commercial satellite imagery published by the UK-based Jane's organisation detected elements of a S-300PMU system on railway cars after being unloaded at the Kerch ferry terminal on 13th March. (20) Additional air surveillance was provided by two Beriev A-50 airborne early warning radar aircraft which were forward deployed at Yeysk air base, south of Rostov, from the 144th Airborne Early Warning Aviation Regiment's home base at Ivanovo air base. (21)

In the wake of its military success, the Russian government moved quickly to consolidate its political control over Crimea. On 15th March it held a referendum on unification with Russia in which some 95% of voters backed joining with their Motherland. The Moscow parliament agreed to admit the Republic of Crimea and Sevastopol to the Russian Federation on 21st March.

This whirlwind campaign seemed to herald a new level of sophistication in the way Russian commanders conducted military operations. The most distinctive feature of the Russian operation was its emphasis on "economy of effort". Unlike previous interventions in Afghanistan in the Soviet era or Chechnya and Georgia more recently - where Russian commanders traditionally relied on mass employment of tanks and artillery - the Crimea intervention featured less than 10,000 assault troops lined up against 20,000 Ukrainian military and security personnel. For much of the operation, the heaviest armoured vehicle employed by the Russians in operation against the Ukrainians was the wheeled BTR-80 armoured personnel carrier.

Once Russian troops had moved to blockade Ukrainian military personnel in their bases, psychological warfare, propaganda, intimidation and bribery were their main weapons to undermine their opponents' will to resist, rather than overwhelming firepower. Russian troops displayed considerable discipline and patience during this phase. They also appeared well equipped, boasting new personnel equipment, body armour and light wheeled armoured vehicles.

This novel approach was necessitated by President Putin's need for the operation to be launched within a very tight time frame after the fall of the pro-Moscow regime in Kiev on 22nd February. There was insufficient time to mobilise a larger force. Russian commanders would initially have to make do with Naval Infantry of the Black Sea Fleet already based on Crimea, backed up by a motor rifle brigade, a couple of battalions of Airborne troops and Spetsnaz commandos flown or shipped onto the peninsula. Economy of force also fitted the political narratives of the campaign - that this was a mission to protect Crimea's Russian- speaking population rather than an invasion.

In just over four weeks, the will of the Ukrainian forces on Crimea was broken and all 190 of their bases had surrendered without a shot being fired by any of the defenders. The Russian armed forces facilitated a political and psychological success, rather than achieving a conventional military victory on the battlefield.

Chapter 2
Putin and his Generals

On 9th May 2014, the Russian President made a triumphant visit to Sevastopol for the first Victory Parade after the return of Crimea to Russian control. A beaming Vladimir Putin watched a flying display, inspected troops and reviewed the Black Sea Fleet as they celebrated the defeat of Nazi Germany in 1945.

Although Russia had been hit by Western sanctions after Putin sent his troops to seize Crimea, at home the President had reached unprecedented levels of popularity. The bloodless return of Crimea to Kremlin control restored the pride of many ordinary Russians in their armed forces. Defeats in Afghanistan and Chechnya had sullied the reputation of the Soviet and Russian armies, so many ordinary Russians were pleased to see their soldiers winning for once under commanders who at last seemed to be competent.

Putin was milking this wave of acclaim for all it was worth but he had not always been on such good terms with his generals and admirals.

To many in the West, Vladimir Putin appears to be the devil incarnate. He is accused of presiding over a bid to restore the Soviet Union and its massive military machine. The Russian President's aggressive foreign military campaigns in Ukraine and Syria and pro-military rhetoric in his mammoth press conferences fuel these perceptions. When combined with his apparent love of Red Square military parades full of tanks and other military hardware, it confirms opinion in the West that Putin is a "clear and present danger".

Yet inside Russia, the country's President is not viewed as a puppet of the Russian military top brass or a born-again Communist. Putin's rise to power tells us a lot about his relations with the Russian military and its generals.

Despite coming of age under the Soviet Union, Putin never served in the Red Army because he secured a university place and then opted to join the Committee for State Security – or, as it is known in the West, the KGB. In 2019 Putin did claim that he had undergone artillery training as a reserve army officer during his student days. He was posted to work for the KGB in the former German Democratic Republic, or DDR, in the latter half of the 1980s, witnessing first-hand the disintegration of Moscow's East German ally. Yet when the remnants of the KGB leadership and old Soviet military high command attempted to stage a coup in 1991 to restore the former regime, Putin resigned his membership of the KGB and secured work with the reforming mayor of St Petersburg. He appears to have burned his bridges with those who wanted to turn the clock back to the old order. Putin is no Communist.

For most of the next decade, Putin had little to do with Russian's crumbling and increasingly shambolic military. This period was instrumental in developing Putin's dismay at the chaotic (and often drunken) rule of the then President Boris Yeltsin, which was reducing Russia to an international laughing stock and allowing the rise of a class of businessmen who grew fabulously wealthy from buying and selling former state assets. Known as oligarchs, these businessmen were universally loathed among Russians for their contempt for ordinary citizens and apparent immunity from the law. To sell himself to the Russian public, Putin developed what we would call a "political brand" based around not being his predecessor.

After rising to power on 31st December 1999 almost by accident, Putin set about creating his core political narratives. First, he is famously teetotal and revels in taking part in sports, particularly judo and ice hockey. This reinforces his image as a tough guy. Next, he famously took on the oligarchs and organised the jailing of several of them to show the Russian public that these super-capitalists were no longer running the country. Surging oil prices after the turn of the century provided Putin with a windfall and allowed him to spend billions rebuilding neglected public services.

Restoring Russia's great-power status was a more long-term project. His immediate priorities were crushing a new uprising in Chechnya and dealing with a spate of terrorist attacks in Moscow and southern Russia. The Second Chechen War saw Russian troops launch another brutal invasion of the lawless Caucasus republic but, unlike in the earlier invasion in the 1995-96, the operation was better managed. Rather than simply trying to bomb their way to victory, Russia's generals this time bribed key rebel commanders to switch sides and this broke the morale of the resistance. This was a rare success for the Russian military but many of the old Soviet-era generals were still in charge and Moscow's military boasted few modern weapons. For ordinary soldiers life was little different to in Soviet times. The Chechen wars and other scandals involving the death of conscripts in bullying incidents and corruption cases involving rogue officers resulted in the reputation of the Russian military sinking to rock bottom.

Putin was an early supporter of military reform. It was popular with the public who were keen for someone to clear out the ageing top brass. He backed increased defence budgets, military reform and improved professionalism. For the first time since the Second World War, Putin approved the purchase of major new hardware from overseas, including amphibious landing ships from France, surveillance drones from Israel and armoured troop carriers from Italy.

Putin took every opportunity to be photographed with soldiers and military hardware, including famously taking the controls of a Tupolev Tu-160 strategic bomber and sporting naval uniforms when visiting warships, as part of his macho image. But this was all spin organised by the Kremlin public relations machine. The President did not socialise with his generals or admirals who were not very fashionable or popular with the public.

Moscow's top brass, while welcoming Putin's interest in promoting military modernisation, came to fear their new President. Failures that embarrassed Putin were dealt with ruthlessly and a dozen senior naval officers linked to the sinking of the submarine Kursk in 2000 were removed from their posts. In a sign that 21st Century Russia was not Stalin's Soviet Union, the disgraced officers were not shot or shipped to the Arctic gulag on prison trains but were allowed to shuffle off to become bureaucratic functionaries in local government far away from Moscow.

Putin's ambitions to regain Russia's international position as a major power were a key part of his internal agenda, which portrayed him as the leader who had returned stability to the country and made the world respect Russia again. For Putin, the years after the demise of the Soviet Union had been dominated by a litany of attempts by the West, led by the United States, to topple and overthrow Russia's traditional allies. The 2011 intervention against Libya had been the last straw for Putin, as he believed the US and its allies had overstepped their authority from the United Nations Security Council to protect civilians. Instead, the West had overthrown the Libyan strongman Muammar Gaddafi, a long-time Soviet and Russian ally. So when President Viktor Yanukovych was toppled, Putin quickly resolved to strike back.

The men who Putin turned to in February 2014 were not the ageing Soviet-era generals who made such a mess of the Chechyn war almost 20 years before. Russia's defence minister, Sergei Shoigu, was a close political ally of Putin who was closely attuned to what his boss wanted. Despite styling himself as a general and wearing military fatigues, Shoigu, like Putin had never served in the Soviet military.

Shoigu is a classic Putin-era political operative, who has helped in the President's election campaigns and was governor of the Moscow region. Most importantly he had helped craft Putin's macho image and set up several of his iconic "action man" television appearances, the including the famous footage of him wrestling a bear. Despite his professed interest in Russian military history, Shoigu has proved not to be a deep strategic thinker. He benefited immensely from the work of his predecessor, Anatoliy Serdyukov, who began a major programme to make the Russian conventional military more "useable". This saw the disbandment of the divisional level of command in the army, the shutting down of hundreds of bases and the sacking of scores of senior officers to save money. Not surprisingly, Serdyukov was deeply unpopular with many Soviet-era generals and admirals.

For the first time since the Soviet era, Serdyukov instituted a system of equipment procurement plans that brought some order to the chaotic Russian defence industry. This put in place the orders that set in the train the mass production of Kalibr precision-guided cruise missiles, as well as the Improved Kilo-class submarines and Admiral Grigorovich-class frigates to fire them, mine-proof vehicles and surveillance drones. The repair and overhaul of Russia's huge inventory of tanks, artillery, helicopters and fighter jets was put on a sustainable basis. In one of his most important reforms, Serdyukov made major progress in hiring professional or contract rank-and-file soldiers into the army. Under his direction, the army for the first time had more contract soldiers in its ranks than conscripts. Conscription had long been unpopular in Russia because of the brutal and squalid conditions that many conscripts had to endure, so when Putin ordered the period of service reduced to just one year it was widely welcomed by the Russian public. A year was only just about long enough to train a soldier to march, fire his rifle properly and drive a tank. More complex training was not really possible so many Russian generals and politicians saw contract soldiers as away to restore the combat capability of the country's army units. The reduction in time in uniform for conscripts was a real problem for the army or Ground Forces.

Serdyukov's reforms meant the number of professional soldiers was dramatically increased so that at least one battalion in each army brigade was manned by contract soldiers. In some brigades and regiments of elite forces, such as the Airborne Forces and Naval Infantry, all the battalions in brigades were manned by contract soldiers. The need to recruit hundreds of thousands of contract soldiers created its own problems and the Russian army had to launch recruiting campaigns and start welcoming the media into barracks to show how living conditions for soldiers had improved. Like much of the world, the internet is now central to much of Russian life and the country's soldiers are now heavy users of social media. There have been repeated campaigns by the Russian military to try to clamp down on social media use by soldiers to prevent headlines in the media about bad living conditions but there is fear of going too far in case it damages recruiting.

When Shoigu took over as defence minister in November 2012 he was sensible enough to leave the vast majority of Serdyukov's reforms in place, although he did make some token restoration of historic unit titles. Soon after he took over, Shoigu launched a clear-out of old generals and replaced the Chief of the General Staff with a new officer, General Valery Gerasimov. The General had a reputation as a commander who cared about his troops, had rooted out brutality and most importantly he had led an army in the successful Second Chechen war between 1999 and 2000.

Gerasimov was fully signed up to the modernising agenda and pushed ahead with the reform of the military. He famously authored what became known as the Gerasimov Doctrine, which envisaged combining cyber warfare, precision weapon strikes and special forces operations in fast-moving blitzkrieg campaigns to throw opponents off balance. This was just what Shoigu and Putin wanted to hear. There was no going back to the old Soviet days of mass conscript armies that were intended to steam roller enemies into submission. The general was a keen supporter of what was known in the West as anti access, area denial (A2AD) weapons and tactics. This involved the development and deployment of long-range air defence, anti-ship and ballistic missiles to deter and defeat the use of air power and precision weapons of Western air and naval forces. By creating "anti-missile domes" over Russian forces, A2AD weapons would give Moscow the freedom of manoeuvre to secure its interests without interference from Western countries. (1)

Below Gerasimov, a new generation of Russian officers were making their way up the ranks. By 2014, the senior officers who led the armies, fleets, air divisions and military districts across Russia had all been majors, colonels or navy captains when the Berlin Wall collapsed. They had served through the lean years of Yeltsin's rule in the 1990s and most army officers had endured multiple tours in the brutal Caucasus wars. This experience had turned many of these officers into supporters of military reform as a means to restore the prestige and position of the Russian armed forces. There was, however, still a rump of unredeemable Soviet-era officers who still saw military rank as a means to line their pockets and live the good life. Scandals concerning senior officer using their soldiers to build dachas or work as servants for family members were almost routine for much of the first decade of this century.

The arrival of Putin as President coincided with a surge in global oil prices that meant for the first time since the collapse of the Soviet Union the Russian state was able to start of making real increases in government expenditure. Russia's generals and admirals wanted their cut of this action but Putin controlled the flow cash to the Ministry of Defence. He ruthlessly used this power to force the military to follow his directions and policies. So by 2014 when the orders started emanating from the Kremlin demanding troops to head to Crimea, the generals and admirals reacted with some gusto. They roused their troops out of their barracks in hours or days and marched off to war. This was their chance to show their boss in the Kremlin that the money he had lavished on the Russian military was well spent. Putin would not be disappointed.

Chapter 3
Hybrid Warfare – Dial Moscow for Subversion

Even as the Ilyushin Il-76 transports were flying the Russian paratroopers to Crimea late in the evening of 26th February 2014, the Kremlin had embarked on a psychological warfare campaign to prepare the ground for their arrival.

A statement was issued to news agencies in Moscow warning that a "snap inspection drill" was being ordered of 150,000 Russian troops along Ukraine's eastern border. Soon Reuters was reporting that the troops of the Western Military District were "on alert". (1) The Russian Ministry of Defence announced that the aim of the drills was to check the combat readiness of formations and military units of the Western and Central military districts. It said up to 90 aircraft, over 120 helicopters, up to 880 tanks, more than 1,200 units of military equipment and up to 80 ships and vessels were involved. Kremlin spokesman stressed that the drills were pre-planned and not linked to the crisis in Crimea but this did not sound convincing.

We now know from the accounts of Kremlin insiders that this information was put out just as Vladimir Putin and his closest advisors were meeting at the president's Novo-Orgaryovo residence outside Moscow to order the paratroopers to fly to Crimea to seize its parliament building. (2)

The reports of the huge exercise were immediately picked up by the international media and headlines started to appear around the world saying Russia was threatening to invade Ukraine. It was all exaggerated but it served the Kremlin's purpose, reinforcing the strategic message to Ukraine's new government that if they took action in Crimea, there would be military consequences elsewhere. It was a classic psychological warfare play but it was also a total bluff. The Russian military was in no position to march into Ukraine.

Russian Ground Forces deployments in the spring of 2014 meant the Kremlin had very limited options to strike into Ukraine. In the proceeding 25 years the focus of Russian land operations had been the Northern Caucasus, and the Southern Military District had been assigned more than 10 combat brigades to secure this troublesome region. None of the district's combat brigades were based close to the Ukrainian border. The Western Military District was in an even worse position with almost all of its eight combat brigades being based around Moscow, St Petersburg or further east. None of its units were less than a day's drive of the Ukrainian border.

So when the Kremlin announced that 150,000 troops were on alert they were lumping together all the Western Military District's personnel, including logistic and air force mechanics. It probably had no more 32,000 combat troops available, which was hardly an overwhelming strike force. The most high readiness forces available in western Russian were the three divisions of the Airborne Forces based around Moscow, which totalled around 18,000 troops who could in theory be mobilised for any attack on Ukraine. A strong contingent of the 76th Guards Air Assault Division was already on Crimea and the 106th

Guards Airborne Division was still largely manned by conscripts so could not be used in combat operations outside Russia.

The hollow nature of the threat was made clear on 3rd March when Putin travelled to the Kirillovsky training range to see a tank firing exercise. News footage showed the Russian President, flanked by a posse of generals, striding through the snow to watch the proceedings. The range is located some 500 kilometres east of St Petersburg and is more than 1,100 kilometres from Kiev. Putin's troops were not going to be invading Ukraine from Kirillovsky. (3)

Russia's armed forces needed to make the threat to Ukraine real and fast if the Kremlin's posturing was not to be exposed as a bluff. The Western and Southern Military Districts were ordered to start moving troops to a series of field camps along Ukraine's eastern border. The first signs that this mobilisation was underway came when video clips started being posted online by Russian civilians from Rostov-on-Don northwards to Smolensk showing troop trains loaded with armoured vehicles and artillery pieces on the move. Road convoys of low loaders carrying tanks were also filmed, as well as columns of Airborne Forces BMD armoured vehicles moving close to the Ukrainian border and a regiment of attack helicopters in a field base near the eastern city of Belgorod.

By the end of March commercial satellite imagery was starting to emerge showing the extent of the Russian deployment. There appeared to be three major concentrations of Russian forces. The first one was near Belgorod, opposite Ukraine's north eastern border, the second was at Nonochekassk, north of Rostov-on-Don, and the third was at Golovinka to the west of the southern Russian city. A far smaller camp was detected in imagery at Kilomovo on Ukraine's northern border.

The three main camps each appeared to be home to four or five battalion-sized units, containing up to 30 or 40 tanks, around 100 armoured personnel carriers and some 30 artillery pieces. Nonochekassk camp also appeared to house a battalion of special forces, or Spetsnaz, troops who could be identified by their distinctive troop carriers and artillery. Scores of tents were set to accommodate the 3,000 to 4,000 troops at each of the three main camps.

Soon after the satellite imagery emerged, Ukrainian online campaigners started to find social media posts on the Russian version of Facebook, the VK social network, from the soldiers in the camps. They posted selfie pictures of themselves, their comrades and their vehicles. Many of these pictures contained embedded GPS location data which allowed the Ukrainian cyber warriors to pinpoint the position of several Russian army units and their field camps. (4)

Thousands of these pictures eventually emerged and they showed that the Russian troops were living in very basic conditions with open latrines and very shabby looking canvas tents. It was possible to identify the main types and quantities of armoured vehicles and equipment the Russian army had sent to the Ukrainian border region. Insignia on the vehicles allowed their parent units to be identified and tracked.

While the Russian hardware looked like it was in good working order and the troops appeared to be happy, it seems that their commanders were not convinced these units were ready for action. Soon after the troops arrived they started to be rotated to artillery and tank firing ranges further east along the Volga River to be put through their paces in a series of live firing drills to hone their combat skills. Many of these units were conscripts, not contract soldiers, so needed as much training as they could get.

From the social-media posts, it was possible to work out that the battalions at the field camps were all drawn from different brigades. The units and their commanders thrown together at these camps had never worked with each other before. It would be several weeks before the Russian units would be ready for action.

The way the troops and their vehicles were positioned in these field camps appeared to be done in such a way to make it easier to identify them in satellite imagery. There was no attempt to hide vehicles or artillery under camouflage nets or inside the many forests around Ukraine's borders. The Kremlin wanted the world to think their army was poised to strike.

The troop deployments were just one element of the Russian intimidation campaign aimed at keeping the Ukrainians off balance as the Crimea operation reached its climax. A team of British military intelligence operatives arrived in Kiev in the first week of March to assess the situation and establish links with the new regime in the Ukrainian capital. A senior Ukrainian officer told them that the Russian military was continually probing their borders and air space. At this time a Russian military Il-76 transport aircraft penetrated Ukrainian air space and started a night time approach to land at Kiev international airport without making any radio contact with its air traffic control. The Ukrainian air defence command detected the aircraft, which was not "squawking" normal identification transponders, and directed air defence radars at it. Without making radio contact, when the Russian aircraft realised it had been detected, it turned tail and flew back into Russian airspace. (5)

"Clearly the Russians were probing the Ukrainians' air defences to see if they are still working after the fall of the old regime," recalled one of the British intelligence officers. "This was possibly either as precursor to air attacks in case of war or for an air landing by paratroopers to seize the main airport in Kiev. It was the most serious incursion into Ukrainian air space proper since the start of the Crimea crisis a week or so before. The Ukrainians were convinced that Putin was ramping up psychological warfare against the new Kiev government to intimidate them into not attempting to disrupt Moscow's Crimea referendum. He wanted to keep the threat of all-out war going."

The Russian President hosted Crimea's new political leaders to a lavish ceremony in the Kremlin on 18th March to mark the signing of the treaty to transfer the territory to the Russian Federation. As Russia's political and business elite mixed to celebrate Putin's triumph, speculation moved to what would happen next in the Donbass region of eastern Ukraine.

Discerning Putin's intentions at this point is a far from easy business as the

Russian leader was keeping his cards close to his chest, even in his dealings with his closest advisors. There is considerable dispute among observers about how Putin runs his government and how key decisions are made. One view has him an absolute ruler, who makes all key decisions himself and is surrounded by sycophantic aides who just do his bidding. At the other end of the spectrum, Putin is portrayed as indecisive leader who sits atop a regime of quarrelling oligarchs, bureaucrats, military commanders and intelligence chiefs. These power brokers spend their time manoeuvring events and facts in such a way that Putin has little option but doing what they want. It is not impossible that both views are correct or that Putin operates in different ways depending on the issues or personalities involved.

There are conflicting accounts on how key decisions were made and when during those fateful days in the spring and summer of 2014. Ukrainian and Western accounts paint the picture of Putin as an evil mastermind or super-villain who was rolling out a pre-prepared master plan for the conquest of the Donbass from April 2014 onwards. Accounts from Kremlin insiders and pro-Russian figures in the Donbass describe a confused and less linear decision-making process on the Russian side. Since 2014 several recordings of eavesdropped telephone conversations between pro-Russian figures in the Donbass and their allies in Russia have been made public and they provide some useful context and background. By building up a detailed timeline for actual Russian troop movements and military actions, it is also possible to validate some of the theories about Kremlin decision-making.

Several Kremlin insiders told the respected Russian journalist and commentator, Mikhail Zygar, that in April 2014 Putin had not made up his mind about the way forward in Ukraine. The Russian President was determined to try to retain Russian influence over its neighbour but there seemed no obvious way to do this. (6) After the new government came to power in Kiev in March and the US and the European Union offered it political and economic support there seemed little prospect of re-installing Yanukovych or a similar pro-Russian figure as President. Another device would be needed to gain influence on Kiev. Moscow retained strong economic leverage because of Ukraine's dependence on Russian natural gas supplies to heat homes and fire the country's industry.

To get more influence over Kiev, the Kremlin looked to stir up trouble in the Donbass around the cities of Donetsk, Luhansk and Kharkov. This industrial or "rust belt" region had a majority of Russian speakers and it was a stronghold of the recently ousted Viktor Yanukovych. Several high profile Russian or pro-Russian Ukrainian oligarchs controlled major business interests in the region and they feared the new government in Kiev could soon move against them. Russian nationalist politicians and media commentators were also becoming increasingly vocal, complaining that Russian speakers in the Donbass needed protection from what they called the "anarchy" in Kiev. There was also considerable political and social instability in the Donbass as the population tried to work out how their region would be ruled.

How to turn this unrest to Moscow's advantage was the issue. Putin appeared not to be keen on a direct invasion and occupation, with the financial costs, military risks and diplomatic fall-out that would follow. A more discreet approach was needed.

Putin made comments in public and private at this time, to the effect that the Russian speakers in Ukraine would be helped by Moscow but they had to publicly ask for it. This was a repeat of the power play at the Simferopol parliament in February 2014, where Moscow used its troops and political influence to put pro-Moscow politicians in charge. Repeating that exercise in the Donbass was a more difficult proposition. There were no Russian troops garrisoned in the Donbass and established pro-Russian political groups in the region were in disarray because of the downfall and discrediting of Yanukovych. There were numerous grass roots pro-Russian groups across the Donbass but many of these were outside Moscow's control. The unpredictability and nationalist fervour of these groups meant that at several occasions over the coming months, Moscow would take action to rein them in.

The pitiful resistance put up by the Ukrainian military on Crimea convinced many in the Kremlin and in pro-Russian groups in the Donbass that the Kiev government would not be able to summon up the will to use force to regain control of eastern Ukraine. There was also a feeling among several Kremlin figures that the loss of the Donbass would lead to the total collapse of the Kiev government.

As events unfolded over the next three months, the situation in Ukraine would become a major international crisis, which attracted huge attention from the world's media. Soon there were hundreds of international journalists on the ground in the eastern Ukraine and on the Russian side of the border. There were many more local journalists watching and reporting on events for Ukrainian and Russian media outlets. Adding to the torrent of information, social-media posts, images and video footage from the crisis zone were uploaded in considerable quantities by ordinary people who were observing events around them. The Donbass crisis soon became one of the most reported events in the world.

All the participants in the crisis were very aware that almost everything they did would be observed. Militia commanders and politicians from across the Donbass became media celebrities as they routinely held press conferences and allowed journalists to observe their daily activities in a bid to boost their popularity among their supporters. This meant even minor events were escalated into major crises. The ludicrous extent of this was exposed when a Ukrainian army convoy was blockaded by a pro-Russian crowd in the Donbass during April. As a couple of dozen civilians tried to drag the Ukrainian soldiers from their troop carriers, a crowd of journalists, photographers and people with mobile phone could be seen in the background of video footage filming the proceedings. The crowds of observers seemed to outnumber the actual participants, creating the impression that this was just a "made for television" moment.

If the pro-Russian separatists were embarked on some sort of secret or covert operation it not carried out in a very professional manner. Within days of the start of the uprising across the Donbass, its leader's cell phone conversations were routinely hacked by the Ukrainian security agency, the SBU, and recordings were handed over to the international media. Yet time and again over the next four months the separatist leaders repeatedly discussed the most sensitive information over the same cell phones. These conversations regularly ended up in the media. It was as if the separatists did not care or were too stupid to notice. (7)

Even when the two sides started shooting at each other at the end of April, the media circus continued with both sides still allowing international journalists to observe events relatively uninterrupted. As the Donbass war started to became more violent and dangerous in June and into July, international journalists were less willing to venture close to the frontlines. In these circumstances, local journalists, cameramen and social media operatives took centre stage. Their content became a new theatre of war, as rival narratives were pumped online by digital warriors. This was a new phenomenon that would soon have major geo-political implications. Russian government-funded news organisations, such as Russia Today (now RT) and Sputnik, took centre stage in the Kremlin's information strategy, promulgating its view of the conflict. For the first time in a major crisis, the established international and Western news organisations had rivals that produced high quality video footage of events that they did not have access to. The Western news media appeared to be just as wrong-footed by the Donbass crisis, as the governments in London, Berlin, Paris and Washington. It added to the impression that the Kremlin was setting the agenda - politically, diplomatically and militarily.

While all the players in the Donbass crisis were vying for "information advantage" no one had anything that could defined as "control" of events, both on the ground or in the virtual realm. There was everything to play for in this anarchic and ungoverned space that was the Donbass in spring 2014.

The first moves to create new facts on the ground in the Donbass got underway in early April 2014. This was a very much an "outsourced" or "sub-contracted" operation, in which pro-Russian oligarchs across the Donbass were the key players. Scores of the Russian self-defence militia fighters who had played a minor role in the Crimea operation started to move to the Donbass, where they linked up with private security operatives in the pay of pro-Moscow oligarchs and former Yanukovych-era police officers. Pro-Russian political groups funded by the oligarchs then sprung into action.

All across the Donbass during April 2014 there were pro-Russian demonstrations outside government buildings and police stations. On 6th April the first of these buildings was seized when the Ukraine security service, SBU, headquarters in Luhansk was overrun by demonstrators. The regional government building in Donestk was seized later that day, followed by a declaration of independence by the so-called People's Republic of Donetsk. (8) There were unsuccessful attempts to seize government buildings, security headquarters and television stations in Mykolayiv, Donetsk and Kharkov but these were rebuffed by police personnel who stayed loyal to Kiev.

A week later another wave of seizures was launched with some two dozen police, security and government buildings being captured in a series of raids by groups of heavily armed men. Simultaneously crowds of civilians were mobilised to blockade Ukrainian military bases and harass government army convoys trying to move around separatist-controlled areas.

News and social-media imagery from across the crisis zone suggests that the paramilitary groups were led and organised by a small number of highly trained and well equipped combat soldiers. Videos of assaults on police stations in both Sloviansk and Kramatorsk, showed groups of between 10 and 15 well-armed men wearing military uniforms, operating in a co-ordinated manner, using close-quarter combat tactics. (9) Both groups apparently arrived at their objectives in buses, painted in military style colour schemes. The Sloviansk assault team used their green-painted minibus to pull off the metal grill on a window to gain access to the police station. Another team led by several heavily armed and well-trained combat troops that assaulted Kramatorsk police station using very professional-looking tactics.(10)

Social-media imagery of one of the Sloviansk attackers appeared to indicate that he was also present in Crimea in March during an operation to capture Ukrainian soldiers. Images allegedly taken in Sloviansk on 12th April showed the man had the same style of uniform, webbing and silenced sniper rifle as the man photographed by the French AFP news agency in Simferopol on 18th March. (11)

The Ukrainians and Western governments accused Moscow of being behind the seizures. Putin described the new claims as "nonsense" during a press conference on 17th April but he did admit Russian troops has assisted local "self-defence forces" during the occupation of Crimea that began on 27th February. (12)

The Ukrainian government consistently claimed their country had been a target for infiltration by operatives of the Russian state intelligence agency, the FSB, and the Russian General Staff's intelligence branch, the GRU, since the start of the Crimea crisis. In April 2014, Kiev's security service, the SBU, claimed to have arrested 14 Russian operatives and published a series of photographs on its website of arms caches, lists of local contacts, forged documents, credit cards and fake IDs. In one case it posted a copy of one of its prisoners social media profile, showing her posing in a military uniform with sniper rifles. (13)

The most compelling evidence Kiev revealed were two sets of recordings of telephone conversations between Russian operatives in the separatist stronghold of Sloviansk and men described as their controllers in Moscow. Although they were not independently verified, some aspects gave the tapes credibility. Those operatives, who all have melodramatic code names, such as "Shooter", "Nose" and "Eagle", spoke with distinctive Russian accents and also discussed events that had then not been in the public domain, such as the identity of

Ukrainian intelligence personnel killed and wounded in an ambush on 13th April. Also, they discussed the political narrative that local pro-Russian spokesmen should promulgate in media interviews. (14)

On the ground in eastern Ukraine, evidence painted a picture of collusion between pro-Moscow protestors, paramilitaries and private security companies linked to political supporters of the Yanukovych.

Several local and international journalists who visited towns around Donetsk controlled by the paramilitaries witnessed shadowy figures - again dubbed 'little green men' - in smart camouflage uniforms directing assaults on government buildings, organising defences and blockading Ukrainian military convoys. They appeared to be wearing similar uniforms to the assault teams that overran police stations in Sloviansk and Kramatorsk on 12th April. A number of these men confirmed to at least two British journalists that they were Russians, who were involved in military operations on Crimea. (15)

Photographs of 'signature' Russian weapons, including AK-100 series assault rifles, also appeared in eastern Ukraine. These newly introduced weapons, which had not been recorded as being exported by Russia, suggest that either Moscow's had men on the ground or it was directly supplying arms to the paramilitary fighters. (16)

Ukrainian SBU security service Spetsnaz troops south of the occupied town of Sloviansk were involved in a fire-fight with armed men on 13th April which left one SBU officer dead and five wounded. After the armed men who fired on the troops fled, local media reporters visited the scene and they identified the men's SUV as being registered to Ukraine's largest security company, Vayir-2000. A Ukraine member of parliament subsequently linked the company's owner, Yevgeniy Lykhozhon, to Volodymyr Sivkovych, who was deputy secretary of the National Security and Defence Council under the former PresidentYanukovych. The company's website said Lykhozhon was a member of Coordinating Council at the Ministry of Internal Affairs of Ukraine during the former President's time in office. (17)

A man, later identified as Igor Bezler, was filmed posing as a self-proclaimed "Russian colonel" addressing policemen who had just defected to the pro-Moscow cause in Kramantorsk on 13th April. The Ukrainians accused him of being a Russian GRU officer. (18)

In nearby Sloviansk, another Russian declared himself as the commander of the region's self defence unit. This man soon shot to world-wide fame as Igor Strelkov, which was a pun on the Russian translation of his surname. He soon became known as "The Shooter". Journalists later broke his cover and identified him as Igor Girkin, as former Russian FSB officer with links to Russian nationalist politicians, military re-enacting groups and Ukrainian oligarchs. He was subsequently identified as a security officer for a pro-Yanukovych politician from Donetsk. The Ukrainian security service accused Strelkov as being an operative of the Russian GRU but as the Donbass crisis escalated his links to Moscow got more strained. (19)

The picture that emerged from eastern Ukraine was of Russian operatives, supported by their close political and business allies in the region providing strategic direction and co-ordination of the campaign against the Kiev government. The majority of the rank-and-file fighters and protestors in the towns seized by pro-Russian forces appeared to be local men and they had a significant level of support from local people - who were providing food, building barricades and assisting in mass blockades of Ukrainian army columns and bases. However, at key moments in the crisis Moscow's men appear to have made decisive interventions.

On the ground in eastern Ukraine, the pro-Russian operatives did not appear to be making much effort to hide their identities, apart from donning balaclavas. Even during the 12th April police station assaults, Russian media teams were invited to witness the events. The reasons for this appeared to be psychological and it seemed to have a significant impact. First of all, it sent a message to Moscow's supporters inside Ukraine that they had Russia's backing, to motivate them to continue with their campaign. Secondly, it demoralised hapless policemen and soldiers loyal to Kiev by suggesting that they were now facing elite Russian troops and they would be the next target. For audiences in Russia, it put Moscow's seal on another "successful" intervention to help Russian speakers under threat; while in the West it reinforced the perception that eastern Ukraine was already a lost cause so it was not worth doing anything to help Kiev. Moscow's local allies were determined to keep Kiev's troops and police at bay long enough to allow the self-declared People's Republic of Donetsk to successfully hold its referendum on independence from Ukraine in May. (20)

Ukrainian army and security forces struggled to co-ordinate and launch a coherent response to the uprising by armed pro-Russian paramilitary groups. After the armed paramilitaries began seizing police, security and regional government buildings across the Donetsk region in eastern Ukraine on 12th April, large crowds of civilians began blockading and harassing Ukrainian army convoys. Reports were also emerging of defections of police units and commanders to the pro-Russia groups. (21)

Ukraine's acting President, Oleksandr Turchynov. and interior minister. Arsen Avakov, announced on 13th April that "anti-terrorist operations" against the armed groups had begun. Ukrainian army aviation Mil Mi-24s and Mi-8 helicopters were filmed flying over the city of Sloviansk later that day in a show of strength. (22) The Ukrainian ministry of interior then announced the mobilisation of a battalion of the newly formed National Guard to be dispatched to the crisis region to bolster the offensive.

When the separatists first began seizing state buildings across the east of the country on 6th April it prompted the Ukrainian army to begin reinforcing its 25th Airborne Brigade, which had been positioned around Donetsk since mid March. An artillery battalion equipped with 152mm D-20 towed howitzers arrived by road in Donetsk on 9th April. That day social media footage was also posted showing a column of BMD-2 armoured vehicles of the airborne brigade attempting to drive into Donetsk being blocked by angry civilians. (23)

These blockades escalated after the armed seizure of Sloviansk with a convoy of National Guard troops being overwhelmed on 12th April near Artemovsk and at least one lorry looted of a quantity of small arms. Social-media footage showed the soldiers voluntarily handing over AK-47s and other weapons to civilians who then loaded them into cars. The following day, another convoy was blockaded and three lorries seized, including one carrying at least 48 122mm Grad rockets. Social media imagery showed armed paramilitaries inspecting the vehicles. (24)

The loyalty of police units in eastern Ukraine was also being tested by the uprising, with the chief of police in Donetsk resigning and handing over his police station to a crowd of protestors on 12th April. Later that day, international media visited the town of Izjum and found many police officers sporting St George ribbons, which had been worn by pro-Russian paramilitaries in the Donetsk and Crimea regions. (25)

A more determined Ukrainian operation against the separatists got underway on the afternoon of 15th April. A small Ukrainian force flew to an abandoned airbase at Kramatorsk in two Mil Mi-8 transport helicopters and meet no initial armed resistance. (26) The assault force was made up of the interior ministry's Omega Spetsnaz battalion and the SBU's Alpha Group. Both units were manned by professional personnel and they were expected to put up more resistance than the locally recruited conscripts serving in army units elsewhere in the Donbass. A crowd of some 150 local civilians and armed paramilitaries gathered after the helicopters landed. This incident ended in a scuffle and three people, at least one of whom was armed, were shot and wounded by Ukraine troops.

The Ukrainian counter-offensive suffered a major setback on 16th April when two columns of troops from the 25th Airborne Brigade were blockaded by pro-Russian civilians and armed men. These incidents culminated in six BMD-2 armoured vehicles being surrendered by the Ukrainian troops and the other column of 14 vehicles retreated after handing over its ammunition to the civilians. (27)

By the third week in April, the rebel fighters and their supporters had seized control of at least 10 towns and cities across the Donetsk region. They set up a ring of checkpoints around the territory they controlled and there were daily skirmishes with troops and police loyal to Kiev. These incidents became increasing violent, particularly around Slavyansk and the neighbouring town of Kramatorsk. Here separatist fighters had begun to use heavy weapons, including mortars and crew-served machine guns, according to the Ukrainian government. The Ukrainian military decided to launch a major operation against the towns, which they identified as being the epicentre of the resistance. When the Ukrainians advanced, supported by Mi-24 attack helicopters firing rockets and cannons, they were met by fierce resistance and two of the gunships were shot down by shoulder-launched man-portable surface-to-air missiles, also known as MANPADs. Two crew members were killed and one of the pilots was captured to be paraded in front of television news crews. (28)

The battle continued for several days and the Ukrainian Ministry of Defence confirmed that a Mi-24 gunship was badly damaged on 5th May, reporting that it had been hit by heavy machine gun fire. The crew were reported to be unhurt. (29)

Social media footage of one of these engagements appeared to show the use of a 9K310 Igla-1 or 9K38 Igla MANPAD. The Kiev government claimed the use of MANPADs and other heavy weapons was a sign that the separatists were receiving military support from Russia. (30)

At this time, Strelkov and other rebel leaders were recorded in hacked telephone calls to their allies in Moscow repeatedly criticising Putin for not sending troops to fight off the Ukrainians. The role of the Russian military and intelligence agencies in support the rebels in the Donbass was a source of considerable controversy. Despite denials from Moscow that no Russian arms or troops crossed into Ukraine it seems pretty clear that the Kremlin approved escalating support from late April onwards.

During the early days of the conflict there were probably not more than a few dozen Russian military specialists who crossed the border to operate the MANPADs and get some idea of what was going on. Imagery of Russian Spetsnaz soldiers and reconnaissance troops from regular units in the Donbass in May was posted on Russian social media networks later in 2014 and picked up by Ukrainian cyber activists. During this period media reports started to emerge of small convoys of trucks and minibuses loaded with arms moving via back roads across the border from Russia into separatist-held areas. (31)

Russian media was covering the conflict in the Donbass extensively and the tone was overwhelmingly sympathetic, mirroring Kremlin lines about the Kiev government being illegitimate and run by pro-Nazi groups. The view from inside the Kremlin was rather more complicated. While Putin and his senior aides did not want to see the Ukrainian government reclaim control of the Donbass - hence the small-scale arms supplies and technical support - it seems they were not convinced that the various pro-Russian political groups and militia bands were fully following the Kremlin line. In particular, Strelkov and other militia leaders repeatedly, and in public, called for the Donbass to be incorporated into Russia, just like Crimea. Putin was not ready to do that so in May he turned to his trusted fixer, Vladislav Surkov, to bring the rag-tag collection of self-appointed political leaders and administrators in Donetsk under control. This was a forlorn hope.

The city, along with nearby Luhansk, was in anarchy. The militia fighters were out of control and operated their own street justice, including imprisoning Kiev supporters and murdering several of them. The oligarchs who had funded several of these groups and militias were getting worried that the escalating war could devastate their property. The most famous Donbass oligarch, Rinat Akhmetov, fled Donetsk in May for Kiev. His mansion was destroyed in the fighting and several of his companies were subsequently seized by separatists. The two separatist states, the People's Republic of Donetsk (DNR) and its twin, the People's Republic of Luhansk (LNR), had a Ruritanian feel about them with all their political office holders and officials being self-appointed. Surkov attempted to clear out many of those who were not following the Moscow line, including drafting in a Russian-born journalist and public relations executive, Alexander Borodai, to be the prime minister of the DNR.

Many of the hard-line nationalists in Donetsk instinctively suspected Surkov of wanting to sell them out as part of a deal between Moscow and Kiev because of his regular visits to negotiate with the Ukrainian President. Their suspicions ultimately proved to be correct as Putin never incorporated the Donbass into Russia, leaving it in political and diplomatic limbo as only one country, the breakaway Georgian region of South Ossetia, ever recognised the DNR and LNR. Not even Russia formally recognised them as independent countries.

Strelkov, who now styled himself as the "DNR defence minister", and his militia commanders proved equally hard to control. He staged a series of bombastic press conferences in which he boasted of turning Donetsk into a new Stalingrad. Moscow's displeasure with Streklov and his associates would become clear later in the summer when they fled the Donbass after the arrival of Russian regular troops. Their services were no longer required.

In Russia, popular support for the separatists was widespread thanks to dramatic media reports from the battlefields in the Donbass. Strelkov and other militia leaders were media celebrities so they could not immediately be purged. With fighting escalating each day it was not the time for the Kremlin to abandon the militia groups fighting the Ukrainians. The militias were the main leverage Putin had over the Ukrainians, even if subsequently they could be "traded away" as part of any deal with Kiev. This was cynical power politics at it worst.

On 22nd May later separatists mounted four co-ordinated attacks across the east, each involving groups of between 100 and 200 fighters. The most successful attack overwhelmed a Ukrainian checkpoint, south of Donetsk, killing 13 and wounding 33 Ukrainian soldiers. Less than 24 hours later, the separatist Vostok or 'East' Battalion attacked and routed the Ukrainian National Guard Donbas Battalion. The Ukrainians suffered five dead, 20 wounded and lost an unconfirmed number of prisoners, as well as abandoning at least one BMP armoured vehicle. The Vostok Battalion was made up of Russian Spetsnaz veterans of the Chechen war and local men from Donetsk city and would be one of the most high-profile rebel units over the next few months. (32)

An audacious attempt by more than 200 rebel fighters of the Vostok Battalion to seize Donetsk airport sparked fighting that eventually escalated to involve fixed -wing air strikes and a helicopter-borne landing by Ukrainian paratroopers. The fighters occupied the terminal building at Sergei Prokofiev International Airport in the early hours of 26th May to try to pre-empt the arrival of the recently elected Ukrainian President, Petro Poroshenko, on a visit to the war-torn east of the country. (33) He subsequently, vowed to continue the "anti-terrorist operation" against rebel fighters in Donetsk and Luhansk regions as well as offering to open talks to resolve the crisis with President Putin.

By the early afternoon of 26th May a force of five Mil Mi-8 transport and three Mi-24 attack helicopters had delivered a ground assault force to begin an operation to clear the airport of rebels. Two Ukrainian Sukhoi Su-25s carried out rocket attacks on rebel positions and the Mi-24s strafed targets with their cannons. A MiG-29 fighter was also filmed by news media flying over the airport. Fighting continued during the night and by the morning of 27th May the Ukrainian Interior Ministry claimed their troops had regained control of the main airport buildings.

International media representatives confirmed that the main airport buildings were in Ukrainian hands, although there were continuing reports of fighting elsewhere across Donetsk city. News media footage of the aftermath of the battle showed at least two Kamaz trucks of the Vostock Battalion riddled with bullets and surrounded by pools of blood in the airport car park. A rebel spokesman in Donetsk claimed that more than 30 of their fighters had been killed during the battle at the airport.

The Ukrainian seizure of Dontesk airport set in train a further expansion of Russian military aid through June and into July, as fighting continued to escalate. Heavier weapons started be spotted moving across and it was becoming increasingly difficult for the Kremlin to deny the accusations it was running a secret weapons pipeline.

A convoy of four new-looking BM-21 multiple launch rocket launchers were photographed weaving through the traffic on the outskirts of Luhansk city on 10th June. The weapons looked as if they had been well maintained with clean canvas covering their rockets launch rails. Interestingly, they sported the markings of the Russian Ground Forces 18th Motor Rifle Brigade. (34)

Early in July, a brand new-looking 9K35 Strela-10 self-propelled surface to air missile (SAM) launcher vehicles was photographed in the centre of Donetsk city by the Reuters news agency. Another of these vehicles was filmed with separatists south of the city a few days later. The improvements in the separatists' air-defence capability was demonstrated in June when Ukrainian aircraft, including one Antonov An-26 and a Ilyushin Il-76, were shot down near Luhansk airport by missiles, with the loss of nearly 50 crew and passengers. The rebels were trying to cut off the Ukrainian garrison at Luhansk from outside support. (35)

The Ukrainian government decided to launch a major operation in early July to clear out the separatists from the Donbass. This was to be the biggest offensive yet by Kiev's army with tanks, artillery and other heavy weapons massed around rebel enclaves. Units of the newly formed Ukrainian National Guard joined the operation to help out the regular military.

The chaotic and poorly armed separatist militia groups were unable to hold back the Ukrainian tank columns. By mid July, Donetsk and Luhansk were increasingly isolated and the Ukrainians were threatening to cut their supply routes to the Russian border. In response, the arms pipeline was opened wider to allow tanks and artillery to flow across.

In the first week of July, Girkin and Borodai visited Moscow to try to drum up more aid for their revolution. When Borodai returned to Donetsk on 10th July, he told a press conference, "I was [in Moscow] for political consultations, which, in my opinion, went fairly successful. With respect to the people I met, I will certainly not reveal that. This secret, if you will, belongs to the area of military intelligence. However, I consider these consultations to be very successful, and I am very much counting on the assistance of the Russian Federation in the nearest possible future." (36)

It appears that Moscow still had cold feet and a few days later Borodai telephoned Putin's senior advisor, Surkov, to try to free up the extra military assistance. The conversation was taped by the Ukrainian intelligence agency, the SBU, and subsequently released as part of the investigation in to the downing of Malaysian Airlines flight MH17. Surkov told his man in Donetsk, "So, I had a conversation with fellows back home, well, you know, the ones who are in charge of this whole military story. And they said: "Yes, we're up to speed on everything don't worry, we're aware," but steps that will turn the tide... I have already spoken much about it back there: "...we understand, we're preparing..." But honestly, Sasha, I can't really vouch that those answers can be relied upon. Because although I know all of them very well, there's no... to trust them to whether or not they're preparing something." (37)

Borodai was not impressed, saying, "Yes, I completely understand that. We've managed to hold out for a week already – it's hard, but we can hold out some more." Surkov told him to hold on, saying, "Well, yes Sasha, that's about what you'll have to try to do."

The investigative website Bellingcat, revealed that a high level meeting between DNR and LNR military commanders and senior representatives of the Russian military agency, the GRU, took place in the town of Krasnodon on 14th July to organise the transfer of more arms and equipment from Russia. (38) By 15th July the problems were overcome and a convoy of several T-64 main battle tanks, three 2S1 122mm self-propelled guns and one BTR wheeled armoured personnel carrier was filmed by civilians near Luhansk as it moved in broad daylight from the direction of the Russian border and then headed westwards towards Donetsk city. (39) The vehicles did not carry any Ukrainian army markings and looked as if they had just been driven out of a storage depot, reinforcing the impression that they had come from a Russian military stockpile.

The Ukrainian offensive continued through early July with strong air support from Sukhoi Su-25 ground attack jets, which were engaged by separatist's missile teams who shot down two of the jets. These attacks shocked the separatist leaders and they stepped up their calls to allies in Russia for more help to counter Ukrainian airpower. Dutch investigators into the MH17 crash revealed another transcript of a phone call from a pro-Russian militia commander to a contact in Russia on 16th July, claiming the Ukrainian air strikes were threatening to break the morale of this troops. (40)

This led on 17th July to a low loader being sent across the border carrying a Russian Ground Forces 9K37 Buk surface to air missile (SAM) system. It weaved its way through separatist-held territory to a site to the south east of Donetsk, where the weapon system was activated. Later that day its crew detected a large aircraft flying high and heading towards Luhansk airport. It appeared that another Ukrainian supply mission was underway so the Buk crew prepared their missile and fired. Separatist leaders initially boasted about shooting down another Ukrainian aircraft but the missile crew had made a tragic error and engaged the Malaysian Airways Boeing 777, flight number MH17. It detonated in front of the jet's cockpit and sent it heading earthwards. All of MH17's 283 passengers and 15 crew died. (41)

The result was understandable outrage across much of the world. The pro-Russian separatists became international pariahs. The Russians were accused of supplying the missile used in the attack. Rather than own up to the attack and admit it was a accident caused by the fog of war, the Kremlin ordered everyone involved to deny it had anything to do with Russia or the separatists. Putin was not willing to own up to the arms pipeline as the Kremlin was still claiming the separatists were just local people who were defending themselves. While the incident was given great prominence in the West, on the ground in Donbass the war continued as if little had changed.

Chapter 4
The Russian Army Rolls

"If nothing changes in military terms, we won't last two weeks," commented Donetsk People's Republic prime minister Alexander Borodei in late July 2014 to the Russian oligarch, Konstantin Malofeev, who had been funding rebel fighters in the Donbass. The telephone conversation was recorded by the Ukrainian SBU intelligence agency and then revealed to the Kiev media. (1)

The separatist enclaves in Donetsk and Luhansk were in a precarious position in July 2014 and this was soon recognised in Moscow. President Putin's misgivings about the separatist political leaders were put to one side. As far as the Russian leader was concerned, he was not going to oversee the defeat of pro-Russian groups in the Donbass. This would boost the Kiev government just at the time he wanted it weakened. The half-hearted approach of out-sourcing the war in the Donbass to the separatist militias was not working and Putin soon had to bite the bullet and commit Russian regular armed forces to the battle. Years later, the Kremlin still has not publicly acknowledged the role played by Russian troops in the Donbass conflict. This is perhaps one of the Kremlin's worst kept secrets. The Russian journalist, Mikhail Zygar, recounts how in September 2014 the German Chancellor, Angela Merkel, telephoned Putin to complain about the presence of his troops in the Donbass. "Do Russian soldiers always go on holiday with weapons and military equipment?" she exclaimed. "Oh, there's so much corruption in Russia you know. They must have stolen it from warehouses along the way," answered Putin without batting an eyelid. Merkel hung up. (2)

From July 2014 onwards, the role of Russian regular troops in the Donbass escalated but the Kremlin still tried to hide their role. Evidence of Russian involvement in the Donbass is overwhelming. Scores of international journalists recounted sighting Russian troops in the Donbass or heading towards the border. Local people in the Donbass immediately identified them as Russians rather than local Russian speakers. These troops drove in Russian vehicles, which sported the markings of Russian Ground Force, Airborne Forces and Naval Infantry/Coastal Forces units, wore Russian uniforms and carried weapons only used by the Russian military.

Commercial satellite images showed the location of Russian army camps close to the border with Ukraine. Some of the most compelling evidence of Russian involvement came from Moscow's soldiers themselves. Like most Russians of their generation, these young men just could not resist posting photographs of what they were doing on the VK social-media network, showing them on duty in field camps near Rostov-on-Don and then inside Ukraine. Many of these photographs were geolocated with position data enabling the movements of soldiers to be tracked to within a few metres. These soldiers then posed for "selfie" photographs in front of recognisable landmarks and road signs in the Donbass.

During the summer of 2014, Russian civilians in the countryside around Rostov began posting online imagery of Russian rocket launchers firing into Ukraine. Then more Russians were filmed driving around the Donbass in large convoys. When Russian soldiers started to be killed, wounded and captured in fighting the game was up for Moscow's denials of Russian involvement. The pretence became even more difficult to sustain when Russian generals turned up to ceasefire talks with the Ukrainians and the Organisation for Security and Co-operation in Europe (OSCE) in September and October 2014 to speak on behalf of the separatist militias.

Since the war, more and more information has come to light about Russian involvement, as a stream of Moscow's soldiers have been awarded medals and other honours for their bravery in the fighting in the Donbass. Perhaps the most telling evidence of Russian military involvement is the contrast between the shambolic and chaotic war run by the separatist militias between May and July 2014 with the professional, well organised and ruthless operation that unfolded in August and September 2014. The war in the Donbass had entered a new and more deadly phase.

The retreat of separatist forces led by Igor Strelkov from the besieged town Sloviansk on 5th July set in train the escalation of the conflict. Ukrainian columns were pressing hard to surround the separatists inside Dontesk and Luhansk cities. Across the border in Rostov-on-Don, in the Southern Military District headquarters, senior Russian officers were making the necessary plans for their troops to intervene. First the troops based in the field camps at Nonochekassk, to the north of Rostov-on-Don, and at Golovinka to the west of the city, would have to be brought up to full combat readiness. One by one the Russian battalion tactical groups (BTGs) started to move out of the field camps to take up positions in a series of assembly areas some five or six kilometres from the Ukrainian border. These were hidden away in large forests in a bid to protect them from satellite surveillance. Camouflage nets were erected over vehicles and artillery weapons to further confuse observers.

If this force was to go into battle, then an operational or field command structure would be needed. This mission was too complex and big to be run by telephone from the headquarters of the Southern Military District in downtown Rostov.

Commercial satellite imagery from late July detected a large field headquarters hidden under camouflage netting the village of Malaya Kamenka, some six kilometres from Ukraine. A Mil Mi-8 could be seen parked in the field, further giving away the game that this was an important site.

Ukrainian intelligence subsequently identified Major General Andrey Gurulev as the commander of Russian ground forces operating inside Ukraine in the summer of 2014. He was then the commander of the 58th Combined Arms Army based in the Northern Caucasus at Vladikavkaz; but in the run-up to the 2014 conflict he was implicated in a public scandal for ordering conscripts to do building work on his home. State prosecutors were investigating him for abusing his rank. After the war in the Donbass he was promoted to lieutenant general and assigned to a new high profile job as deputy commander in the Southern Military District headquarters, indicating he was no longer in disgrace. This was most likely as a result of his combat successes. (3)

The assignment of the 58th Army's headquarters to run the war in the Donbass was not the only indicator that the Russian military was preparing for war. The Southern Military District received additional reinforcement and specialist capabilities to allow it to intervene in the Donbass.

Although several thousand Russian soldiers were already in field camps to the north and west of Rostov-on-Don in the early summer of 2014, these were not the most suitable, trained or equipped units to take on the Ukrainian army in a stand-up fight. Most significantly, six BTG of professional paratroopers drawn from airborne or air assault units were dispatched to join the troop build-up. These were the most highly trained and motivated Russian combat units and it was not surprising the Russian General Staff wanted them to be ready to lead any operation in the Donbass.

The Russian air force dispatched a helicopter group, with six Mil-8 transports and two Mi-24 gunship helicopters, to Milerovo airbase to the east of the Donbass to stand ready to support the ground forces, in attack, troop movement or casualty-evacuation roles. Satellite imagery of Milerovo airbase from the summer revealed the helicopters, along with the presence of Israeli-designed but Russian-assembled Forpost unmanned aerial vehicles. These drones were able to transmit live video imagery of targets back to ground stations, up to 300 kilometres away, putting all of the Donbass in range of the system. One of the drones could be clearly seen in satellite imagery parked on the Milerovo ramp near the helicopters.

Another Forpost detachment was also detected in satellite imagery at Taganrog airbase to the west of Rostov-on-Don, bringing even more of Ukrainian territory in range and potentially doubling the surveillance coverage available to Russian commanders. Two Forposts would be lost over the Donbass in the coming months and their distinctive remains, including Israel Aeropsace Industries manufacturers' plates, would be photographed by the Ukrainian media.

The Russian 4th Air and Air Defence Forces Command had more than 200 combat aircraft and helicopters based at more than a dozen airfields across southern Russia so it did not really require significant reinforcements to take on the Ukrainian air force. However, its aircraft were not the most modern in the Russian inventory so seven Su-30SM fighters were dispatched to Primorsko airbase to the south of Rostov-on-Don to bolster its air-combat capability.

With so many troops gathering in field camps across around Rostov-on-Don, Russian commanders wanted to protect them from Ukrainian air attack so tactical air defence batteries were moved to the region to set up a "surface-to-air missile umbrella".

Even before most of these reinforcements and additional capabilities were in place the Russian military began intervening across the border to help the separatist militias. Telephone conversations between militia commanders and their contacts across the border in Russia were hacked by the Ukrainian SBU and subsequently passed to Dutch prosecutors investigating the downing of Malaysian Airlines flight MH17. (4) The Ukrainians apparently tapped into the mobile phone network across the Donbass to monitor the conversations of the separatist leaders. The ease with which the Ukrainians were able to hack into the high-level conversations of the separatists and their contacts in Russia suggests they either didn't care having the communications monitored or were too careless to realise about their communications were compromised.

In these conversations it emerged that the requests for artillery and rocket fire were co-ordinated by the self-declared DNR defence minister Igor Strelkov, who collated calls for help from his unit commanders. Strelkov then telephoned a contact in the Russian military with the target co-ordinates. One on occasion, Strelkov was recorded organising a Russian artillery fire mission against a Ukrainian unit positioned on a hill top near the village of Dibrivka, some three kilometres from the Russian border. (5)

Russian artillery commanders did not just fire blind against the map co-ordinates provided by the separatists but systematically carried out their own aerial surveillance activity to confirm what their guns and rockets were firing at.

At this point a string of Ukrainian border guard posts were in still in place at road crossing points from the Donbass into Russia. They were supported by some two dozen Ukrainian army forward operating bases several kilometres back from the border. Each base contained a Ukrainian army battalion or companies and they launched regular patrols from these bases to try to observe and then close down the separatists' supply lines.

At the start of July, these Ukrainian army units started to see mini-unmanned aerial vehicles flying over their bases. These appeared to be little more than remote-control model aircraft but the Ukrainians soon came to fear these drones. The Ukrainian army did not try to camouflage their bases as they wanted to show off their presence to local people to reassure them that Kiev was not giving up any land to the separatists. So it was not very difficult for the Russian drone operators to find and then identify the Ukrainian bases. Just over the border, Russian artillery batteries had moved out of their field camps to firing positions in fields and were waiting for the order to open fire.

The first significant fire mission took place in the early hours of 11th July when a barrage of BM-21 rockets struck the Ukrainian camp on a hillside outside the Zelenopillya village. In the space of a few minutes the camp was transformed into an inferno as vehicles and ammunition were consumed by fire across an area of some 450 metres by 150 metres, setting off a string of secondary explosions. Red-hot shrapnel tore through the unit's tents leaving them shredded. As the fires died down, some 30 soldiers were dead and more than 100 were wounded. Almost every T-64 tank, BTR armoured personnel carrier and truck caught in the strike zone was destroyed or badly damaged. The survivors were left shell-shocked and could do little but try to tend to their wounded comrades. The 1st Battalion of the Ukrainian 79th Air Assault Brigade was effectively destroyed as a fighting unit.

Further attacks unfolded over the next two weeks as half a dozen Ukrainian bases were targeted in the south east corner of the Donbass with more Russian rocket and conventional artillery fire. Satellite imagery showed fields around the Ukrainian positions cratered with hundreds of shell and rocket craters. The Ukrainians soon realised it was very unhealthy to stay inside their fixed bases and started to move out into the countryside.

An artillery strike on Sverdlovsk on 25th July caught the Ukrainian 72nd Motorised Brigade in its base. This left more than half a dozen BMP-2 infantry fighting vehicles and BM-21 rocket launchers as burning wrecks.

A video of one of these artillery and rocket attacks was subsequently posted online by a Russian civilian living near the village of Gukovo. It showed a battery of BM-21s launching salvos of rockets westwards into Ukraine. Satellite imagery from the location showed that during July and August the Russian military progressively reinforced the site at Gukovo, which dominated the south east of the Donbass. Earth revetments for artillery pieces and rocket launchers were built, along with ammunition storage dumps and tents for soldiers to live in.

Soldiers from the Russian 200th Motor Rifle Brigade's artillery battalion posted a video on a social-media account showing them firing from the site with BM-21s and 2S3 152mm self-propelled guns. In the imagery, the artillerymen appear to have taken over a farm shed to use as an assembly line for 122mm rockets, fitting fins and warheads.

Further to the west, Russian artillery batteries operated "shoot and scoot" tactics, moving to firing positions close to the Ukrainian border before retreating after they had conducted fire missions. The movement of the Russian batteries could be tracked from satellite imagery by the damage they caused from driving into wheat fields, which were close to being harvested.

Weapons used in this sector included 152mm MSTA-B towed howitzers, 2S19 Mista-2 152mm self-propelled guns, as well as BM-21, BM-27 Uragan and BM-30 Smerch rocket launchers. Batteries from the 291st Artillery Brigade, 17th Motor Rifle Brigade and 7th Military Base took part in these operations, according to images posted on social media by their soldiers. This imagery showed the artillery occupying firing positions, surrounded by huge piles of ammunition. In several of these images, the artillery men can be seen cooking meat on improvised barbeques around their guns. This suggests that they spent several hours or days in position waiting for calls to fire. Fire missions came from their own headquarters, where intelligence experts analysed the video imagery from the Russian mini drones or Forpost UAVs.

Separatist leaders were also becoming increasingly worried by the stepping up of air attacks on their positions by Ukrainian strike jets and attack helicopters. Ukrainian air strikes were not very accurate and did not inflict many casualties but they seriously weakened separatist morale and disrupted operations as their fighters had to take cover whenever Kiev's jets appeared overhead.

Several 9K35 Strela-10 self-propelled surface to air missile (SAM) systems were supplied to the separatists and they were credited with downing a Ukrainian Su-25 on 2nd July near Donetsk. A separatist missile crew also shot down a second An-26 near Lugansk on 14th July.

Two days later another Su-25 was downed near the Russian border while flying at 6,000 feet. The Ukrainians claimed it had been hit either by a Pantsir SAM fired from inside Russia or an air-to-air missile launched from a Russian fighter jet. Another Su-25 was reported damaged by a SAM the same day but it was able to return to its base.

This spike in air activity occurred the day before the Malaysian Airlines flight number MH17 was shot down by a 9K37 Buk SAM system to the south east of Donetsk city, with the loss of all 283 passengers and 15 crew onboard. Several separatist leaders, including Strelkov, had lobbied the Russian military to supply the Buk systems to bolster their air defences. Immediately after the incident Strelkov boasted on social media that the missile crew had engaged a Ukrainian transport aircraft. (6) As the truth emerged, the separatists and the Kremlin quickly backtracked and come up with some implausible excuses to avoid blame.

Despite the international outcry created by the incident and the need to mount a major effort to recover the remains of the dead, the war in Donbass continued. Five days after the MH17 incident two more Ukrainian Su-25s were downed close to the Russian border. The Kiev defence ministry blamed Russian fighters for shooting down one of its jets with long range air-to-air missiles. No Russian-linked sources, Ukrainian cyber warriors or Western military sources have so far stood up the claims that Russian fighter aircraft were involved in the Su-25 shoot-downs during July 2014. But the deployment of Su-30SMs – Russia's most advanced air supremacy aircraft - to Primorsko airbase could be linked to the incidents.

The Russian artillery raids and the shooting down of Ukrainian aircraft brought some respite to the separatists during July but the Kiev government soon reacted. It re-organised its forces and brought in reinforcements to bolster its offensive in the Donbass. Three large columns, made up of regulars equipped with tanks and artillery, as well as newly recruited National Guardsmen, were organised to spearhead the new offensive.

The first group was positioned north west of Luhansk city and it pushed southwards to widen a corridor to Ukrainian troops isolated in the city's airport. This would then allow them to push eastwards and cut off Luhansk from the Russian border.

To the south west of Donetsk city, as a 2,000-strong Ukrainian combat group was built up and its mission was to drive due east to first surround Donetsk and then continue towards Luhansk. Another group of Ukrainian troops was north of Donetsk and they were driving south to link up the column driving eastwards around the city's southern boundary. These two columns were set converge around the town of Illoviask.

These were the strongest forces that the Ukrainian military had mustered so far in the war and Kiev hoped this new offensive would deliver a decisive blow against the separatists. The separatist leaders in Donetsk and Luhansk shared this view and started to make desperate calls for help from their backers in Russia. The transcript of the telephone call between the DNR prime minister Alexander Borodei and Russian oligarch Konstantin Malofeev quoted at the start of this chapter is one of many from this period.

The Russian military was also watching the situation in the Donbass with growing concern. Convoys of arms supplies continued to cross across the border and they included T-64 tanks, 2S1 122mm self-propelled guns and BTR troop carriers. (7) One report suggested 12,000 AK-47 assault rifles were also sent to the separatists at this time. (8) Contingents of Russian special forces or Spetsnaz went with these weapons to operate or direct them. These soldiers subsequently posted social-media images of themselves in the Donbass dressed as DNR and LNR fighters. As well as helping the separatists, these Spetsnaz troops had the mission of identifying Ukrainian troop positions and possible routes for Russian regular troop columns to move into the Donbass.

The trigger for the Russian intervention was the Ukrainian advance on Illoviask. Halting the advance on this town was seen as the key to preventing the link up of the Ukrainian columns trying to encircle Donetsk city. Ukrainian spearheads were moving rapidly eastwards, bypassing Illoviask to the south. During the first two weeks of August the Ukrainians and separatists battled for Illoviask, devastating much of the town. By 19th August Ukrainian troops were pushing into the town's centre.

It is not clear when President Putin took the decision to intervene but it must have been some time during the second week of August as Russian troop movements across the border started to be observed at this time.

By early August, the Russian attack force was in position and prepared to strike. It was grouped into three main assault forces. The Western Group was positioned to the north west of Rostov-on-Don in a series of tactical assembly areas around the town of Kuybyshevo. It was given the objective of defeating the Ukrainian columns advancing on Illoviask. To spearhead its advance were four battalion tactical groups of paratroopers, three battalion tactical groups from motor rifle brigades and two companies of T-72M3 tanks from the 6th Tank Brigade. The 291st Artillery Brigade was brought forward to provide fire support. Gathering in a series of assembly areas in forests around the border town of Malaya Kamenka was the Northern Group and its task was to defeat the Ukrainian forces around Luhansk. It had a battalion tactical group of paratroopers, four battalion tactical groups from motor rifle brigades and a group of Naval Infantry. Armoured support was provided by T-90A tanks of the 136th Motor Rifle Brigade. A strong artillery group of tube and rocket weapons was concentrated to support its advance. A smaller group of Russian troops was massed to the west of Taganrog, on the Sea of Azov coast, to launch a launch a diversionary operation toward the Ukrainian city of Mauripol. This was based around a battalion tactical group of paratroopers, backed by artillery from the 17th Motor Rifle Brigade. It mission was to try to divert Ukrainian reserves away from the main operation further north.

Over the next three weeks the Russian operation unfolded across the Donbass. It has been possible to build up a detailed understanding of Russian troop movements and combat operations from a variety of sources. Russian vehicles and troops could be tracked by their unit insignia and tactical markings. These vehicles were often photographed in front of distinctive landmarks and signs that could be matched to those on Google's Street View. Russian soldiers also helpfully uploaded geo-tagged images of themselves in the Donbass onto their social-media accounts.

Several Russian units committed to the Donbass operation also used very distinctive equipment, such as T-90 tanks, BMD-2 airportable armoured vehicles and 2S9 Nona self-propelled guns that made it possible to track their progress. The Russian troops made a half-hearted effort to disguise the identity of their vehicles by paining over original unit markings and applying the insignia of LNR and DNR militia units or slogans supporting the separatist cause. These efforts often failed to cover up all their markings or the paint was applied in such a haphazard way that the original markings could still be seen. This deception exercise was fatally undermined when the Russian soldiers posted images of their repainted vehicles lined up in their assembly areas near Rostov-on-Don. Many of these vehicles later showed up in media images from inside the Donbass. The efforts made by these troops to match their vehicle's markings to those used by specific separatist militia units also illustrates that Russian commanders had thought closely how they would deploy their units once inside the Donbass.

The desperate situation around Luhansk prompted the early commitment of the Northern Group of Russian troops. Little effort was made to hide their movement across the border into the Donbass. At a railway crossing south of the Russian town of Kamensk-Shakhtinsky early on the morning of 15th August a group of international news reporters and photographers watched as a column of more than a dozen BMD-2 vehicles, sporting the tactical markings of the elite 234th Guards Air Assault Regiment, approached. The vehicles then crossed the railway and headed westwards towards Ukraine. This was would be a very public "secret" military intervention.

Three days later a citizen of Shosseynaya Street in Lugansk took out his smartphone and started to film a Russian column driving eastwards. He subsequently uploaded a video clip onto YouTube which showed 15 green painted Kamaz-53501 trucks towing eight D-30 122mm howitzers. They were accompanied by a BMD-2, two Ural trucks and a military minibus. The D-30s were from the 1140th Guards Artillery Regiment, the 234th Regiment's sister unit in the 76th Guards Air Assault Division. A company group of 13 T-72B3 tanks of the 35th Motor Rifle Brigade accompanied the paratroopers.

The Russian Airborne Regiment was in action soon after this in the fields to the south west of Luhansk city. After an artillery barrage the paratroopers advanced with tank support and ran into a solid defensive line. The Ukrainians called up air support to try to drive back the Russians. A pair of Mil Mi-24P helicopter gunships approached the battlefield at low level and were greeted by a barrage of man-portable surface-to-air missiles. One successfully dodged the missiles but the other was hit and crashed in flames. Despite their success shooting down the Mi-24P, the Ukrainian defence was too strong and the paratroopers had to pull back into Luhansk, abandoning two BMD-2 vehicles. When the Ukrainian troops examined the vehicles they found that they sported 234th Regiment tactical insignia that had been very badly over-painted, proving the presence on the battlefield of the Russian paratroopers.

This indicated that in the space of a week the Russians appeared to have been able to manoeuvre a battalion tactical group of 234th Regiment, backed by an artillery battery and tanks, into Ukraine, by-passing the bulk of the Ukraine troops positioned around Luhansk airport and then engaging the Ukrainian forces on the western edge of Luhansk city.

To capitalise on the manoeuvre of the 234th Regiment, the Russian military next sent a convoy of more than 100 heavy goods vehicles into the city on 22nd July. The Kremlin public relations machine heralded the convoy as a humanitarian gesture to help the citizens of Luhansk who had been effectively under Ukrainian siege for more than a month. The Russian 69th Logistic Brigade provided vehicles and drivers for the convoy, even though the vehicles had been painted white for this "made for television" event. Once across the border at the Izvaryne checkpoint, which was now under Russian control, they followed the same route as the paratroopers into Luhansk city.

Now the main bulk of the Northern Group of Russian units began to move into Ukraine, heading from the Izvaryne crossing towards Luhansk airport. The motor rifle troops clogged up the roads around the town of Krasnodon, with units of the 15th, 74th and 136th Brigades being photographed and filmed by residents. The social media imagery showed hundreds of armoured vehicles were involved in this operation, including main battle tanks, tracked armoured vehicles and self-propelled artillery.

Once past Krasnodon the Russian column divided into two, with battalion tactical groups of the 15th and 200th Motor Rifle Brigades, backed by the T-90A tanks of the 136th Brigade, heading north along the route taken by the paratroops into Luhansk city. To the south, battalion tactical groups of the 15th and 74th Motor Rifle Brigades advanced directly towards Luhansk airport.

On the northern axis there was some brief skirmishing in which a reconnaissance detachment of the 18th Motor Rifle Brigade lost a BTR troop carrier. The advance appeared to be largely unopposed.

As the Northern Group was establishing itself around Luhansk, to the south west the Western Group of Russian forces was also on the move. From its assembly areas in the forests and farmland around the town of Kuybyshevo, the Western Group was tasked with destroying the Ukrainian forces operating south and east of Illoviask. Russian drones and special forces teams of the 2nd Spetsnaz Brigade operating with the separatists were all active in this region in the first three weeks of August, trying to pin down the strength and location of the Ukrainian troops. One Forpost drone was even caught on satellite imagery overflying the region just over the border from Kuybyshevo on 15th August.

Ukrainian commanders were focused on capturing Illoviask and pushing east to Luhansk and did not give any priority to watching their southern flank. Apart from isolated border guard and police units the region was largely devoid of Ukrainian troops. So on 23rd August residents of the border town of Amvrosiyivka were surprised to find very polite but heavily armed Russian troops guarding a nearby crossroads. These were the advance reconnaissance troops of the Russian force.

Just south of the border were three main contingents of Russian troops, positioned along a 50-kilometre front. On the western flank was the battalion tactical group of the 247th Guards Air Assault Regiment, in the centre were battalion tactical groups from the 31st Guards Air Assault Brigade and the 331st Guards Airborne Regiment, and to the east was 137th Guards Airborne Regiment.

A second echelon force of four battalion tactical groups, from the 8th, 17th, 18th and 21st Motor Rifle Brigades, backed by two companies of T-72B3M of the 6th Tank Brigade followed on behind the central column. The headquarters vehicles of the 18th Brigade were photographed in the combat zone at this time, suggesting it was acting as the command centre for this operation.

For another day the Russian columns pushed north west towards Donetsk city and Illoviask meeting minimal resistance. They entered several Ukrainian towns and villages where they were photographed taking over police stations and government buildings and removing the flags and insignia of Kiev government and state. The Russian columns were pushing into the open and undefended flank of the Ukrainian army.

This situation came to an abrupt stop on 24th August when the Russian paratroopers stumbled into the first Ukrainian positions some 10 kilometres south of Illoviask on the road from Amvrosiyivka. The paratroopers' lightly armoured BMD-2 troop carriers were engaged by Ukrainian anti-tank missile teams, knocking at least one out and damaging others. A squad of surprised paratroopers from the 331st Regiment took cover in a hedge row as the rest of their platoon pulled back to re-organise. Ukrainian troops quickly followed up their success and took 10 paratroopers prisoner. They were soon paraded on Ukrainian television to prove Moscow's involvement.

Over the next four days, all the Russian columns started to run into the Ukrainian positions south of Illoviask. Ukrainian commanders desperately tried to disengage their troops fighting in the town to move south to bolster their defences against the Russian columns. Three other Russian soldiers were captured during these engagements and several killed and wounded.

These successes were trumpeted by the Ukrainian army and media but they were small engagements and they ultimately proved short lived. As the fighting was taking place along the Illoviask-Amvrosiyivka axis, the 247th Regiment, backed by the 8th Brigade, was continuing to advance to the west of Iloviask. Meeting little resistance, this column pushed northwards and by 27th August, the Ukrainian troops were trapped in a pocket south and east of Iloviask. Drawing on an analogy with World War Two encirclement battles, both the Russians and Ukrainian called this a Kessel, cauldron or boiler, battle.

During 28th August, the Ukrainian and Russian commanders opened negotiations to evacuate the pocket, after President Putin agreed to allow a "humanitarian corridor" to be set up. Talks went on all day and into the night, with the Ukrainians demanding that they be able to take their heavy weapons with them. The Russians wanted them to leave behind heavy weapons and would not allow militia units that were not part of the regular Ukrainian army to be covered by the deal. Both sides accused each of reneging on the deal. By early hours of 29th August the Ukrainian commanders decided to try to break out anyway. A column of some 1,000 Ukrainians headed due west and another, some 600 strong, headed south and then west.

In the gloom just after dawn the convoys were spotted by Russian troops who started engaging them with tank, machine-gun and mortar fire. The Ukrainian columns drove directly through the Russian lines to try to escape the fire. Most of the Ukrainian troops lucky enough to be in tanks and armoured vehicles managed to get through to safety but hundreds riding on tanks, vans and police cars were killed or wounded. The southern column had some successes knocking out two T-72B3Ms of the Russian 6th Brigade and capturing one of their tanks, as well as two tank crewmen, but a large group of Ukrainians was soon trapped near the village of Chervonoselsky. Some 250 Ukrainians eventually surrendered in the village on 30th August.

The Battle of Iloviask was a disaster for the Ukrainian army. The Kiev government admitted that some 366 of its soldiers were killed in the break-out battle, 429 injured and 300 captured, along with significant losses of weapons and equipment. This was probably an underestimation. The Russians had achieved their objective and rendered several of the Ukrainian army's best units combat ineffective. This opened the route to Donetsk. It would not be the last defeat for the Ukrainian army.

Further to the south, the Russian diversionary column started advancing on Mauripol on 26th August. The paratroopers of the 51st Guards Airborne Regiment and their supporting tanks and artillery pushed westwards over the border meeting minimal resistance. They reached the outskirts of the city in a couple of days and then started to trade fire with a scratch force of Ukrainian troops who had been rushed to protect it. Again, the Russians had confused and confounded the Ukrainian high command.

The finale of the Russian operation would now take place around Luhansk. After the debacle at Iloviask, the Ukrainian commanders at Luhansk airport were getting increasingly concerned about the two Russian armoured columns approaching from the east. The airport was being pounded by massive artillery barrages that added to the feeling that the position was untenable. They decided to withdraw, rather than stay and risk being encircled. Over the first two days of September, the Ukrainian troops started to pull out of their positions at the airport and move to the north of Luhansk city.

Russian troops of the 200th Motor Rifle Brigade moved into the airport on 3rd September and found it completely devastated. The airport terminal was in ruins and the runway, taxiways and nearby fields were peppered by hundreds of craters, according satellite imagery taken a few days after the battle. To their north, the 74th Motor Rifle Brigade linked up with Russian paratroops on the western fringe of Luhansk city. The Asiatic soldiers of the 74th Brigade were easily identifiable in video clips of the link-up.

If the Ukrainians had thought they had escaped disaster, they were mistaken. Russian drones were already looking for their retreating columns and found them hiding in forests north of Luhansk. In two strikes by BM-30 Smerch rockets on 3rd and 4th September, units of one Ukrainian brigade and two territorial defence battalions were rendered combat ineffective. One strike alone destroyed a Tochka-U missile launcher, nine tanks, 14 BMP infantry fighting vehicles and BTR armoured personnel carriers, as well as thirty trucks. One Ukrainian battalion commander was reported to have been left alone wandering around the devastated site looking for his dead soldiers. At least eight tanks were knocked out in the other strike.

With the defeat of the Ukrainian troops around Luhansk, the Kiev government had little choice but to sue for peace. Ukrainian and Russian delegations met in the Belarus capital and signed the Minsk 1 peace accord on 5th September. It "froze" the conflict in a ceasefire that was to be monitored by the Organisation for Security and Co-operation in Europe.

As the diplomats were putting the finishing touches to this deal, the Russian combat troops were being pulled out of the Donbass to rest, tend their wounded and bury their dead. Columns of Russian armoured vehicles were photographed crossing out of Ukraine with cheering and waving troops sitting on the turrets. Paratroopers and tank units were the first units to pull out, leaving the contingents of motor rifle and Spetsnaz troops to secure the front lines and begin trying to the transform the separatist militias into an organised army.

There would be no victory parades for the troops because President Putin still wanted to keep the Russian intervention secret. They received numerous medals in secret ceremonies and successful officers would soon be promoted. But the Russian people would not get to celebrate the success of their soldiers. The Russian dead could also not be honoured in public. There has been a lot of speculation that the Russian regular military suffered hundreds of fatalities in the summer of 2014. Russian units started to unveil their own memorials to their fallen comrades in their garrisons and local newspapers in their home town published obituaries of the fallen soldiers, although the exact locations and circumstances of their deaths were couched in euphemisms. The dates of the soldier's deaths coincide with the Russian intervention in the Donbass, giving away their role in the conflict.

Ukrainian social-media activists set about collating photographs of these memorials from social media posts and Russian media reports about them. By early 2017 they had complied names of between 70 and 107 Russian soldiers who had been killed in action in the Donbass during 2014, with a further 378 wounded soldiers being identified. This is perhaps the most accurate total to emerge so far and it demonstrates that the Russian military paid a heavy price for their victory, although it is only a fraction of the losses suffered by the Ukrainians.

Chapter 5
Frozen War - The Battle for Debaltseve

The column of around 40 cold and dejected Ukrainian soldiers appeared at the edge of the bombed-out town. A handful of pro-Russian militia fighters could be seen escorting them to a patch of open ground. Abandoned tanks and burnt-out armoured vehicles could be seen nearby, along with trenches surrounded by piles of spent cartridge cases.

A television crew was waiting to film the prisoners as they stood in the snow shivering, while a local militia leader harangued them about their defeat. They were then herded onto a convoy of buses and trucks to carry them away from the battlefield.

The images were evocative of the images filmed by Red Army cameramen in the ruins of Stalingrad some 72 years previously of German soldiers emerging from bunkers to surrender. The snow and landscape of ruins looked similar to the iconic battlefield on the Volga, where the might of the Nazi Wehrmacht had been broken in January 1943.

In February 2014, the Ukrainian prisoners looked exhausted but they did not appear terrified like the Nazi prisoners in Stalingrad. Unlike the Germans who suffered more than a decade of brutal captivity in Stalin's gulag, within a week the Ukrainian prisoners were exchanged for pro-Russian militia men held in Kiev.

The Ukrainian defeat at the Battle of Debaltseve in February 2015, like the victory at Stalingrad was a battle of encirclement. Both the Russians and Ukrainians called the town in the Donbass a "boiler", which is a translation of the German phrase "Kessel" or "cauldron" battle. This was a tactic used by both sides on the Eastern Front in World War Two to first trap their opponents in pockets or Kessels. Then the pocket would be squeezed until the trapped troops were killed, surrendered or broke out. The Battle of Debaltseve was the second Kessel defeat suffered by the Ukrainians in six months and this secured Russian control over the disputed Donbass region.

The events that led to the Battle of Debaltseve originated in the Minsk 1 ceasefire agreement that paused the fighting in the summer and autumn of 2014. Ukrainian defeats in August and September at the hands of Russian troops had caused both sides to take a breath but neither side saw the Minsk 1 ceasefire as any sort of permanent ending of the conflict.

Along the so-called ceasefire line in the Donbass, there were routine firefights and artillery exchanges between Ukrainian forces and pro-Russian militia fighters. This fighting steadily escalated during the final months of 2014 and culminated in a major battle for the control of Dontesk airport in December 2014 and early January 2015.

Although Russian regular troops had been to the fore during the battles in August and September 2014, once the Minsk 1 agreement came into effect and the frontlines started to stabilise, the Russian combat troops pulled back into reserve positions to rest and recuperate. The locally recruited militia units were pushed up to man the ceasefire line, with the Russians providing specialist support such as flying surveillance drones, artillery fire and electronic eavesdropping. Other Russian units and teams of officers arrived to set up a training programme to try to mould the local recruited militia fighters into some semblance of an organised army.

This coincided with major political changes in the pro-Russian mini-states in the Donbass - the Donetsk and Luhansk People's Republics, or the DNR and LNR respectively. The Kremlin's point man on Ukraine, Vladislav Surkov, made several trips to the Donbass to organise the replacement of the first wave of pro-Russian leaders. (1) These characters had become famous since the start of the pro-Russian revolution in April, including the self-declared Dontesk defence minister, "Colonel" Igor Strelkov. Within days of the arrival of regular Russian troops in the Donbass, Strelkov found himself redundant and on his way back to Moscow. He soon became an embittered figure as he tried to fend off attacks in the Western media and from Dutch criminal prosecutors about his role in the shooting down of the Malaysia airliner over the Donbas in July 2014. (2) He gave a series of media interviews in which he lambasted Surkov for selling out his fighters in the Donbass for the sake of securing a political deal with Kiev.

Strelkov's political counterparts in Donetsk and Luhansk also soon found themselves out of favour with Moscow and had to find new employment. More reliable placemen were found to take over running Europe's newest states. Strangely, despite the blood and treasure expended by the Kremlin to bring them into existence, the two Donbass republics were not even recognised as independent country by the Russian government.

Moscow's military footprint in the Donbass could be tracked by the social media posts of Russian troops serving the region, commercial satellite imagery, and the first reports of the Organisation for Security and Co-operations in Europe (OSCE) monitoring missions set up in the Ukraine as part of the Minsk agreement.

The bulk of first wave of Russian units that fought in August and September, were pulled back to their field camps to the north and west of Rostov-on-Don. A handful of battalion tactical groups remained in the cities of Donetsk and Luhansk immediately after the September ceasefire to act as tactical reserves, setting up bases in abandoned industrial sites. Late in the year, new units rotated into the field camps to give Moscow the option of surging forces across the border in time of crisis. With the winter approaching the conditions in these camps worsened as the troops had little shelter beyond tents. To help with the logistic re-supply of troops inside the Donbass, Russian military engineers built a series of ferries and bridges over the River Donets near Luhansk city, which could be identified on satellite imagery. This created a new route to Luhansk from the large Russian field camp at Milerovo airbase.

Teams of Russian officers and trainers were now dispatched across the DNR and LNR to try to re-organise the dozens of militia groups that had been formed during the early days of the rebellion. Several of these teams were provided by Russian Spetsnaz brigades, who set up outposts in most of the region's major towns. These Russian special forces operatives were soon posting images on their social media sites, showing them drinking in bars or posing with local women.

Larger teams were provided by Russian motor rifle brigades and they began trying to organise major field training exercises or parades of the militia fighters. Video clips and photographs of these events showed how awkward this activity was with the local fighters sporting beards, ill-fitting uniforms and driving around in graffiti-covered vehicles. They did not look much like an army, at that point.

Despite the claims from Moscow that it had no troops inside the borders of Ukraine the Russian military did not make much effort to hide its presence in the Donbass. In October it appointed a senior officer, Lieutenant General Alexander Lentsov, who was deputy commander of the Russian Ground Forces, to be its representative to the OSCE's Joint Centre for Control and Co-ordination, which was delineating the Minsk agreement ceasefire line. General Lentsov soon became a well-known figure in the local and international media from his appearances at events across the Donbass. The Ukrainian military accused him of being the commander of what it called the Operational Command Donbass, which controlled both regular Russian and locally recruited militia forces in the disputed region.

More and more regular Russian officers started appearing with Lentsov in meetings with the OSCE and Ukrainians. Across the Donbass, the militia forces were metamorphosed into new organisations. Fighters in the Dontesk region became the 1st Corps of the DNR armed forces and those in the LNR were dubbed the 2nd Corps. They were in turn combined into the joint armed forces of New Russia or Novorossiya.

Ukrainian internet activists soon started to match the photographs of the officers leading the new 1st and 2nd Corps with social-media profiles of Russia military personnel. All the senior officers of the DNR and LNR military were Russian regular officers, said the activists. The presence of General Lentsov in the Donbass and his obvious power and influence over militia units across the region, appeared to confirm the view that the 1st and 2nd Corps were under the control and direction of the Russian military.

In the autumn of 2014 and spring of 2015, the military capacity of the DNR and LNR was limited. Russian controlled territory was devastated by war, economic activity had all but ceased, public services had collapsed and lawlessness was rampant. Service in the LNR and DNR military was one of the few sources of regular income for its population. To try to further military reform, Russian contract soldiers started to appear in the ranks of the militia forces as part of Moscow's drive to try to improve their effectiveness. LNR and DNR personnel also started attending Russian military schools and training depots. This was definitely a long term project.

In the winter of 2014/2015 regular Russian forces were still needed in considerable numbers to bolster the local forces in the Donbass. The biggest contribution was providing a command-and-control system to co-ordinate all the militia units and integrate them with regular Russian units. Ukrainian activists hacked a Russian military document that described how the Russian motor rifle brigades based in the field camps over the border had dispatched groups of unmanned aerial vehicle operators into the Donbass to provide surveillance coverage along the ceasefire line.

As 2014 drew to an end, the ceasefire was increasingly frayed with heavy fighting underway to control Donetsk airport on the north western side of the city. Through December and January, the airport terminal buildings changed hands on a number occasions. Both sides called down increasing volumes of artillery and rocket fire to aid their advances. This battle took on a meat grinder quality as more and more troops were fed into the fight with little effect. There was increasing concern among the Western powers that the Minsk process was breaking down and full blown conflict could soon break out. A new round of talks were called in the Belarus capital in mid-January 2015.

In this environment, the Kremlin decided to escalate its involvement in the war to achieve a tactical victory that would significantly enhance its bargaining position in the new round of peace talks. Moscow wanted peace on its terms and that depended on a new defeat being inflicted on the Ukrainian army. The target was the Debaltseve salient that penetrated between the Russian-controlled cities of Donetsk and Luhansk. The salient cut the main road and rail lines between the two cities and forced Russian forces in Donetsk city to take a convoluted route back to the Russian border. Perhaps more importantly, the point of the salient was occupied by some 3,000 Ukrainian troops who manned a series of fortified strong points around the town of Debaltseve. A similar number of troops held open the neck of the salient. These were some of the best troops in Ukraine's depleted army and their defeat would magnify the political impact of any Russian victory.

Since the battle, a vast amount of information from both Ukrainian and Russian participants has emerged about the course of the fighting and the role Moscow's troops played. It has also been possible to cross reference and verify the accuracy of these accounts with social media-video and commercial satellite imagery. A key factor in understanding the battle is to appreciate that the conditions faced by the troops of both sides were atrocious. Temperatures rarely rose above zero in daytime, snow or freezing rain fell every day and there were no more than six hours of daylight. The weather meant Russia's Forpost and Orlan 10 unmanned aerial vehicles or other air reconnaissance were of limited use. Ground commanders had to move forward to the frontlines to find out what was happening on the battlefield.

These conditions meant the Ukrainian defenders of the salient were in a very precarious position. They were deployed in a network of strong points, protected by deep bunkers and trenches. While these earthwork defences provided protection against Russian artillery and rocket fire, without open lines of communications to regularly bring in fuel, ammunition and food the Ukrainian troops would soon lose the ability to keep warm and fight back. Once cut off, it would only be matter of time before the Ukrainians ran out of supplies, leaving them at the mercy of both the Russians and the freezing weather. Survival would be measured in days.

Debaltseve town itself lay at the centre of a shallow valley and the Ukrainians positioned their strong points to hold a series of woodened ridgelines to the north, east and south of the town. These strongpoints protected the main supply road out to Artemivsk to the west. At its widest point, the salient was little more than 30 kilometres wide so it was easily swept by Russian long range artillery and rockets positioned on either side of the Kessel's neck. This vulnerability would be exploited to the full during the upcoming Russian operation.

As the build-up to the Minsk negotiations started in January, General Lentsov began moving his troops into position ready for the denouement. The frontline was held by militia men from the 2nd LNR Corps on the north and east flanks, while to the south the 1st DNR Corps held the ring. Their mobile reserve contingents were mobilised from their garrisons in Luhansk and Donetsk cities respectively to join the offensive. Their Russian advisors went with them to help mobilise the first wave of the attack because of fears about their motivation to carry out full-frontal assaults. The LNR troops were bolstered by advisors from the 200th Motor Rifle Brigade of the Northern Fleet and private military contractors of the Wagner Group.

The heavy punch for the assault was provided by two groups of Russian artillery and multiple-launch rocket systems, which moved across the border into the Donbass. To the north, a battalion of Mista-S self propelled 152m howitzers and BM-21 rocket launchers moved into position in to support the 2nd LNR Corps. To the south, the 1st DNR Corps was provided with batteries of BM-27 Uragan. BM-30 Smerch and BM-21 rocket launchers were positioned north east of Donetsk city ready to rain down fire across the length and breadth of the salient. Russian artillery observers equipped with GLONASS satellite navigation and data transmission devices to speed the identification of targets and requests for fire support moved into position with the frontline troops. All these moves were caught on imagery posted on social media during the battle by Russian troops or local civilians.

During late January, a battalion tactical group of the Russian 5th Separate Tank Brigade was moved north from the Kuzminsky field camp into a hold area in Donetsk city. This included some 31 T-72B2 tanks and a dozen BMP infantry fighting vehicles of the 5th Brigade from Ulan Ude in Russia's far east, supported by a dozen or so T-80 tanks of the 4th Kantemirovskaya Guards Tank Brigade from Moscow. They were supported by a 2B16 Nona-K mortar battery of the 138th Motor Rifle Brigade.

Serving with the 5th Brigade was a 20-year-old T-72 tank gun loader, Private

Dorzhi Batomunkuev. He remarkably gave an interview to a Russian newspaper while recovering from serious burns suffered during the battle. Other soldiers of the brigade posted many photographs of their role in the fighting and several citizens of Donetsk videoed the brigade's convoys as they moved to the front. A photographer from the Getty news agency was invited to report on the battle and his pictures showed the brigade's tanks and personnel in frontline positions. The tank crews of the 5th Brigade were immediately recognisable in photographs and video taken during the Battle of Debaltseve because their vehicles retained their distinctive tactical markings. Many of the brigade's soldiers were locals from the Ulan Ude region so had Asiatic facial features that made them stand out amongst the European fighters of the DNR and LNR militia.

The Russian offensive proper got underway in the final week of January with extensive artillery and rocket fire being launched against the Ukrainian strongpoints. This was sustained for the next four weeks as the battle grew in intensity. Ukrainian soldiers reported the Russian fire was not very accurate but it did keep them awake and prevented them sleeping for days on end. It also made it impossible for their supply trucks to move up to resupply the strongpoints. As the battle unfolded, the Ukrainians became increasingly tired and a lack of supplies added to their feeling of isolation. Soon the strongpoints started to be abandoned or surrendered by demoralised Ukrainian soldiers.

The first direct attack was made by the 2nd LNR Corps troops against two strongpoints holding the northern neck of the salient. Wagner Group armoured vehicles and LNR T-64 tanks advanced across open ground on 23rd January before being engaged by Ukrainian tanks and anti-tank-guided-missile teams. The attack was pressed over two days but it soon got bogged down, with 14 tanks and armoured vehicles left burning on the battlefield.

The Russian attention then switched to the south-eastern side of the salient where strongpoints in the village of Nikishyne and Chernukhino were relentlessly bombarded. Russian rocket and artillery fire left more than a dozen Ukrainian tanks, armoured vehicles and trucks destroyed and smashed the defenders trenches and bunkers. LNR militia fighters moved forward into the woods around the two villages on 1st February. When they moved into Nikishyne and Chernukhino the following day, the Ukrainians had already left.

At the same time as this attack was unfolding the 1st DNR Corps started its attack on the southern flank of the salient at Vuhlehrs'k. Russian artillery and rocket fire was employed on a lavish scale to hit Ukrainian strongpoints in this section of the front. It took the DNR militia fighters three days to clear Vuhlehrs'k village and the surrounding areas by 3rd February.

Over the next five days, this axis became the main effort of the operation as the DNR militia and their Russian advisors rolled northwards to capture Kalynivka. Russian tanks now started to shoot up Ukrainian traffic moving along the main road from Debaltseve to Artemivsk. This effectively reduced the neck of the Kessel to only some six kilometres. Inside the salient, the Ukrainian troops were becoming increasingly demoralised as they realised that the Russians

might close the neck of the Kessel and trap them inside.
This was the moment that General Lentsov made his decisive move. The 5th Brigade was called forward from its base in Donetsk city to lead the advance to close the Kessel on 8th February.
Private Batomunkuev described the scene in their base. "The captain of our group simply went out and said: everything, guys, we're going, readiness number one. Readiness number one - we are sitting in a wound-up tank. Then the column extends [onto the road]." (3)
The tanks of the 5th Brigade moved forward across their start line on 9th February with DNR militia fighters riding on BMPs in their wake. Several hours later the attack force captured the village of Logvinovo and crossed the main road from Debaltseve to Artemivsk. During the fighting two of the 5th Brigade's T-72s were hit by Ukrainian fire and crews had to abandon their vehicles, including Private Batomunkuev and his battalion commander, who were both seriously injured. The capture of Logvinovo was a surprise to the Ukrainians and several of their vehicles drove into the village later in the day and were ambushed by the DNR militia fighters and the 5th Brigade tanks.
Hundreds of miles to the west in Minsk, the peace talks were reaching a conclusion on 11th February with the arrival of President Putin of Russia, President Francois Hollande of France, Chancellor Angela Merkel of Germany and Ukrainian President Petro Poroshenko. After a marathon overnight negotiating session, a deal was agreed the next day which included an OSCE-observed unconditional ceasefire from 15th February, withdrawal of heavy weapons from the front line, release of prisoners of war, and constitutional reform in Ukraine.
The Ukrainian government hoped the 15th February ceasefire would save their troops in Debaltseve from defeat and the Russians would cease their offensive. Kiev ordered its troops outside the salient to stop providing artillery support of the troops trapped inside the Kessel. It was wishful thinking and made no difference. The Russian offensive continued.
The 5th Brigade continued its advance northward towards the Ukrainian Moisha and Kopio strongpoints, on the ridge line overlooking the road to Artemivsk. Heavy artillery and rocket fire tormented the isolated Ukrainian troops and by the afternoon of 17th February they raised the white flag after firing off their last ammunition. Some 107 Ukrainians them marched out of their strongpoints to surrender.
On the southern edge of Debaltseve, DNR militia fighters were pushing into town and rounding up their first groups of prisoners, as recounted at the start of this chapter.
For the remaining 2,000 Ukrainian troops trapped on the northern edge of Debaltseve town there was little time to lose. If they did not escape from the town that night they would be either captured or killed. In the early hours of the morning of 18th February, the Ukrainian convoys set off to try to escape across country to skirt past the Russian outpost at Logvinovo and then head to Artemivsk. Soon they were detected by Russian tanks and came under fire. Dozens of

vehicles were hit and hundreds of Ukrainian soldiers were killed or wounded. By dawn the first columns made it through to the Ukrainian lines at Artemivsk. Across the battlefield the Russian troops and their militia allies rounded up 150 Ukrainian troops, who were exchanged for captured pro-Russian fighters a few days later. The Kiev government later admitted that 267 of its troops had been killed in the battles. A UN aid agency later said some 500 bodies were discovered in the ruins of the Debaltseve, many of them civilians who were killed by artillery and rocket fire.

The Russian operation to seize Debaltseve had achieved all its aims. The Minsk 2 agreement effectively froze their control over the Donbass. The Ukrainian garrison of Debaltseve had been defeated and abandoned almost all of its equipment in the town. Nearly 10% of the Ukrainian troops in the Kessel had been killed and hundreds more wounded. Those who managed to escape were demoralised and their units effectively ceased to exist as fighting forces.

Chapter 6
War against Ukraine Assessed

The year from launching of the operation to seize control of Crimea to the fall of Debaltseve in February 2015 saw an unprecedented series of military operations being launched by Moscow. Some Western political leaders, military analysts and commentators have been keen to portray this as a pre-ordained march forward by Russia's military to execute Vladimir Putin's master plan for global domination. More than six years on from these events it is possible take a more insightful look at what actually happened, when important decisions were made and how the policies they set in train turned out.

Operation Crimea Spring was hailed a triumph for Russia's military. In a matter of days the Ukrainian garrison in Crimea surrendered without a shot being fired. The operation led to the emergence of the phase "little green men" to describe Russia's troops who blockaded the Ukrainians in their bases. These soldiers were well equipped, well led and motivated. Success in Crimea appeared to put to bed 25 years of Russian military decline.

The use of psychological warfare and political intimidation by the Russians in Crimea was heralded by some Western commentators as a sign that Moscow was putting into action the so-called Garasimov Doctrine of hybrid warfare. From the evidence we have about the rapid formulation of the Russian plan to seize Crimea ascribing this to the adoption of some new military doctrine is perhaps a step too far. In a matter of hours and days, Russian commanders on the ground pulled together an improvised operation and just made it work. There was no off-the-shelf contingency plan that had been rehearsed or built using a doctrine handbook.

The most important thing the Russian political and military command got right was their assessment that the Ukrainian military personnel in Crimea would be unwilling or unable to mount organised resistance. This strategic call ensured that the operation rapidly gained momentum and Russian commanders had the confidence to press on with their high risk operation.

From the start to the finish of the operation, the Russian military were in the driving seat. Its personnel and senior officers dominated the operation and the won major kudos for their success. During the Crimea operation reports emerged of the presence in the region of Russian nationalist operatives, private military contractors working for oligarch-controlled businesses and nationalist militia groups. They appeared to show their loyalty to President Putin's key advisor, Vladislav Surkov, and to have links to Russia's intelligence agencies, including the military intelligence branch, the GRU. These shady operatives took part in a couple sieges of Ukrainian bases in Crimea, including one in which a Ukrainian serviceman was killed. They were, however, never more than bit players during the Crimea operation.

The war in the Donbass could be described as the complete mirror image of the Crimea operation. From the start, Surkov and his political operatives were in the driving seat. Many of the hybrid warriors that had gathered in Crimea in March 2014 soon migrated to the Donbass and were in the forefront of the so-called April Revolution. Within weeks the Donbass was in flames. The GRU and its Spetsnaz brigades were then moving across the border to help the pro-Russian militias. This set off a drip feed of arms supplies to the militias in the Donbass. During July it escalated to include cross-border artillery and rocket-fire support. This was a piecemeal and incremental approach. At the heart of it was a flawed assessment of how the Ukrainians would react. In the Donbass the Ukrainians mobilised their army to fight back. By August the Donbass revolution appeared to be on the brink of collapse.

To reverse this dire situation, a major operation was launched across the border to defeat the Ukrainian army. In a three-week period, the Russians out-manoeuvred and then ruthlessly defeated the main Ukrainian units in the Donbass. Russian commanders manoeuvred their troops to trap one of the main Ukrainian combat groups at Illoviask. They were surrounded and destroyed in a "Kessel" battle. A few days later, two large groups of Ukrainian troops were wiped out in saturation rocket strikes near Luhansk.

While the Russian military intervention attracted a lot of attention in the west, it is now clear that the Kremlin was far from happy at this turn of events. The war in the Donbass is still not officially acknowledged by Moscow. Its servicemen received many honours for their part in the war but they cannot publicly say where they won their medals. At the heart of this official denial is considerable unhappiness in the Kremlin with the nationalist and covert operatives who ran the war in the Donbass between April and August 2014. This was an unmitigated disaster for Russia. The Ukrainians did not surrender the Donbass without firing a shot, the West imposed further sanctions on Russia's economy and the shooting down of the Malaysian airliner in July 2014 has become a political albatross around the Kremlin's neck. One Kremlin source suggested direct economic support for the Donbass republics was running at $85 million a month in 2016, excluding the cost of electricity and gas which was supplied free-of-charge by state-owned Russian companies.

Hybrid warfare in the Donbass proved to be a liability not a panacea. The clearing out of the original group of political operatives from the Donbass in the autumn of 2014 was clear evidence that the Kremlin wanted to put control of the situation into more reliable hands, in the shape of the regular Russian military who moved in to take control of the militia forces across the region.

The intervention of the Russian military in February and March 2014 in Crimea and in the Donbass in August 2014 and again in February 2015 proved decisive in achieving the political and diplomatic outcome desired by the Kremlin. The ruthlessness displayed in these operations showed that Russian land forces have returned to Soviet-era levels of efficiency. In many ways, the new professional Success in the Crimea and Donbass indicated that Russia's current generation of generals have crafted a new stiletto rather than resurrected the old Soviet steamroller.

Chapter 7
The Syria Express

On a rainy morning in October 2015 the huge silhouette of a 4,000-ton Russian Navy tank-landing ship could just be seen in the gloom of the Bosphorus Straits. A Turkish Navy cutter guided the Russian vessel - loaded with arms and supplies destined for Syria - through the ferries and merchant ships which criss-cross the busy waterway that divides Asia and Europe.

The Aleksander Otrakovskiy was one of six Russian ships to head south to Syria over the previous week, putting flesh on President Vladimir Putin's rhetoric of support for Bashar al Assad in the Kremlin only days before. The relentless shuttle of supply ships prompted the Turks to nickname the armada the "Syria Express".

Russia's intervention in Syria in 2015 came at a critical point in the then four year old civil war. After the 2011 street protests against the Assad government, the country had quickly degenerated into all-out civil war. Tens of thousands of army conscripts had defected rather than follow orders to open fire on demonstrators and soon whole city neighbourhoods and country districts had fall under the control of armed opponents of the Damascus government.

As the civil war ground on, the fighting and brutality intensified. Jihadi groups had proliferated and some of them eventually morphed into the group that became known as Islamic State. It would control more than a third of Syria by 2015.

Other rebel groups took control of large parts of Syria's major cities, including Aleppo, Homs, Hama and suburbs of Damascus. Assad's government responded by imposing medieval type sieges on these rebel enclaves, including using poison gas against the East Ghouta enclave in Damascus in 2013. To try to turn back the rebel advance, Assad turned to Tehran and its allies in the Lebanese Hizbullah movement but their intervention did not prove decisive.

By the early summer of 2015, the Assad government appeared to be teetering on the brink of a strategic defeat. An alliance of rebel groups had captured a huge swathe of north western Syria and was poised to advance on the coast to cut the government's links to the Mediterranean and its only means of importing food, fuel and arms.

At the same time, Islamic State fighters were advancing across the desert from the east, capturing the ancient city of Palmyra and staging a mass execution of captured Syrian soldiers in its iconic Roman theatre. Assad's days seemed numbered. In Moscow in July 2015, Putin and his senior advisors met a delegation of top Iranian officers, led by the famous Iranian Islamic Republican Guard Corps commander Major General Qassem Soleimani, to plan how to reverse this tide and ensure that Assad not only survived but won the war. Weeks later the Syria Express would be underway.

At the heart of Putin's decision to intervene in Syria was a major logistic operation to set up and sustain the Russian military contingent in the country, as well as provide the Syrian military with new arms and equipment. This complex logistic operation was one of the most visible aspects of the Russian mission to Syria thanks to a mix of open-source monitoring tools, such as live air-traffic control websites. Photographs, apparently posted by Russian military personnel in Syria, added further details of the logistic build-up that had been underway around Latakia in Syria.

The build-up of Russian forces in Syria was also recorded in detail by Turkish amateur ship-spotters, who began posting photographs and videos of Moscow's ships online. In July 2015 only two supply ships headed south but in August one of the ship photographers, Yörük Işık, started to post pictures showing trucks, cargo containers and other military kit hidden under camouflage nets on the decks of seven Russian ships. Işık described the ships as "packed to the gunnels with military equipment".

In September, the number of ships heading south reached 12 and during October it surged to 17, rising to 74 in total by the end of the year. "The pace of this traffic has revved up our hobby - we almost can't keep up with all the ships," said Işık.

Although Turkey had vigorously denounced Putin's intervention in the Syrian war and incursions in its airspace by Russian jets, it was powerless to stop the Syria Express because of international treaties guaranteeing free navigation through the Bosphorus Straits.

The Russians made little effort to hide their power play, with sailors and soldiers on the decks of the ships in the Bosphorus using selfie sticks to take pictures with Istanbul's historic landmarks as the background. Moscow's soldiers also uploaded pictures online from the port of Tartus in Syria, showing hundreds of troops, scores of vehicles and tons of hardware being off-loaded.

British military sources said the Syria Express quickly had an impact, with deliveries of munitions and spare parts for the Syrian air force allowing the regime to increase its rate of air strikes by 40% during October 2015.

With the war in Syria escalating as the Russian-backed offensive against rebel fighters gained momentum, the demand for arms grew so much that the Russian Navy began to hire civilian cargo ships to bolster the Syria Express. It had bought two ex-Turkish freighters, the Alican Deval and Dadali - renamed respectively, Dvinista 50 and Vologda 50 – and they were soon flying the flag used by Russian Navy auxiliaries. Shipping industry sources said the purchase of these ships was needed because much Russian ammunition and artillery propellant charges was so unstable that they would fail international health and safety rules and could not be carried on chartered vessels without invalidating their insurance cover.

While Russian supply ships had begun moving during the summer months of 2015, the major airlift operations involving Russian, Syrian and Iranian aircraft only got in to high gear in mid-September.

The Russian Aerospace Force (RuAF) established an airbridge to sustain its military contingent in Syria with 39 flights by a variety of transport aircraft in September and some 44 flights the following month. These flights passed through controlled civil airspace in Iran, Iraq and Syria and so were visible on live air traffic control monitoring websites, which used open-source ADS-B transponder-based tracking data.

There were almost daily flights by cargo-carrying Antonov An-124 Ruslan and Ilyushin Il-76 transport aircraft into Lakatia and every three or four days a passenger-carrying Tupolev Tu-154 made the hop to the main hub for Russian combat aircraft in Syria. A number of Tu-154s also staged via airports in Tehran, suggesting they were moving Iranian personnel into Syria.

This huge logistic operation was aimed at delivering the RuAF's air group of strike jets to Bassel al Assad International Airport in Latakia province, which as well as being the regional civilian airport for Syria's coast region was also home to the helicopter squadron of the Syrian Navy. After the arrival of the RuAF was re-named Hmeinyan airbase.

In late August and early September satellite imagery showed the Russians were installing hundreds of prefabricated buildings, new air traffic control facilities, aircraft fuel stores, maintenance hangers and ammunition bunkers. Imagery from inside the Russian airbase, posted on social media in September and October, showed the widespread use of prefabricated building to accommodate Russian military personnel. A ring of earthwork defences was also thrown up around the base. Fuel trucks and other vehicles needed to support the aircraft were unloaded at the Russian-controlled section of the port at Tartus, just down the coast.

More than a dozen T-90 tanks and around 30 BTR-82 troop carrying vehicles soon arrived to protect the base, along with hundreds of Russian marines from the 810th Naval Infantry Brigade of the Black Sea Fleet. These were the very soldiers who had spearheaded the seizure of Crimea from the Ukrainians the year before and became famous as Putin's "little green men".

On 18th September the first Russian combat aircraft began arriving at Hmeinyan airbase. It was now almost exclusively a Russian base – the Syrian Navy had to move their helicopters to a newly constructed heliport a few miles away and civilian flights were temporarily halted to free up landing slots for Russian military aircraft.

The Russian jets arrived in three waves. First were four Sukhoi Su-30SM fighters on 18th September which took off from an airbase in southern Russia, flew over Iranian and Iraqi airspace, and were refuelled in flight from an Ilyushin Il-78 tanker to allow them to reach Latakia. These were Russia's most powerful fighters and they immediately changed the balance of air power over Syria and the Eastern Mediterranean.

The next day, a squadron of a dozen Sukhoi Su-25 ground-attack jets, known as Rooks by the Russian aviators, flew into Hmeinyan airbase after a refuelling stop at an airbase in Iran. A Russian Ilyushin Il-76 transport shepherded each cell of four Su-25s on their ferry flight to Syria. This was the first time foreign aircraft had operated from an Iranian airfield since the 1979 Islamic Revolution and it demonstrated in graphic form that Moscow and Tehran were united in their endeavour to support Damascus. On 20th September, the next contingent of Russian jets, some 12 Sukhoi Su-24Ms made the journey to Hmeinyan airbase, again with the aid of air-to-air refuelling from Il-78s.

The Russian strike force was completed on 26th September when four Sukhoi Su-34s arrived at Hmeinyan airbase. These jets were capable of dropping Western-style "smart" munitions and they gave the Russian Air Group in Syria a precision-strike capability. While each squadron of aircraft came from a specific airbase, the pilots were drawn from the across the Russian Aerospace Force to ensure the most experienced personnel were involved in the most high-profile operation ever undertaken by the service.

When President Putin hosted a glitzy Kremlin ceremony in March 2016 to decorate veterans of the Syrian campaign it became clear that many of the pilots of the first squadrons deployed to Hmeinyan airbase were instructors and test pilots. A strong contingent of technical experts from the Sukhoi enterprise and other Russian aerospace companies also went to Syria to make sure there were no technical glitches.

A number of the ferry flights of the Russian jets to Hmeinyan airbase were filmed by rebel activists in north-west Syria as they flew overhead in formation with the Il-76s and Il-78s. This footage was quickly posted online. The transport and tanker aircraft shepherding the jets also showed up on the Flightfinder Radar 24 website as they moved across Iranian, Iraqi and Syrian air space. Within days, satellite images had appeared on major media outlets around the world showing rows of Russian fighter jets at Hmeinyan airbase.

This was a very public display of Moscow's air power and it appeared to have been deliberately done to demonstrate to the United States and its allies across the Middle East that Russia was a player again in the region. The fact that Iraq, nominally a major US ally in the Middle East, had granted the Russians overflight rights, probably at the behest of Tehran, was a very public slap in the face to Washington.

Only days before, the US State Department had requested US allies in Europe and the Middle East not allow Russian aircraft overflight rights.

As the Russian fighter jets were making their way to Syria and generating huge headlines, giant Antonov An-124s delivered more than a dozen Mil Mi-24P attack helicopters to Hmeinyan, along with five Mil Mi-8AMTSh transport helicopters. The Mi-24Ps had been the mainstay of the Russian attack helicopter force since the 1970s and had achieved fame in the Afghan campaign in the 1980s. Known as the "Crocodile" or the "flying tank" to its crews, the Mi-24 ws heavily armoured and can fire unguided rockets and guided anti-tank missiles. It has a 30mm cannon fitted in a turret under its nose.

The final elements of the Russian Group of Forces in Syria began arriving between mid-September and early October, with an artillery and rocket contingent from the Russian Ground Forces unloading its equipment at Tartus. Built around the 120th Artillery Brigade, but with sub-units from a number of other artillery brigades, this force boasted an array of powerful weapons, including a battery of around eight 2A65 MSTA-B 152mm towed howitzers, a battery of half a dozen BM-21 multiple-launch rocket launchers and a battery of a dozen D-30 122mm towed howitzers. The brigade also had several TOS-1A rocket launchers that were fitted with thermobaric warhead-tip rockets and a handful of BM-30 Smerch long range rocket launchers. While the D-30 guns would be positioned to defend Hmeinyan airbase, the remainder of the brigade's weapons, as well as several teams of artillery spotters and a number of command-post vehicles, started to move away from Tartus in early October and began moving towards front-line positions in Latakia and Hama provinces to support the Syrian army.

Across Syria in September, small teams of Russian officers started to spread out to Syrian army headquarters to set up liaison teams. They worked to establish a "ground truth" of the battlefield and pass on requests for air support. Small detachments of Russian Special Forces, or Spetsnaz, and Russian Airborne Forces were also sent out to act as advisors and trainers to Syrian army units in key sections of the front-line. They were accompanied by forward air controllers to direct air strikes onto their targets. Photographs of these Russians and their GAZ Tigr utility vehicles became increasingly common on social media sites linked to the Syrian military at this time. The Russian soldiers all appeared to have very new uniforms, helmets and body armour.

In Damascus, the commander of the Russian Group of Forces in Syria, Colonel General Alexander Dvornikov, set up his headquarters in the Ministry of Defence building in the centre of the city to work with his Syrian and Iranian counter-parts. Dvornikov had been personally selected by Putin over an air force officer, despite the mission being heavily dependent on air power. Apparently Dvornikov first met the Russian President in Berlin in the final days of the Soviet presence in East Germany and had gained his trust. He had also served with some distinction in the North Caucasus operations between 2000 and 2003.

To help make their coalition with the Iranians and Iraqis work smoothly, military liaison teams headed by senior generals were also sent to Tehran and Baghdad to work in the Russian embassies there and establish contact with the Iraqi and Iranian governments and military. Securing and co-ordinating overflight rights was vital to the Russian operation and these teams also included intelligence operatives to pick up information on Syrian rebels and Islamic State. The Baghdad liaison team would also have the job of telling the Americans when the first Russian air strikes were to begin, although the timing of this was a closely guarded secret.

By the end of September the Russians probably had around 5,000 military personnel in Syria. All of them were professional, known to Russians as contract soldiers. Many of the officers were veterans of the conflicts in the Caucasus in the 1990s and early 2000s but few had any experience of the type of operation they were about to participate in. During the 1970s the Soviets launched intervention missions in Ethiopia, Angola and Afghanistan with mixed results. Only

a handful of the veterans of these operations were left in uniform.
The Russians had participated in UN and NATO peacekeeping missions in the Balkans and had closely studied US-led interventions in Iraq and Afghanistan. Russian military literature was full of articles analysing the lessons of these missions. The Russian operation in Syria seemed to copy many aspects of Western intervention forces, such as prefabricated accommodation and mess halls, media briefings and a focus on humanitarian aid to the civil population. But the Russians also applied an important lesson from recent Western interventions and their own failed Afghan campaign. They did not put a big force of conventional troops on the ground in Syria.
The reaction of the US and its allies to this ramping-up of air and naval movements, as well as the surge in construction activity in Syria, was very low-key. Western intelligence and surveillance assets easily picked up the Russian and Iranian activity but it seems there was considerable confusion about Moscow's and Tehran's intentions. The Israelis had also been watching the Russian and Iranian build-up with some concern, including sending up special missions by Gulfstream G550 AWACS radar surveillance planes to monitor the arrival of the Russian air group.
Soon, plane and ship spotters across Europe and Turkey were tracking what the Russians were doing. In the first week of September several media reports appeared describing the first phases of the Russian deployment. US diplomatic and military sources criticised the Russian moves but they did not offer any firm conclusions about Moscow's intentions.
The build up at Hmeinyan airbase could just be a move to facilitate the delivery of more arms to the Syrian military or to set up a base for 1,000 Russian military trainers and advisors, said senior US sources in response to journalists' questions. The possibility of a major Russian intervention was given little prominence. US intelligence also picked up the visit of Soleimani to Moscow in July, but this was also not linked to any Russian-Iranian military planning for intervention in Syria. In comments to the New York Times, Soleimani's visit was attributed by US government sources to dealing with fallout from the international agreement to limit Iran's nuclear sector. (1)
The then US Secretary of State John Kerry, met his Russian counterpart Sergey Lavrov twice in early September 2015 and efforts to kick-start peace talks to end the Syrian conflict were top of the agenda. If the US was concerned about the possibility of Russian intervention, Kerry did not use the press conferences after his meetings with Lavrov to issue any sort of public demarche or warning. US allies were asked in early September to deny Russian aircraft heading to Syria overflight rights but this was a routine reiteration of established US policy rather than as part of a co-ordinated new effort to thwart Moscow's build up.
It has been suggested to me by senior Western intelligence sources that US and British intelligence agencies could not agree on what the Russians were up to, so Kerry had conflicting advice. America's top diplomat apparently did not feel confident enough to issue any warning to the Russians on the basis of uncertain

intelligence assessments.

The US National Security Agency and British GCHQ eavesdropping agencies have a major facility on the island of Cyprus, some 200 kilometres from Syria, and, according to documents released by the whistleblower Edward Snowden, they had considerable success in cracking the communications of the Syrian and Iranian militaries, including breaking into the video transmission links of Iranian unmanned aerial vehicles to enable the British and Americans to watch what the drones were filming. This generated over-confidence in London and Washington about the ability of their intelligence agencies to monitor events in Syria, and possibly led to a misunderstanding of the situation.

Putin and other Russian leaders are - with some justification - notoriously paranoid about eavesdropping by Western intelligence agencies so conduct much of their business in face-to-face meetings, and only issue orders for sensitive missions to senior military commanders in person. This makes it very difficult to monitor what they are doing by using technical means, such as listening to cell phones or tapping email and video conferencing links.

This appears to have been what happened with the high-level planning of the Russian deployment to Syria, making it difficult for Western intelligence to determine Moscow's strategic intent. The Russian commander in Syria in late 2015 and early 2016, General Dvornikov, boasted that the deployment of the Russian air group was a "bolt from the blue" that took the West by surprise. Russian commanders and units had regularly practiced no-notice deployments in a series of exercises in 2014 and 2015, so the air force was ready to dispatch aircraft to Syria at a few days' notice, said the general, in one of his few media interviews.

On top of this, senior Russian leaders, including Putin and Lavrov, made a series of public comments in early and mid-September, suggesting that the early signs of the Russian deployment were little more than a continuation of the long-established policy of supplying arms and technical advisors to the Syrian military.

So, when the first flights of Russian fighter aircraft were picked up on the radar of a US Air Force Boeing E-3 Sentry AWACS aircraft monitoring Iranian, Iraqi and Syrian airspace, it was news to coalition military commanders and Western leaders. The Russian move into Syria had kept everyone guessing until the very last minute. More surprises were in store.

When the news broke of the first Russian air strikes against targets in Syria on 30th September, US leaders claimed were taken by surprise. Kerry later described the events of that day, saying, "The Russians told us they were sending their military into Syria in a typical Russian manner – which is to say, they didn't tell us at all. President Obama and I met with President Putin in New York the day before their strikes were launched. We discussed Syria at length. Putin gave us no indication of what was coming. The next morning, as soon as I learned the news, I caught up to Sergei Lavrov in the hallway of the UN [headquarters in New York]. I said, 'Sergei – you guys are now bombing in Syria and moving troops? What's up?' he looked surprised and at first said, 'No way – what do you mean?' I showed him the media reports. He blanched slightly and hurried off, [and was] subsequently seen talking on his cell phone."(2)

Chapter 8
Air War Russian Style

High over the Euphrates valley a line of six Tupolev Tu-22M3 supersonic bombers approached the last Islamic State stronghold around the Syrian town of Abu Kamal. One after another, the aircraft, which in the Cold War were know to NATO pilots as the Backfire, took turn to unload their cargo of six FAB-500-62 505lb bombs in rapid succession.

The whole manoeuvre was filmed from the cockpits of a pair of Sukhoi Su-30SM fighters that were flying in formation alongside the big bombers. Once the Tu-22M3s had delivered their deadly cargo they turned for home. A few days later, social media video footage emerged from a ground-level observer which showed huge explosions throwing up earth and debris hundreds of feet into the air. These pillars of debris then moved across a field as the stick of bombs landed in quick succession.

During November and December 2017, the Tu-22M3s made this foray over eastern Syrian on 14 occasions to pound what remained of Islamic State to allow Syrian government troops and their Hizbullah allies to take Abu Kamal and a string of towns along the Euphrates. This was more than two years on from the initial Russian deployment of its air force to Syria and the incident illustrated the central role played by air power in Moscow's intervention.

When the first Sukhoi Su-30SM fighters began their final approach to Hmeinyan airbase in Syria's Latakia province in September 2015 they were making history in more ways than one. The Russian intervention in Syria would soon change the course of the Middle East country's civil war, but the way Moscow chose to intervene in the war was also very unusual.

Russia - and before it the Soviet Union – has traditionally been a land power and its army has borne the burden of its foreign wars. Never before had a major Russian military campaign been so dependent for its success or failure on the country's air force.

President Vladimir Putin was turning over a new leaf in Russian military history when he put his trust in the Russian Aerospace Force (RuAF) backed up by cruise-missile-firing warships and submarines to win the war in Syria. In a further military first, the Russian Navy's only aircraft carrier would launch bombers off its deck on combat missions for the first time in Russian military history.

Soon after the Su-30SMs arrived in Syria, more waves of jets touched down at Russia's newest airbase. Russian and international news crews were invited to the base to see the aircraft and crews preparing for action. It was a great show, with jets roaring down the runway and Mil Mi-24 attack helicopters circling overhead to add to the impression of military might. Some Western observers noted that the bulk of the Russian aircraft seemed to date from the 1970s or 1980s and few boasted the precision guided "smart" bombs that adorned Western jets. The red stars on the jets' tails suggested this was just "another failed Soviet intervention", or so said the critics. The presence of the Mi-24s just added to the impression that this was going to be a re-run of Afghanistan in the 1980s.

The "Russian Air Group in Syria", as the contingent at Hmeinyan airbase was formally titled, eventually boasted more than 30 fast jets and was supported by over 4,000 support and security personnel. This was the largest air force contingent dispatched overseas by Moscow since Soviet times and it was meant to showcase the Russian armed forces at their best. The ground technicians and repair crews all had new uniforms. They lived in brand-new prefabricated housing units and ate in purpose-built mess halls. Bomb stores, maintenance hangers, fuel dumps and air-traffic control radars had all been installed at the base ahead of the arrival of the jets themselves.

The composition of the air group showed that Russian air commanders wanted to have a balanced force, with fighters, strike bombers, ground attack jets and attack helicopters to cover multiple tasks. This was a force designed to be able to look after itself.

As with other branches of the Russian military, the air force in 2015 was a mix of old and new. The vast bulk of Moscow's air force flew jets built in the 1980s but there were new aircraft around that had comparable capabilities to advanced Western combat aircraft. The best jet on the ramp at Hmeinyan airbase was the Sukhoi Su-34. Its crew sat side-by-side in the jet's cockpit and were able to monitor computer screens displaying radar returns and video images from heat-detecting thermal cameras. The crew could then dial the co-ordinates of targets into their precision-guided bombs and missiles. This was the main Russian jet sent to Syria that could deliver Western-style "smart" bombs, so it was used for raids that needed pin-point accuracy, such as strikes on suspected rebel commanders. The Su-34 was one of the most recent aircraft to enter Russian service so only eight could be mustered to head to Syria; and the Sukhoi company sent a contingent of engineers and technicians to ensure nothing went wrong during the combat debut of the jets.

According to biographic data on the Su-34 pilots sent to Syria collected by the Ukrainian internet monitoring group InformNaphalm, the majority were senior majors, lieutenant colonels and full colonels with several decades of cockpit experience. The 47th Independent Composite Aviation Regiment, which operated the jets from its home at Baltimor Airbase, near Voronezh, was clearly considered an elite unit and it was expected to play a key role in the coming operation.

To make sure the American, Turkish or Israeli air forces did not interfere with the Russian operation a contingent of top-line fighters was sent to Syria. First to arrive were Sukhoi Su-30SMs and then a quartet of Su-35Ss. These are Russia's classic "super fighters," known as Flankers by NATO, which boast a fearsome reputation for close-range dogfighting, as well as supersonic performance and beyond-visual-range missiles to engage targets from dozens of miles away. Although not in the same class as US Lockheed F-22 Raptor stealth fighters that were already flying over Syria, the Russian jets were more than a match for anything else flying around the Middle East. As with the Su-34 regiment sent to Syria, the Su-30s and Su-35s were piloted by veterans with plenty of fight experience.

The real burden of the looming bombing campaign would fall on the crews of the RuAF Sukhoi Su-24 strike jets and the Su-25 ground-attack jets. Both jets were originally designed in the 1960s and the airframes in Syria were probably built in the mid- to late-1980s. A dozen or so of each type of jet was sent to Syria. The Su-24 is broadly equivalent to the early models of the European Tornado jet, featuring swing wings and pylons to carry bombs on its wings or underneath its fuselage. The Su-24 regiment sent to Syria came from the 2nd Guards Composite Aviation Regiment at Shogol Airbase, near Chelyabinsk in the Urals, and it was equipped with the SM variant of the jet, which allowed it to drop a limited number of "smart" munitions. The jets also benefited from an avionics upgrade that included the incorporation of a new navigation computer, as well as having handheld satellite navigation devices mounted on their cockpit's dashboards. This all meant that the "dumb" or "iron" bombing accuracy of the aircraft had been dramatically improved, with some reports suggesting the new variant could put bombs within 25 metres of the aim point compared to 200 metres with the old system. The US-made Paveway laser-guided bomb, by comparison, is accurate up one metre. While the Russian jets were obviously not as precise as their Western counterparts, their accuracy was good enough to hit a street of houses or an artillery battery position.

The Su-24 regiment in Syria had a far wider age and experience spread than other units, with a mix of veteran majors and colonels as well as young captains and lieutenants. The two-seat Su-24 allows for less-experienced crew to be paired with seasoned veterans.

The Su-25 is of a similar vintage to the Su-24 but is meant for a very different job. In World War Two the Red Air Force's most famous aircraft was the Sturmovik, which was built to find and kill German tanks. The Su-25 was meant to be the successor to the Sturmovik and the Cold War equivalent of the American A-10A Warthog tank-buster jet. It had an armoured cockpit, reinforced fuselage and a canopy with a bigger field of view so the pilot could look for enemy tanks to attack. As with the Su-24, the Rook's cockpit had been upgraded and the latest variant could hit targets with far greater accuracy than older models. The Rook's most devastating weapons were its 23mm and 30mm nose-mounted cannons and under-wing unguided rocket pods. If a Su-25 pilot could line up a target and then dive at it, a salvo of rockets and a ripple of cannon fire would inflict heavy losses on enemy tank columns, artillery positions or infantry trench lines.

The Rook pilots of the Russian air force were an elite group. The 960th Attack Aviation Regiment, from Primorsko Airbase in southern Russia, that provided the Su-25 detachment in Syria contained many combat veterans. Several of its pilots had served in the Caucasus conflicts in the 1990s and in Georgia in 2008 but the Syria operation was a new endeavour for them.

Over the next five years, almost every RuAF fast jet, helicopter and UAV unit, as well as several units from Naval Aviation, took turns to serve in Syria to ensure that as many pilots and specialist personnel got a chance to gain combat experience.

While the Moscow government's propaganda machine went into overdrive to show off the air group in Syria to the Russian and international media, other parts of Russia's armed forces were also being readied to support the war in Syria. A major objective of the intervention in Syria was to project Russia as a global superpower with armed forces and weapon systems that could rival those of the United States and its close allies, Britain and France. This would also have the secondary benefit of boosting sales of Russian military hardware in export markets around the world.

The high commands of both the Russian Aerospace Force and Navy had studied recent intervention operations by the US military in Kosovo, Afghanistan, Iraq and Libya and were keen to show they had similar power-projection capabilities.

Russian Long Range Aviation (LRA) was put on stand-by to strike at Syria with its manned Tupolev Tu-22M3, Tu-95 and Tu-160 heavy bombers. These bombers were classic Soviet-era nuclear war machines which had been re-roled for conventional warfare. The Tu-95 was perhaps the most famous of the bombers and was known in the West as the Bear. Its four counter-rotating engines and swept-back wings gave it a distinctive silhouette.

A Tu-95 famously dropped the most powerful ever thermo-nuclear bomb, the Tsar Bomba, in 1961. In the later years of the Cold War the Tu-95s were re-equipped with long-range cruise missiles to fire at targets from outside NATO air defences. By 2015, the Tu-95 force was re-equipped with conventionally armed variants of the Kh-55 cruise missile. Although the Bears had regularly been intercepted by NATO fighters over the North Atlantic during the Cold War, the Tu-95 had never been used in action before the Syria conflict. Just under 40 were in frontline use with the Russian air force in 2015.

The Tu-95's big brother was the Tu-160, or as it was code-named by NATO, the Blackjack. This was a supersonic bomber, known to the Russians as the White Swan, that was designed to penetrate NATO air defences at low level. It first entered Soviet service in 1987 but only just over two dozen were actually built before the Berlin Wall collapsed and production ground to a halt. By 2015 some 16 remained airworthy and were the pride and joy of Russian LRA. President Putin famously once took the controls of Tu-160 during a training mission and he liked the experience so much he approved plans to re-start production of an upgraded version.

The most numerous Russian heavy bomber in 2015 was the Tu-22M3. It was originally designed to make low-level raids into NATO airspace to launch cruise missiles at land targets or ships. They had been used to drop bombs on Afghanistan in the 1980s, Chechnya in the 1990s and South Georgia in 2008. Between 60 and 70 were in service in 2015.

In the decade up to 2015, the LRA force had undergone renewed investment with more money being spent on spares, maintenance and training for strategic strike operations with conventional weapons. The Tu-95s and Tu-160s concentrated on strike operations with long-range, air-launched cruise missiles, while the Tu-22M3s would focus on carrying out "carpet bombing" strikes with "iron" bombs against area targets. This recreated the "Arc Light" strikes of the Vietnam War by the US Air Force B-52 bombers.

The commanders of LRA had been progressively stepping up the operational readiness of their bomber squadrons by holding a series of short-notice or snap scrambles or by sending aircraft on long-range patrols in the North Atlantic, Arctic or Pacific regions.

After the start of the Russian mission in Syria, the Tu-95s and Tu-160s were held at their home bases in central Russia and used air-to-air refuelling to reach their targets. But the shorter-range Tu-22M3s did not have air-to-air refuelling so needed a base closer to Syria to be effective. To give the Tu-22M3s the legs to get to Syria, Mozdok airbase in the Caucasus was prepared to host a detachment of the bombers.

Russia's Navy was also keen to enhance its conventional strike capabilities and since 2012 had been progressively equipping its surface fleets and submarines with the 3M14 Kalibr cruise missile. It reportedly had a range of up to 2,500 kilometres and Moscow touted it as a rival to the US Tomahawk Land Attack Missile. One version could be launched from an Improved Kilo-class submarine's torpedo tube and another from the vertical-launch tubes of a frigate or corvette. For Putin, the Kalibr was the ultimate military machismo symbol, with only the US and Britain ever using such weapons in combat before. As part of the build-up to the Syria operation, a number of warships and submarines of the Black Sea Fleet and Caspian Sea Flotilla equipped to fire the Kalibr were put on alert.

Co-ordinating bringing together aircraft, missiles and warships across several times zones and arranging diplomatic clearances for aircraft and missiles to overfly a number of neighbouring countries, as well as international sea and air routes, was a complex task that fell to members of the Russian General Staff's new National Defence Command Centre in Moscow. This was opened in December 2014 as the nerve centre of Russia's armed forces and it boasted a network of computer links to airbases, naval vessels and army bases across Russia and outside the country. During the Syria crisis, the command post would become famous as the venue of media briefings by top Russian generals. Photographs from inside the command centre showed scores of Russian staff officers at work behind ranks of computer screens. It also had wall-sized computer screens able to display maps and drone imagery, as well as allowing video conferencing with commanders at remote locations to take place.

Once the Syrian campaign got underway, Russian generals began to appear at almost daily media briefings in Moscow. Behind them would be slick Microsoft Powerpoint presentations of maps, photos and video clips of the Russian air force's "greatest bombing hits". Some of the videos also appeared to have been recorded by the Sukhoi Su-34's thermal-imaging cameras.

The Russian air campaign in Syria evolved into a number of distinct phases as the operation to support the Damascus government developed. After the deployment and initial operations in late 2015 and early 2016, Russian air operations began to be focused on specific sectors across Syria. Early 2016 saw a major drive to support the recapture of the historic city of Palmyra in the central desert region. In the latter half of 2016, Russian air power played a major role in the battle to recapture Aleppo.

The focus during 2017 was on supporting fast-moving Syrian operations across northern, central and eastern Syria to defeat Islamic State fighters. In the following year, the Russian military concentrated on rolling up the last rebel-held enclaves in East Ghouta near Damascus, Qalamoun and Rastan pockets in Central Syria and Dara'a in the south. As these operations unfolded, the Russian military became involved in wider confrontations with the Western and Israeli air forces. The withdrawal of US troops from much of north-eastern Syria saw Russian troops, backed by strong airpower, move quickly to occupy their vacated bases. The first months of 2020 saw a renewed Syrian offensive against the final rebel enclave around Idlib in north west Syria and this brought Russian forces into direct confrontation with Turkish troops who were moving to back rebel fighters.

Russian air operations in Syria during the final three months of 2015 underwent rapid evolution as new units and commanders started to bed down in their new bases and gain experience of operating in Syria. The identities of senior Russian air commanders in Syria remain a closely guarded secret and none of these officers have been named in the Moscow media. Nor have senior Russian air force officers discussed the evolution of their air campaign in an open forum. To build up an accurate picture of events it is necessary to piece together accounts of Russian pilots and forward air controllers, conduct analysis of video of Russian air operations, and look at open-source tracking of Russian and Syrian aircraft.

The first six weeks of the air campaign were characterised by tightly controlled air strikes, with the majority of targets being pre-selected by the Russian headquarters in Syria for attack. According to multiple accounts by pilots, they were briefed at Hmeinyan airbase before their missions and then would take off to head out to attack their targets.

These strikes would generally be carried out from medium altitudes of around 10-15,000 feet using their aircraft's bombing computers to calculate bomb release points. Except for the Su-34s, which used a number of precision guided weapons, all the other strikes were carried out with unguided bombs. All the strikes were carried out under tight direction from a ground-control centre at Hmeinyan airbase. There appear to have been occasions when Russian jets were directed to attack targets of opportunity but all these involved hitting co-ordinates passed to the pilots from the ground-control centre. During the early months of the campaign, Russian strike-jet pilots did not have much freedom of action to find and engage targets.

Attack helicopter pilots who operated at low level over battlefields were given permission to engage targets that popped up or were located by forward air controllers on the ground.

One Russian Su-25 pilot based in Syria described his regiment's tactics in a media interview, saying: "In the Western press, there are sometimes reports that, they say, Russian pilots somewhere hit a peaceful object. All this is a lie. We use weapons only on the co-ordinates that come from the higher headquarters, and, therefore, have already been clarified, reconciled. Therefore, if I strike, I am convinced: this is a blow to terrorists."

An account of the Su-25 regiments' operations in Syria in late 2015 and early 2016 appeared in the Russian media in 2017. It said the "main method of conducting combat operations by the Su-25SM crews in Syria was the successive infliction of air strikes against pre-determined land at a fixed time in the navigational bombing mode."

It revealed that surveillance aircraft first scouted out the targets and then groups of between two and six aircraft would be sent to attack one or two minutes after the targets were detected. The attack wave would circle over their targets at between 3,500 and 4,000 feet for up to 40 minutes at a time to keep the enemy's heads down, said the report. During this time, each Su-25 would take turns to drop bombs.

"The hits were made point-by-point - for each air bomb had its own purpose," said the report. "The principle of one bomb, one goal was for the modernized Su-25SM like a law. [The Su-25SM] ensured the accuracy of target destruction of several tens of metres."

Interestingly, the report confirmed that for targeting large groups of enemy fighters the Su-25 crews would drop weapons fitted with sub-munitions.

The next major escalation of the Russian air campaign in Syria unfolded after the loss of a Metrojet Airbus A321 airliner over Sinai on 31st October 2015, just after it had taken off from the Sharm al Sheikh holiday resort. The deaths of 219 Russian, four Ukrainian and one Belarusian tourists and aircrew caused outrage in Moscow. Two weeks later the Russian government accused Islamic State terrorists of planting a bomb on the aircraft. President Putin ordered a military response. This unfolded on the morning of 17th November.

A dozen Tu-22M3 bombers took off from Mozdok airbase in South Ossetia and headed to eastern Syria to unload their cargo of dumb bombs on targets near Raqqa and Dier Ez Zor between 5am and 5.30am. Some four hours later, a second wave of Tu-95 and Tu-160 bombers took off from Engels-2 airbase, the home of the 121st Heavy Bomber Aviation Regiment, in central Russia and headed south towards Iran, before turning west and into Syrian air space. They launched 34 air-based Kh-55 and Kh-101 cruise missiles at targets around Aleppo and Idlib.

The first public indication of the strike came early on the morning of 17th November when still and video imagery appeared on social media showing what appeared to be a Russian cruise missile overflying northern Syria. Images of debris from other large missiles, possibly Kh-55s, also appeared online.

Later that day President Putin strode into the National Defence Command Centre in Moscow to hold a remarkable event. Putin took a seat on the stage and started to issue orders to his military commanders for a series of further strikes in full view of the cameras, live on Russian television. He also ordered the Russian navy cruiser Moskova to co-operate with the French aircraft carrier, Charles de Gaulle, which was to sail for the Eastern Mediterranean on 18th November in the wake of a major Islamic State terrorist attack on Paris that left 130 dead and 368 people injured.

Over four days, the Russian bombers repeatedly returned to targets over Syria, with the Tu-22M3s continuing their carpet bombing and the bigger Tu-95s and Tu-160s firing further volleys of cruise missiles. Smaller strike jets based in Syria also surged their efforts.

After the conclusion of the LRA campaign on 20th November, the Russian Ministry of Defence issued statistics for the bombing effort. It said 101 cruise missiles had been fired, including 18 from naval vessels. When added to dumb bombs dropped by the Tu-22M3s the amount of ordnance dropped ran to 1,400 tons. This was the largest operation by the LRA branch of the Russian air force since the Second World War.

Senior Russian government leaders and military commanders claimed success for their strikes, but independent bomb damage assessment was unavailable. Imagery that appeared on social media showed at least one Russian cruise missile apparently detonating prematurely in mid-air over Aleppo province and another, apparently a Kh-55, crashed in Iran.

Nevertheless, the four days of activity suggested that efforts by its commander, Lieutenant General Anatoly Zhikharev, to rejuvenate the LRA Command had made progress. Equally important had been the ability of the Russians to marry its operations with an information operation to not only project firepower onto targets in Syria, but to reap political and diplomatic benefits from the bombing campaign both at home and abroad.

The four days of intensified bombing demonstrated Russia's long-range strike capability. It also allowed Russia to target Islamic State without distracting its air group in Syria from its core task of supporting the ongoing Syrian ground offensive. In that way, Russia could be seen to be indirectly retaliating for the Metrojet Airbus bombing and demonstrating solidarity with France in the wake of the 13th November Paris attacks, thereby presenting itself as a credible partner in the fight against Islamic State.

There remains considerable controversy over the effectiveness of the Russian air campaign during its first six weeks. The effectiveness of Russian air strikes was only as good as the intelligence they were based on. At this stage in the campaign, the Russians appeared to have not built up detailed understanding of the Syrian battlefield.

Interestingly, there were accusations at this time that the Russian air force targeting officers were harvesting intelligence from online posts by a Russian blogger called Ivan Sidorenko, who trawled through Jihadi posts on Twitter and Facebook and identified military bases and other locations of significance. Several of these locations were subsequently bombed by Russian and Syrian aircraft. This use of what is known as "open-source" intelligence is widespread in Western air forces but it was a new development for the Russian air force and showed they were on a steep learning curve. Breaches in operational security, or OPSEC, by rebel groups through their online postings would continue to be exploited by the Russian military as the campaign unfolded.

At the regular media briefings in Moscow, senior Russian generals routinely boasted of the effectiveness of their air strikes. But still and video imagery posted on social media on both the rebel and government sides, as well as in bomb damage video released by Moscow, suggested that the impact of Russian air strikes was less than optimal in this period of the campaign. The bulk of targets for Russian jets appeared to be fixed buildings, bridges and fortified positions, not moving targets. Repeatedly the Russians described these positions as rebel command posts, ammunition factories or troop concentrations. The imagery of strikes suggested that many of the targets were empty buildings, or otherwise, not what Moscow said they were. On one occasion, the Russian military released imagery of what was described as an Islamic State oil refinery, whereas independent analysts suggested it was a water-treatment plant. There were repeated accusations from rebel sources and Western governments that the Russian air attacks were causing widespread civilian casualties.

The imagery released in Russian media briefings appeared to have been either satellite imagery or cockpit video from the Su-34 jets. There was no live drone video footage, suggesting that the Russians did not have the ability to monitor targets in real time over extended periods. Repeatedly, pictures emerged during this period of crashed Russian Orlan-10 drones in rebel areas - but these were small hand-launched drones that could not transmit their pictures back to the Russian air group headquarters at Hmeinyan airbase. These drones helped frontline commanders but could not be used to plan and conduct what the Western military termed "time-sensitive targeting", or to strike at moving targets. Russian commanders clearly realised this was a major shortcoming and they moved to try to redress this capability gap, to establish what would be known in the West as a working "kill chain".

The best evidence that the Russians had brought a time-sensitive targeting capability online in Syria emerged in early January 2016, when commercial satellite imagery of Hmeinyan airbase started to show large Forpost surveillance drones and their distinctive hangar. During December 2015, Forpost video imagery started to appear in Moscow Ministry of Defence briefings, to illustrate claims of attacks on rebel supply convoys and targeted strikes on senior rebel commanders.

The Forpost drone came to be central to Russian air operations in Syria, in effect becoming Moscow's "ace in the hole". Time after time, Forpost imagery was used in press briefings about Russian heavy bomber and cruise-missile strikes, fighter-jet attacks and ground operations. This before-and-after imagery, revealed that the Russians regularly had Forposts up to find targets for air strikes and then to film their progress, all live while senior commanders watched the imagery back at Hmeinyan. Subsequently, further imagery showed that the Russians had found ways to distribute the footage, so commanders away from Hmeinyan could view it in real time. This was a major advance for the Russians, which gave them an advantage in many battles during the re-mainder of the campaign.

The fact that the Russian military were dependent on an Israeli-supplied drone was not something either Moscow or Tel Aviv wanted to talk up at this point in the campaign. After the poor performance of Russian air strikes against Georgia in the brief 2008 war, Putin had brokered a deal with the Israeli Prime Minister Bibi Netanyahu to buy a batch of Searcher 2 drones from the Israel Aircraft Industry (IAI) company and then to set up a factory in Russia to assemble them. The Israelis had pioneered the use of drones in combat, ironically against the Syrians in the 1982 Lebanon war, and they were the only "Western" country that was willing to share drone technology with Russia. It would have taken Russian scientists several years to catch up with their Western rivals without the help of the Israelis.

The Russian OPK Oboronprom company and IAI subsequently established a UAV partnership which led to the Joint Stock Company Ural Works of Civil Aviation (UZGA) in Ekaterinburg setting up an assembly line to put together the drones from kits supplied by Israel. The drones were renamed the Outpost by the Russians, which translated into English as Forpost.

Moscow has not released much information about its UAV units but it is believed at least five Forpost air vehicles were lost in operations over the pro-Russian separatist enclave in eastern Ukraine since 2014 and another two were lost over Syria in 2018.

The Forpost could beam live video pictures back to the Russian air operations centre from hundreds of miles away, which revolutionised how the Russian air force did business. The new drones and the video imagery they recorded also transformed how the Russian military and the Kremlin carried out information operations – or, as they are better known - propaganda.

In June 2017, the Russians finally unveiled the Forpost base in Syria to the Moscow media. The Russian Ministry of Defence's Zvezda television network sent a team of its reporters to Hmeinyan to talk up the role of the Forpost. For the first time, it showed the inside of a Forpost ground-control cabin at Hmeinyan airbase. This revealed that the cabin was a standard Israel Aircraft Industries MALAT Division Advanced Ground Control Station product, which was likely to have been delivered as part of the original sales contract. An IAI MALAT Division logo could be seen on one of the work stations. The logos of the US computer company APC could be seen on what appeared to be server rack, and one of the computer displays has the logo of the Japanese company

NEC. Flight and sensor controls had English-language markings on them, further indicating they had been supplied by IAI as part of the original Forpost/Searcher contract. A Russian military telephone handset appeared to be the only non-Israeli supplied piece of hardware in the ground station.

Russia's air offensive got off to a slow start but by the end of 2015 Moscow's airmen began to get into their stride. During the first months of 2016, Russian air power would start to swing the balance across several battlefields in favour of forces loyal to the Damascus government.

The bombing surge against Abu Kamal recounted at the start of this chapter was the culmination of a two-year-long campaign by the RuAF's LRA command in eastern Syria. The distances involved in operating in the east of Syria meant jets based at Hmeinyan had limited endurance to give them much time over targets. Although the RuAF moved a handful of Su-25 and Mi-24 to forward bases at T-4 and Palmyra airports during the drive to the east, long-range bombers and cruise missiles filled a crucial role in providing firepower as the battle unfolded in this remote desert region.

A key part in the Russian campaign after 2015 was the occasional activation of what the RuAF termed a Reinforced Air Wing to support tactical and transport aircraft en route to bases in Syria. In Western parlance, Mozdok airbase in North Ossetia was a forward operating base or hub where aircraft on temporary deployment were grouped under a single command. First, the fighter aircraft staged through the base before making the final leg of the trip to Syria with the support of Ilyushin Il-78 air-to-air refuelling tankers. The base's huge flight line and parking pan, as well as extensive fuel and bomb dump infrastructure, meant it was an ideal location for the forward deployment of Tu-22M3s. Imagery released by the Russian Ministry of Defence of Mozdok over the next two years indicated that aircraft from the LRA's two main Tu-22M3 units at Sheykovka (52nd Guards Heavy Bomber Regiment), Belaya (200th Guards Heavy Bomber Regiment) and Olenya/Olenegorsk (40th Composite Aviation Regiment, formerly the Russian Naval Aviation reconnaissance regiment) deployed aircraft to the South Ossetia base. Over the years the jets started to sport "bomb" mission tally markings and one even featured sharks' teeth insignia around its engine intakes.

The second phase of Russian strategic bombing campaign was focused on the besieged Syrian city of Dier Ez Zor in the east of the country. Syrian troops and 100,000 civilians had been trapped in the city by thousands of fanatical Islamic State fighters since early 2014 and relied on a precarious helicopter supply line to bring in food and supplies. In January 2016, after Islamic State fighters launched a ground offensive and captured a large army barracks on the edge of the city, the Reinforced Air Wing at Mozdok was mobilised to turn back the tide. Eight Tu-22Ms were deployed to Mozdok and from 22nd January a series of seven raids against targets around the perimeter of Dier Ez Zor took place over a two-week period. Formations or strike packages of six Tu-22Ms at a time flew in these missions. Russian Ministry of Defence video of these missions showed Tu-22M3s each dropping sticks of up to 24 OFAB-250-270 270kg (595lb) unguided fragmentation bombs in an attempt to "carpet bomb" Islamic State fighters pressing the city's defence lines.

Russian strategic bomber operations paused for the next five months until Mozdok was re-activated again to help an ill-fated Syrian army advance eastwards from Palmyra to try to punch through to Dier Ez Zor. Six waves of Tu-22M3s were launched against targets in central Syria up to mid-August 2016 but Mozdok was in the midst of a major upgrade, including the building of a new runway, and it eventually had to be closed to allow this work to progress. The LRA command wanted a base closer to their bomber's targets so Iran was approached to make Hamadan airbase in the west of the country available. On 15th August four Tu-22M3s and Su-34 strike fighters, as well as Il-76s carrying support equipment, arrived at the desert airbase for a rapid refuel, before taking off to hit targets across Syria. Two days later the Su-34s hit Syria again from Hamadan. When the details of the deployment were leaked by the Russian Ministry of Defence there was considerable disquiet in the Iranian parliament about foreign forces being based in their country. As a result, the deployment was curtailed after the Tu-22M3s flew their last mission on 18th August. Four days later the last Russian aircraft returned home.

In the latter half of 2016, the focus of RuAF operations was supporting the Syrian offensive to capture the rebel held enclave in the north western city of Aleppo. This included an audacious raid by two Tu-95 bombers on 17th November. They were launched from an airbase in Russia's Arctic north, supported by Il-78 air-to-air refuelling tanker aircraft. Their 13,000 kilometre flight took them around the west coast of Ireland and through the Straits of Gibraltar to fire a handful of Kh-101 cruise missiles at targets to the west of Aleppo from over the eastern Mediterranean, before flying over Iraq and Iran to land back in Russia. Again, this was a first, as LRA Tu-95s had never used this type of missile in combat before. The strike caught Britain and other NATO allies by surprise and it took them several hours to work out actually what the Russian bombers had done. A rather bemused RAF press spokesman in Ministry of Defence in London initially laughed at the idea when he was asked questions by reporters about the raid. He had to make apologetic phone calls back to the journalists several hours later to confirm the raids.

In a sign of the deterioration of the situation around Dier Ez Zor, the LRA was mobilised again to strike back and relieve the pressure on the Syrian garrison. The first raid, by six Tu-22M3s, took place on 21st January 2017, with each bomber unloading a stick of between 12 and 24 OFAB-250-270 bombs. Further raids were revealed by the Moscow on 23rd, 24th and 30th January, each involving six Tu-22M3s flying from Mozdok.

The LRA staged another Kh-101 strike against targets near Raqqa, the capital of the Islamic State's self-declared Caliphate, in February 2017, this time launched from Tu-95s flying southwards over Iran and Iraq. This process was repeated in July when Tu-95s fired three more Kh-101s at targets in Hama province.

By November 2017, Islamic State's Caliphate was imploding. Iraqi troops had captured Mosul, US-backed Kurdish fighters had taken Raqqa and Syrian troops had at last lifted the siege of Dier Ez Zor. The last Islamic State fighters had retreated down the Euphrates valley and they staged a final stand around the town of Abu Kamal, just across the border from Iraq.

The LRA now re-activated the Reinforced Air Wing at Mozdok with eight Tu-22M3s to deliver the coup de grace against Islamic State. This would be the most intense period of strategic air and missile attacks since the major four-day-long bombing and missile offensive in November 2015.

On 1st November six Tu-22M3 long-range bombers of the Russian Aerospace Forces flew south from Mozdok over Iran and Iraq to hit targets near Abu Kamal using "iron" bombs. Moscow's defence ministry said the bombers hit "strongholds, ammunition and armament depots of insurgents". Over the next month more than a dozen similar strike packages were launched by the Tu-22Ms, flying some 84 sorties, and on two occasions they were co-ordinated with Kalibr cruise missile strikes, launched from Russian submarines in the Mediterranean. During the final assault on Abu Kamal Syrian and Lebanese Hizbullah troops massed artillery and rocket batteries outside the town. News imagery of the fire base showed Russian command post vehicles and satellite communications dishes, indicating that Russian officers were co-ordinating the complex air support and artillery fire during the battle.

The Russian Ministry of Defence never published any drone imagery of the impact of the Tu-22M3 strikes so it is difficult to assess whether they found their intended targets or what damage they caused. From Russian imagery of the aircraft taking part in the raids, the Tu-22M3, each dropped a stick of six FAB-500-62 unguided high- explosive 500 kilogram bombs. It would seem that the Russians were aiming to put 36 bombs in a small space to shock and disorientate any Islamic State fighters caught in the bomb area. The lack of effective resistance to the Syrian and Hizbullah advance towards Abu Kamal suggests the Tu-22M3 strikes had the intended effect.

On 11th December President Putin flew to the main Russian airbase in Syria's Latakia province to declare victory. He then ordered a winding-down of the Russian air campaign and over the next week several air force units made high-profile returns to their home bases. Tu-22M3 aircraft were given top billing by the Kremlin's public relations machines taking off from Mozdok and then arriving at the home bases at Sheykovka, Belaya and Olenya/Olenegorsk. This was the first time Mozdok had been officially recognised as the forward operating base of the Reinforced Air Wing. The Tu-22M3's role in the Syrian war was now well and truly out of the shadows.

The commitment of LRA to the Syria campaign raised many eye brows in the west. It was not a surprise that Russian bombers had been able to strike so far from their home bases. Long-range flights had been something of an LRA speciality going back to the days of the Soviet Union. What was interesting and impressive was the degree to which LRA assets were integrated with unmanned aerial vehicles and manned strike aircraft based in Syria, as well as cruise missiles launched from warships and submarines. The LRA was well and truly part of a global "kill chain". This was very new for the Russian Aerospace Force and few air arms could pull off such missions. Flying a bomber from the Arctic into the Mediterranean and then firing a cruise missile on the basis of real-time intelligence from a UAV circling over a target in the Syrian desert was quite an achievement.

Chapter 9
Finding a War-Winning Strategy?

Two days after Syrian troops, backed by Russian Special Forces and attack helicopters, retook the desert city of Palmyra from Islamic State in March 2017, television crews from Moscow made their way to film a musical concert amid the iconic ancient archaeological ruins. On hand to provide suitably uplifting and positive sound-bite commentary for the Russia 1 television station was the Commander of Russian Group of Forces in Syria, Colonel General Andrei Kartapolov.

The general was already a familiar face to Russian and international television audiences, after his role in 2015 as the ""media face"" of the Kremlin's intervention during Moscow press conferences about the Syria conflict. The presence of Russia's top military commander in Syria so near to the frontline – Islamic State fighters were still less than two kilometres away skirmishing with Syria troops around Palmyra airbase – was a vivid illustration of the role played by Moscow's senior officers in the Syria conflict.

For outside observers, the Syria intervention offers some important insights into how the Russian military organises and executes expeditionary warfare in the 21st Century.

Although the presence of the Russian Aerospace Force's (RuAF) strike jets and attack helicopters at Hmeinyan airbase in Syria's Latakia province was usually at the heart of media coverage of Moscow's intervention, its military had also established an extensive command-and-control presence across Syria to link up the Russian air contingent with its Syrian counterparts.

The Russian military only provided occasional "snap shots" of its command structure in Syria but it is possible to piece together information from public media briefings, open-source analysis of news and social media imagery from Syria, and analysis of the timeline of Russian military operations. These sources can be used to build up a picture of how Moscow controlled its forces in Syria. Some of these operations were highly complex, involving strategic air and naval forces operating far from Syria, indicating high-level command-and-control linkages across the Russian military.

For many months, the Russians kept the name of the field commander in Syria secret and did not even acknowledge they had a deployed commander. The identities of the senior air force commanders at Hmeinyan airbase have also never been revealed, even in the Russian media.

Several Russian media outlets have reported from Russian bases in Syria between 2015 and 2020, interviewing many mid-level commanders, special forces operatives, and air force pilots. Their accounts give interesting insights into how Russian military operations were organised. Obituaries of senior Russian officers killed in Syria, also add more details.

Still and video imagery from Syria, posted both on social media and available via traditional news media, along with satellite imagery of Syrian and Russian bases, also added much to our understanding of Russian operations. It is possible to identify satellite communication dishes, radio antenna, and command post vehicles and buildings. The footprint of Russian liaison vehicle and personnel deployments is very illuminating. The relationships building between senior Russians and Syrian officers can also be tracked.

From the very start of its intervention, the Russian military had put great effort into creating a command-and-control network that mirrored the Syrian military chain of command. The commander of the Russian forces, usually an officer with the rank of colonel general or lieutenant general was based in Damascus, close to the Syrian Ministry of Defence and the military high command. Senior Russian officers of major general and senior colonel-rank have been photographed visiting Syrian army headquarters across the country, either acting as advisors on a long-term basis or on fact-finding visits.

More junior officers - lieutenant colonels and majors from the Airborne or Spetsnaz - were also recorded deploying in the field with Syrian army brigades and regiments as their advisors and air support co-ordinators. Many of these advisory detachments were routinely photographed operating from light armoured vehicles, including Iveco Lynx and Gaz Tigr. They also appeared to be equipped with multiple communications devices and tablet computers to view satellite imagery and maps.

The Russians have also put considerable effort into the co-ordination of air operations, including setting up an air command centre at Hmeinyan airbase. Liaison teams were based at other Syrian air bases and air force command posts and there also appeared that Syrian and Russian air defence forces had been integrated into a single organisation. Russian Spetsnaz forward air control teams were also deployed with Syrian army units to request air strikes and to monitor their execution.

From the start of the Russian intervention in Syria a senior officer was posted to Damascus as the head of the Group of Russian Forces in the Syrian Arab Republic. The pre-eminence of the Russian military in the intervention, as opposed to the foreign ministry or the intelligence agencies, suggested that the senior military officer in Damascus was the main conduit for Moscow's political direction of the Russian campaign.

The first commander of the Russian mission was Colonel General Alexander Dvornikov, formerly the deputy commander of Central Military District. His mission to Syria was kept highly secret at the time and was not publicly revealed by the Kremlin until the spring of 2016, several months after he arrived in Damascus. He was made a Hero of Russia, the country's highest honour, for his leadership in Syria during a glitzy ceremony in the Hall of the Order of St. George in the Grand Kremlin Palace in Moscow.

After returning from Syria, he was promoted to command the Southern Military District, which was responsible for the sensitive Caucasus region and directs Russia's military support for rebel separatist fighters in eastern Ukraine.

Lieutenant General Alexander Zhuravlev replaced Dvornikov as the Kremlin's

Syria commander in July 2016. He had served in Damascus since the start of the Russian intervention as deputy to Dvornikov and had previously been first deputy commander of the Southern Military District, after commanding a motorised rifle division in the Far East. It is unclear if Zhuravlev was promoted to colonel general rank on his appointment in Damascus, but he was certainly seen sporting the new rank in early 2017.

Zhuravlev took the reins at a key point in the Syria campaign, overseeing the Russian participation in the siege of Aleppo, the deployment of the Russian navy aircraft carrier Admiral Kuznetsov to the eastern Mediterranean, and the re-establishing of military-to-military co-operation with Turkey. He handed over command just after the final opposition fighters departed from east Aleppo. Subsequently, Zhuravlev was appointed as deputy chief of staff of the Russian armed forces and in 2018 was given command of the Western Military District, confirming the impression that service in Syria is proving to be good for the promotion prospects of senior Russian officers.

Colonel General Andrei Kartapolov's appointment emerged after he hosted the Chief of the General Staff of the Syrian armed forces, Ali Abdullah Ayyoub, on a visit to the Admiral Kuznetsov and the nuclear-powered cruiser PyotrVelikiy on 6th January 2017 off the Syrian coast, prior to the carrier group's departure back to its home base near Murmansk.

Kartapolov had been closely involved in the Russian intervention in Syria from its beginning in the summer of 2015, when he was head of the Russian general staff's main operational directorate. During the early days of the operation he routinely conducted briefings for the international media in Moscow. His most high-profile operation after taking command in Damascus was to organise Russian assistance to the Syrian army offensive, which re-captured Palmyra in March 2017.

Since 2015, the Russian military employed a range of strategic weapons systems in Syria, including ship- and submarine-launched Kalibr cruise missiles, air-launched cruise missiles, heavy bomber strikes, land attack missiles, and carrier-launched strike aircraft. The employment of these weapon systems appeared to be co-ordinated by the Russian General Staff from the National Defence Command Centre in Moscow.

The Russian military routinely distributed video imagery collected by unmanned aerial vehicles (UAVs) of both air and missile strikes in Syria. The speed at which this imagery was collected, packaged, and then released to the media in Moscow suggests that the Russian military had developed a capacity of some sophistication to conduct intelligence, surveillance, targets, acquisition, and reconnaissance (ISTAR) operations.

During the Soviet era, Moscow's military routinely deployed to support allies in a range of conflicts from Angola, to Ethiopia and Afghanistan. However, there were few Russian officers left still in uniform who could draw on this experience. After 1991 the Russian Federation's armed forces had found themselves operating mainly at home or in the territory of neighbouring countries.

Russian troops did join a number of UN-authorised peacekeeping missions, including in Bosnia and Kosovo in the 1990s, but these were relatively small-scale affairs and only involved land forces and helicopters, not long-range offensive air power.

So in this context, the Syria operation was an ambitious undertaking for the Russian military. It required the Russian military to come up with innovative solutions to command-and-control challenges it had not faced in living memory. Some of the operational challenges, particularly those involving air activities and strategic missile strikes, were completely new to the Russian military.

The Russians had clearly drawn on many lessons from Western operations in the Balkans, Iraq and Afghanistan. They were keen to adopt and integrate unmanned aerial vehicles into their operations and choreograph them with the employment of precision-guided munitions.

The operation in Syria also for the first time involved significant co-operation with an array of new "allies" including Palestinian militias, Lebanese Hizbullah, Iraqi Shia militia and Iranian forces. Tehran had a similar advisory mission in Syria so it had to be co-ordinated with the Russians. Iranian UAVs and Lockheed C-130 Hercules air-drop missions also had to be co-ordinated with Russian air operations. The co-ordination of strategic air movements and missile strikes with countries neighbouring Syria, including Iraq, Iran, and Cyprus, as well as with the US-led Coalition, was also a new development for the Russian military.

Moscow's intervention in Syria also saw the Russian military blend "hard power" and "soft power" activities into a sophisticated strategy that rolled up several opposition enclaves with little resistance. The sophistication of these operations increased as Russian officers in Syria built up their experience and expertise in the region.

Russian military units organised prisoner and population exchanges; delivered humanitarian aid; brokered political deals and ceasefires with local communities and militia groups; and helped to recruit new fighters to fill the depleted ranks of the Syrian military.

Although early Russian efforts to employ soft power effects in the first months of 2016 were localised in nature, in 2017 and 2018 the operations became more ambitious and central to Moscow's strategy.

The Russian intervention in Syria started as an operation to shore up the faltering forces of the Syrian government of President Bashar al Assad, which had succumbed to opposition advances in the north and south of the country, as well as simultaneous Islamic State offensives in the eastern desert region. After initial operations to stabilise the Syrian frontlines, newly arrived Russian commanders formulated plans for offensive operations to help the Damascus government to re-establish control of the country.

At this point in the war, the Syrian Arab Army (SAA) had been weakened by four years of fighting and mass desertions, and did not have the combat power to launch a nationwide offensive to defeat the opposition and the Islamic State.

The Syrian government had set up a Ministry for National Reconciliation in 2011 headed by the controversial leader of the Syrian Social National Party, Ali Haider, who expounded a "reconciliation strategy". The Damascus government was fighting for its survival in 2014-15, so Haider appeared to be sidelined by army hardliners and paramilitary commanders – such as Tiger Force commander Suheil al Hussein – who advocated scorched-earth policies to eliminate regime opponents.

The Syrian government's internal dynamics are complex and shrouded in secrecy, but the author's contacts with members of the Ministry for National Reconciliation suggest that by late 2015, Haider's influence had begun to rebound as many of the Syrian elite realised that the war could not be won by conventional military means alone, even with Russian firepower in support. In offensives in Hama and Aleppo provinces in October and November 2015, government troops regained some ground but could not break through rebel lines and suffered heavy casualties.

By 2015, the Ministry for National Reconciliation had brokered a series of local ceasefires, the provision of utilities, humanitarian aid deliveries, and prisoner exchanges. These initiatives necessitated contact with opposition militia commanders, community leaders and tribal chiefs. These soon revealed that not all were implacably opposed to the Damascus government. Many communities were war-weary, suggesting that there was a prospect of wider reconciliation deals to win such communities back to the government in a series of piecemeal moves.

The first commander of the Group of Russian Forces in Syria, General Dvornikov, arrived in Damascus in August in 2015 to oversee Moscow's intervention, and rapidly came to similar conclusions as Haider and other exponents of reconciliation. Russia would need to craft a sophisticated strategy to win over the Syrian population to the Damascus government if it was to progress on the battlefield.

Although the Russians adopted the reconciliation brand for their strategy, it was a variation of the classic hearts-and-minds counter-insurgency strategy familiar to Western military theorists. Dvornikov met Haider and Ministry for National Reconciliation officials in late 2015 and early 2016 to fine-tune the adoption and execution of the strategy. With high-level Russian backing, the Syrian government and military were forced to accept the reconciliation approach.

In February 2016, the Russian military unveiled its Centre for Reconciliation of Warring Parties in the Syrian Arab Republic to oversee its soft power activities. Its headquarters was within the main Russian command complex at Hmeinyan air base in Latakia province and had a staff of some 200 personnel, according to a Russian Ministry of Defence announcement.

The Centre's first operations involved the delivery of humanitarian aid to government-controlled areas in Hama, Latakia, and Homs provinces. International media were invited to witness some of these deliveries, observing troops from Hmeinyan delivering food to devastated villages and holding improvised medical clinics in archetypal hearts-and-minds activities that aimed to bolster morale within government territory.

Early steps were taken to spread the Centre's messages, including Arabic-language websites, Arabic-language leaflets, and extensive engagement with the local media across Syria, promoting a message that the Russian presence in Syria was intended to help Syrians. Aid deliveries were small, but enabled the Centre's officers to visit areas close to frontlines to meet community leaders and to build up a picture of local conditions and loyalties.

According to reports in Russian military publications by Russian pilots and forward air controllers, this "human terrain mapping" was rapidly incorporated into Russian military planning. They said the Centre was consulted in real-time by Russian Aerospace Forces commanders on the allegiance of communities before airstrikes were authorised.

In its earliest operations, the Centre did not appear to have its own dedicated personnel and assets. Its first commander, Lieutenant General Sergei Kuralenko - who subsequently became the commander-in-chief for peacekeeping operations in the Russian ground forces - was moved from Baghdad to head up the Centre at short notice. In Iraq he had headed an intelligence centre with Iraqi and Iranian military representatives.

The Centre's first operations were carried out on an ad hoc basis by diverting force protection personnel and units from Hmeinyan air base and Tartus port, predominately members of the 810th Naval Infantry Brigade from the Black Sea Fleet.

The Centre's first major operational test to win back territory from opposition forces occurred in the summer and autumn of 2016. This was a complex operation that involved Syrian ground and air forces, backed by Russian air, naval, and special forces, working to isolate and then seize control of the opposition-held enclave in eastern Aleppo.

At the centre of the Syrian and Russian plan were activities by the Centre to win the heart-and-minds of the approximately 150,000 people trapped inside the enclave. The operation's symbol became the green buses that moved refugees out of Aleppo, but the role of the Centre was often over-looked. In August-September 2016, offers were made by the Russians and Syrians that the enclave's population would be evacuated via what were dubbed "humanitarian corridors". This was a considerable logistic challenge and planning began in parallel with kinetic military operations.

Personnel from the Centre coordinated with the Syrian government and local authorities in Aleppo to establish refugee shelters, bus transport to the shelters, food provision and medical services. Extensive leaflet drops over opposition areas spread information to the enclave's population, and the local Red Crescent, United Nations and other aid organisations were also brought into the Centre's planning. Hundreds of Russian army personnel moved to the Aleppo region to support the Centre's operations, establishing military hospitals and field kitchens to look after the shelters' refugees, and providing force protection.

Once the operation began in late September, the Centre's activities increased as opposition frontlines cracked and civilians left the enclave. By the time the enclave fell in December 2016, United Nations data suggested that a little more than 100,000 civilians had left the enclave and moved into refugee shelters in government-controlled territory.

Simultaneously, Russian negotiators brokered a deal with opposition groups, via the International Committee for the Red Cross (ICRC), for opposition fighters to be evacuated to opposition-controlled territory around Idlib, with ICRC data stating that at least 34,000 opposition fighters, activists and their families were eventually evacuated to Idlib.

The Aleppo operation was cited by senior Russian officers as a major success for the Centre in public speeches and military conference presentations. Russian commanders concluded from the large numbers of refugees that opted to use their shelters meant that the Centre's messaging had resonated with the local population. Moreover, according to Moscow media reports, senior Russian military leaders became convinced that more resources were needed for the reconciliation strategy.

After Aleppo fell, Russian Military Police (MP) battalions began to arrive in Syria and started full-time work for the Centre across the country. In early 2017, four de-escalation zones were established in Dara'a, Eastern Ghouta, Homs-Rastan and Idlib, after negotiations with Jordan, Turkey and the United States.

By mid-2017, four Russian MP battalions had deployed along the de-escalation zones' boundaries, manning observation posts, running checkpoints to enable civilians to move between opposition and government territory, and meeting community leaders to conclude ceasefires. Medical and other humanitarian activities, such as running community health clinics, were organised to establish links with local populations.

According to analysis of news imagery of the deploying troops, each MP battalion boasted around 300 personnel, suggesting that the de-escalation zone operation involved approximately 1,200 troops in total. The battalions drew on personnel recruited in Chechnya and other Muslim areas in Russia to ensure that they contained personnel with the language and cultural awareness skills to operate in soft power roles and to interact with local populations. Their operations were reported extensively by local media in their home regions.

The Russian Military Police are very new organisation. The Soviet Red Army did not have a Western-style MP organisation or service branch for internal army discipline, traffic control, and rear-area security, but instead several distinct organisations carried out these tasks. In 2012 the MP branch was formed and the first operational units were only activated in 2014. Public and political pressure to end the abuse of conscripts was a key driver, requiring the units to be manned by trustworthy and disciplined professional or contract soldiers and officers.

The intended establishment was 20,000 military police personnel, but Russian media reports suggest that only some 6,500 had been recruited by 2018. This indicate the importance of the Syria mission to the new MP branch. However, its small size – and the longevity of the conflict – appeared to be putting it under strain. Reports emerged in the Russian media early 2018 that it was being augmented by troops from the Ministry of the Interior's paramilitary National Guard (Rosgvardiya) operating in Syria.

The MP units deploying to Syria were equipped with some of the most modern vehicles in the Russian army, including Gaz Tigr armoured utility vehicles and Kamaz Typhoon mine-proof heavy vehicles. These vehicles appeared regularly in imagery from Syria, and could be identified by red stripes on their sides.

For the Russian and Syrian governments, the de-escalation zones were an extension of the reconciliation process, aiming to undermine opposition morale and turn wavering communities to the government. The zones also allowed the Syrian military to wind down its operations in the west of the country during 2017 and to concentrate its forces temporarily for a major offensive against Islamic State in the central and eastern desert region later in the year.

Centre personnel also played a role in this large-scale offensive, despite it being predominately kinetic. Russian officers accompanied Syrian advance columns to negotiate with desert Arab tribes, aiming to win them over from Islamic State and US-sponsored Syrian Democratic Front (SDF) fighters. These efforts culminated in at least two high-level meetings with senior commanders of the Kurdish People's Protection Units, which was known as the Yekîneyên Parastina Gel or YPG. Militia. It was the lead military organisation in the SDF.

In one of these meetings, which were reported by Russian and Kurdish media, a Russian major-general from the Centre met YPG military commander Sipan Hemo on 3rd December 2017 in Dier Ez Zor province. The first meeting took place a few weeks earlier near Dier Ez Zor city and involved lower-ranking officers. Although several hundred Arab tribesmen were recruited into the Syrian army, the YPG could not be enticed away from the SDF.

However, these links laid the groundwork for diplomatic negotiations in 2019 with the YPG/SDF political leadership after the US decided to pull most of its troops from north-east Syria to allow Turkish troops to enter to attack Kurdish militia fighters.

With central and eastern Syria largely cleared of Islamic State fighters by the end of 2017, the Russian and Syrian governments turned their attention to the last opposition-held enclaves in western Syria. The recently returned Russian commander in Syria in early 2018, Colonel General Alexander Zhuravlev, had previously masterminded the Aleppo operation and revisited many of those techniques for his second tour.

At the heart of this planning was the inclusion of soft power tools overseen by the Centre. Its commander, Lieutenant General Yuri Evtushenko, and senior staff, along with a number of Russian MPs, were deployed to Damascus to take part in the East Ghouta operation that began in March 2018.

Similar to Aleppo, once Syrian troops had created a breach in opposition defences, Russian officers negotiated with local leaders and aid agencies to open a series of humanitarian corridors to enable civilians to leave. Links established during the de-escalation phase came into play: Russian journalists who accompanied the Syrian troops said that Russian officers had the telephone numbers of necessary interlocutors and knew which communities were susceptible to negotiations.

In the operation, Russian officers organised refugee shelters for civilians leaving government territory and organised the first defections of opposition fighters. In several sectors, this enabled government troops to move forward unopposed and contributed to the collapse of opposition resistance.

The Centre and the Syrian Red Crescent also evacuated around 70,000 opposition fighters and their families to Idlib, representing around a third of the population of the enclave. During the final phase, Centre officers also travelled to the Qalamoun and Rastan pockets, which surrendered in a matter of days. Opposition groups split, with some defecting to the government and others being evacuated to Idlib.

In June, a new Syrian offensive targeted the opposition Dara'a enclave along the borders of Jordan and the Israeli-occupied Golan Heights. Centre officers and military police were again deployed with Syrian assault troops and senior Russian officers – escorted by military police detachments – moving ahead of Syrian forces to negotiate with local communities and militia.

After the US declared that it would not assist the opposition, local leaders across southern Syria were eager to switch sides in return for protection against reprisals and to receive humanitarian aid. Syrian troops swept through the Dara'a enclave in less than a month, with around 10,000 opposition fighters opting for evacuation and many more defecting to the Syrian government.

The central role played by the Centre for Reconciliation of Warring Parties in Russia's Syria campaign illustrates a degree of sophistication that was absent in Soviet operations in Afghanistan in the 1980s and 1990s, and Russian campaigns in Chechnya and Georgia. Such campaigns were characterised by heavy kinetic operations, with brute force being a defining feature. The Russian repertoire now includes more nuanced strategic and tactical options, characterised by economy of force.

Kuralenko's rise to the head of Moscow's peacekeeping forces showed that the Russian military is more alive to the integration of soft power with kinetic operations. The general has advocated soft power operations at international defence conferences using Syria as a case study. However, the success of such soft power may be unique to the particular geopolitical context of the Syrian conflict.

In winning the Syrian population's hearts-and-minds, Russia was aided by French, UK, and US policies of non-intervention against the Syrian government that implied a lack of active support to opposition forces. Russia's 2015 intervention shifted the conflict's central narrative substantially, and opposition defeat could be portrayed as inevitable.

With repeated Syrian government victories, the opposition was on the back-foot, and Russian offers of reconciliation and assistance were the best offer for survival.

Chapter 10
The Mediterranean Squadron

In 2010, the then Russian President Dmitriy Medvedev summoned several mid-ranking military officers to his country residence outside of Moscow to find out for himself the "ground truth" regarding the state of the country's troubled armed forces.

According to a report of the meeting leaked to the Moscow media, officers from all branches of the military were handpicked by their service chiefs to make a good case to the Russian president for enhanced defence spending. When Medvedev asked the naval officers present what was needed to bolster Russia's maritime power, top of their list was the re-establishment of a network of foreign bases to enable warships to be sustained on operations around the world. (1)

Medvedev indicated that this would not be easy, saying, "As you know, bases on the territory of foreign states aren't created on the order of the President of the Russian Federation. For this, it's necessary to conduct complex political diplomatic work … I won't hide from you that we have some ideas on this issue, but I won't say them out loud for understandable reasons."

From his comments, it was clear that Moscow's political and military elite were keen to expand the horizons of Russian naval power, but it would be two years before these ambitions were realised. Syria's civil war provided the opportunity for Russia to make its move.

The Soviet Navy famously maintained a significant naval presence in the Mediterranean for much of the Cold War. Many observers see the recent deployment of Russian warships to the Mediterranean region as a re-boot of the old Soviet presence.

However, Russia's new naval foray into the Mediterranean is very different in nature and takes place in a very different geo-strategic context.

The first Soviet naval presence in the Mediterranean involved the dispatch of a contingent of diesel submarines to Albania in 1958, but the high command in Moscow showed little interest in establishing bigger bases for surface ships in the region. This changed dramatically in the aftermath of the 1967 Arab-Israeli War when the Soviet Union realised it would need to send warships to demonstrate support for its allies in the Middle East.

The next decade was the high-water mark of Soviet presence in the Mediterranean, with air and naval bases being established in Egypt, Libya, and Syria. When Egypt opened peace talks with Israel in 1978 the centre of gravity of Soviet naval activity switched to Syria, and Moscow began building up the port of Tartus as the headquarters for its 5th Mediterranean Squadron of Warships, or Fifth Eskadra. A treaty was signed with Damascus to guarantee Soviet access in return for arms supplies to help the Syrians in their conflict with Israel.

Ships and submarines from the Black Sea and Northern Fleets rotated through duty in the Mediterranean during the Cold War to monitor NATO naval activity. The main focus was to have units on hand in the Mediterranean to neutralise

US carrier battlegroups and Polaris ballistic missile-firing submarines should the Cold War ever turn "hot".

This naval stand-off continued in a predictable pattern until 1989 when the Berlin Wall came down. When the Soviet Union was dissolved two years later it was decided to abandon the naval base in Tartus – the new Russian Federation had neither the money nor the will for foreign military adventures. The last Russian personnel eventually left Syria in December 1992.

The descent of Syria into civil war in 2011 led Moscow to consider returning to Tartus. As outside powers decided to back rival sides in the conflict, the Russian government became increasingly determined that Syrian president Bashar al Assad would not be driven from power by Western-backed rebels.

Russia's involvement in the Syrian conflict was small-scale at first, with the delivery of limited quantities of weapons and equipment starting in 2013. Later that year, the Russian Navy returned to Tartus to re-open facilities to receive cargo-carrying ships dispatched from Black Sea ports.

In mid-2015 Vladimir Putin stepped up military involvement in the Syrian conflict. This saw the Russian Navy take on a key role to enable and protect the deployment of the Russian Air Group to Syria, as well as its ground protection force of around 1,000 army soldiers and naval infantry.

August 2015 saw the activation of what became known as the Syrian Express through the Bosphorus, to and from the port of Novorossiysk. Black Sea Fleet amphibious landing ships, augmented by civilian cargo vessels chartered by the Russian Ministry of Defence-owned logistics company Oboronlogistika, shuttled to Syria, delivering cargo and personnel to Tartus more than 180 times during the second half of 2015, according to data collected by amateur ship observers in Istanbul. To protect this deployment several Black Sea Fleet surface units were dispatched to patrol off Syria, including the Soviet-era Project 1164 cruiser Moskva.

The initial phase of the Russian deployment to Syria appeared to be a relatively conventional power-projection mission, but within weeks the Russian Navy embarked upon some very innovative combat activity.

Following the terrorist attack that brought down a Russian airliner over Egypt's Sinai Peninsula in October 2015, Putin ordered a large-scale air and missile strike campaign to be launched in Syria. This involved the first-ever combat use of a land-attack cruise missile fired from a Russian warship in the Caspian Sea. During the 7th October attack, a Project 11661 Gepard-class frigate and three Project 21631 Buyan-M-class corvettes launched 26 Novator Kalibr 3M-14 cruise missiles at 11 militant targets in Syria.

On 8th December, the Russian Project 636.3 Improved Kilo-class diesel-electric submarine Rostov on Don, of the Black Sea Fleet, deployed in the eastern Mediterranean fired four Kalibr cruise missiles at a target in Syria. This was also a milestone for the Russian Navy, marking the first time that it had used submarine-launched deep strike cruise missiles operationally.

Through 2016 and into 2017, surface units from the Black Sea Fleet operating in the eastern Mediterranean also joined the Kalibr strike operations. These included Project 11356M Admiral Grigorovich-class frigates and Buyan-M-class corvettes.

Russian naval presence reached a high point in the second half of 2016 as the battle to capture the rebel enclave of Aleppo neared its climax. This included the deployment of the Russian Navy's sole Project 1143.5 aircraft carrier, Admiral Kuznetsov, supported by a naval task group, including the Project 1144.2 nuclear-powered battle cruiser Pyotr Velikiy, to the Mediterranean.

Once on station, the carrier's embarked air group participated in combat operations for the first time in Soviet or Russian military history. The coastal defence missile brigade of the Black Sea Fleet also carried out a combat first at this time, firing NPO Mashinostroyeniya Bastion-P missiles in the land-attack mode.

During 2016 and 2017, the Russian Navy established a rotation plan to ensure that Kalibr-firing warships and submarines were always on station off Syria. Two Improved Kilo-class submarines were forward-based in Tartus due to the requirements of the Montreaux Convention preventing routine transits through the Bosphorus. This meant it was easier to rotate surface ships from the Black Sea Fleet and almost all of its ships have spent two or three months at a time on Syria duty.

In 2018, the Russian Mediterranean Task Force was centre stage in a major strategic power-projection exercise, dubbed Ocean Shield. This was the first of what has become an annual naval exercise but it has not since returned to the Mediterranean.

Exercise Ocean Shield kicked off in September 2018 and saw the first large-scale practice of power-projection operations by the Russian Navy. In the scenario, a large force of warships and submarines, backed by long-range aviation, defeated a foreign naval force to enable a naval infantry brigade to carry out an amphibious landing to assist a friendly ally under attack by insurgents.

Russia moved a naval task force to the Mediterranean from the Baltic, Black Sea, and Northern fleets in late August 2018 for the manoeuvres, which started on 1st September. From analysis of ship movements through the Bosphorus and Strait of Gibraltar, and imagery released by NATO's Maritime Command, it was possible to identify 13 warships, two patrol craft, possibly two Improved Kilo-class submarines, three amphibious landing ships, and six support vessels participating in or supporting the exercise. These assets participated in training events in exercise areas stretching from eastern Libya to the coast of Syria up to 8th September.

Russian news imagery from Hmeinyan Air Base in Syria's Latakia province early in September identified several Russian Naval Aviation aircraft deployed at the base for the drills. These included at least two Sukhoi Su-33 fighters and six Su-30SM jets from bases in Crimea. Tupolev Tu-142 maritime patrol aircraft of the Northern Fleet also participated, operating from their home base in northern Russia. Up to four RuAF Iluyshin Il-78 air-to-air refuelling aircraft were also seen at the base participating in the exercise, while Tupolev Tu-160 heavy bombers flew from their home base in central Russia to carry out simulated strategic strikes with air-launched cruise missiles in support of the naval task force.

The drill culminated on 8th September with an amphibious assault on the coast of Syria, south of the city of Latakia, involving the landing of several BTR-82AM wheeled armoured personnel carriers, flying Naval Infantry flags, manoeuvring ashore from an Alligator-class landing ship. Other troops came ashore by landing craft and helicopters. Two Alligator-class landing ships and a Ropucha-class assault ship could be seen close to shore launching the landing force.

After the exercise the three Russian landing ships returned to home base in Sebastopol, but the surface combatants and support ships remained in the Mediterranean.

The inclusion of an amphibious landing phase at the end of Exercise Ocean Shield was a new development for Russian naval manoeuvres in the Mediterranean. It had been well over 40 years since the Soviet Navy had carried out an amphibious exercise in the region, when Moscow was actively supporting Egypt, Libya, and Syria at the height of the Cold War.

Only nine days after the conclusion of Exercise Ocean Shield, the regional impact of the presence of the Russian naval task force in the eastern Mediterranean was highlighted in the aftermath of the shooting down of a RuAF Iluyshin Il-20M signals intelligence gather aircraft in a friendly fire incident involving Syrian air defence missile batteries. Moscow closed off a large chunk of the Eastern Mediterranean to air activity, citing "ongoing exercises", and effectively created a barrier to Israeli air incursions into Syria from the west.

While the conflict in Syria appeared to reduce in intensity during 2019, with only minor offensives undertaken by government troops against the last remaining rebel enclave in Idlib province, Russia continued to maintain its naval task force in the eastern Mediterranean as a key component of what Western observers call an anti-access, area denial, or A2AD, umbrella in the region. The Russian military don't use the term A2AD but talk about "anti missile domes" in their internal publications and policy statements.

During 2019 and into 2020, force levels remained at around 15 to 20 Russian vessels of all types, according to sighting reports from Turkish ship spotters in the Bosphorus. There were usually two or three large frigate/corvette-sized surface units, two Improved Kilo-class submarines, and two mine countermeasures vessels in hand. The warships were supported by two tankers, one or two tugs, a repair vessel, and an auxiliary intelligence-gathering ship. The number of support ships increased if the Northern or Baltic fleets provided surface vessels for Mediterranean duty that required en route logistic support for the cruise to the operational area.

Tartus naval base was provided with its own naval security detachment, including three or four inshore patrol craft. The port was also protected by a detachment of RuAF surface-to-air missile batteries and electronic warfare jamming units. Naval Aviation Il-38 aircraft were also present at Hmeinyan Air Base on a near continuous basis, along with a shore-based Bastion-P missile battery from the Black Sea Fleet.

The logistic support infrastructure at Tartus port was upgraded to function on a long-term basis. Improvements included the construction of a new ship repair workshop during 2019, complete with newly delivered lathes and metal machining equipment. The workshop was built in six months by Russian construction teams, enabling navy personnel to carry out a full cycle of post-warranty repair and re-equipment of small- and medium-sized vessels.

The 2019 and 2020 iterations of Exercise Ocean Shield were held in the Baltic, so there was no major surge of naval surface and air assets into the Mediterranean during these years. The focus of non-Syria-related Russian naval activity in the Mediterranean was to support diplomatic engagement. Russian warships made port visits to Algeria, Cyprus, Egypt, and Greece during 2019, as well as sailing through Tartus en route to deployments to Sudan, the Indian Ocean and the Pacific.

In the space of just over five years, the Russian Navy had become an important player in the eastern Mediterranean. It contributed to the Russian campaign inside Syria that saw the Damascus government defeat almost all of its opponents and take back control of most of its territory from rebel militias.

Thanks to its naval presence, Moscow had expanded its influence in the region, helping to boost arms sales to key states, giving it political leverage on several important issues as well as opening up opportunities for Russian oil companies and defence equipment manufacturers in new markets.

The Syrian campaign enabled the Russian Navy to make use of several new capabilities in combat, including submarine- and ship-launched land-attack cruise missiles, embarked carrier aviation and UAVs. It also co-ordinated their use over digital communication networks to establish a functioning "kill chain". The co-ordination of naval forces, air power, and land-based anti-ship missiles also enabled the Russian military to establish an A2/AD umbrella over and around Syria.

However, the enduring Russian presence in the eastern Mediterranean was characterised by economy of effort. Fewer than 20 ships were deployed to the region at any point after 2015, and usually less than five of these ships were major surface units.

For much of the time, the majority have been newly built Admiral Grigorovich-class frigates or Buyan-M class corvettes. Although armed with Kalibr cruise missiles, these vessels were a fraction of the size and weight of their Western counter-parts. By comparison, the old Soviet 5th Squadron dispatched large surface units to hunt down US Polaris submarines across the Mediterranean and nuclear-tipped cruise missile-armed submarines to take out the US 6th Fleet's aircraft carrier battlegroups. At its peak in the mid-1970s, the Soviet Mediterranean Squadron boasted more than 44 vessels, including around 10–12 major surface units. Putin appeared to be satisfied with his investment in naval operations in the Mediterranean between 2015 and 2020 so the Russian Navy looks set to continue to sustain a presence in this strategic region for the foreseeable future.

Chapter 11
A2AD and Douma Crisis

During the morning of 14th April 2018 the residents of the Syrian capital Damascus were woken by the sound of explosions around the city. Looking out of their windows, they could see missiles arching into the sky. Within minutes the international media was broadcasting footage of the action.
This looked very reminiscent of the opening hours of the air battles over Baghdad, Tripoli, Belgrade and Kabul since 1991. Later that morning events took a new twist. Colonel General Sergei Rudskoy strode onto a stage in the Moscow Ministry of Defence and started to give a detailed account of the action. (1)
Rudskoy described how the attack unfolded, the number of cruise missiles fired – he said 103 - and the types of aircraft involved, where US warships fired their cruise missiles from and their flight path. Three hours later, a US General gave the Pentagon's account of the allied operation and in most respects it chimed with that given by the Kremlin. (2)
He said the allies launched 105 cruise missiles, only two more than the Russian estimate. The only serious bone of contention was whether or not Syrian surface-to-air missiles successfully shot down any of the in-bound allied cruise missiles. The propaganda war was now in high gear.
What was new about this "war of missile claims" was that it now seemed to be a "war of equals". Both the Russians and Americans clearly had situational awareness of Syria's battlefields in a way that was never seen in previous air wars over the past 30 years. The Russians also showed themselves to be adept at getting their story out first.
After 2015 Moscow made several moves to reinforce its anti-access, area denial (A2/AD) umbrella, or anti-missile dome, over and around its troops in Syria.
The Russian military had already invested considerably in A2/AD weapons systems and technology to protect key regions around its border, including the Black Sea, the Baltic, the Kola Peninsula, High Arctic and the Pacific coast. These included the Almaz-Antey S-400 Triumf and S-300 air defence systems, KDP 96K6 Pantsir S1 self-propelled gun/missile systems, Zvezda Bal and NPO Mashinostroenia Bastion-P coastal anti-ship missiles, KB Mashinostroyeniya Iskander tactical ballistic missiles, Kalibr cruise missile-equipped ships and submarines, Sukhoi Su-30SM fighters with beyond-visual-range-air-to-air missiles, enhancements to Ilyushin Il-38 maritime patrol aircraft and Beriev A-50 airborne early warning radar aircraft.
These capabilities were packaged and based in a way that was intended to keep Western military forces at arms length and limit their ability to launch precision strikes or insert ground and naval forces.
The capabilities of these advanced Russian weapon systems caught the attention of Western military commanders several years earlier and when they started to appear in Syria they changed the rules of the game in the Middle East.
After 2015 the Russian A2/AD umbrella evolved and expanded dramatically.

The first S-400s arrived in Syria after the shootdown of the Su-24 in November 2014 and then further A2/AD systems followed, including Iskander ballistic missiles that could hit most NATO airbases in southern Turkey and the British airbase on Cyprus with runway and bunker-busting warheads. When Syrian and Russian forces massed in late 2016 to attack eastern Aleppo, the Russian Northern Fleet's carrier battle group led by the Admiral Kuznetsov was dispatched to the eastern Mediterranean to deter US intervention.

Amid all the public-relations fire and fury of early 2018, the capabilities and performance of the Syrian Air Defence Force (SyADF) took centre stage. Israeli, US, British and French air forces were locked into deadly duels with Syria's missile and radar crews, who were being actively assisted by their Russian allies. Air defence crews of the Russian Aerospace Force (RuAF) were present in Syria in some strength and Moscow confirmed in early 2018 that they had been re-equipping , re-organising and re-training the SyADF over the proceeding 18 months.

It is possible to build up a picture of the capabilities of the SyADF in 2018 by pulling together multiple sources of information. There is very high-definition commercial satellite imagery available on open sources that allows SyADF missile and radar sites to be pin-pointed with some accuracy. The Syrian and Russian media were taken on visits to several SyADF sites in April and May 2018, giving an unprecedented view of equipment, deployments and personnel. The Russian military have also held several briefings during 2018 describing the operations of the SyADF in some detail.

Since 1969, when the SyADF was established along Soviet lines it had been an independent branch of the Syrian Armed Forces. The SyADF's responsibilities include operating the country's integrated air defence system (IADS), which comprised an early warning radar network, surface-to-air missile (SAM) and anti-aircraft artillery (AAA) batteries, and the command-and-control network to link them all together, as well as providing ground control intercept (GCI) services for Syrian Arab Air Force fighter aircraft.

The SyADF in 2018 was clearly a shadow of its pre-civil war organisations with many of its missile and radar sites overrun by rebel forces or destroyed in fighting since 2011. Analysis of satellite imagery from 2011 suggested that the SyADF boasted some 130 active SAM sites. In May 2018, this had dropped to around 60 active SAM sites with possibly some 500 individual missile launchers and scores of radar sites. However, around a quarter of these involved new Pantsir gun/missile systems or Buk SAMs, which had been supplied since 2008. A Russian news agency reported that Moscow had supplied 40 new Pantsir systems in early 2018, effectively doubling the numbers in service with the SyADF.

The laydown of the SyADF was also very different from its pre-war deployment, according to satellite imagery. Some 75% of the SyADF SAM sites were now in the Damascus area and they included nine of the 11 equipped with new Pantsirs and four of the six Buk sites. The north and east of Syria had been denuded of SyADF missiles and radars because of heavy rebel attacks over the previous seven years. This coverage had effectively been replaced by the RuAF's arrival in Latakia province, on Syria's Mediterranean coast.

The Russians positioned at least one of the S-400 SAM batteries on the top of the Latakia mountain range, as well as two long-range radar sites and a ground-control intercept command post, linked into the country-wide air defence network by satellite communications. This allowed Russian air defence commanders to monitor huge tracts of airspace, and those parts of Syria shielded by other mountain ranges could be observed by the RuAF's Beriev A-50 airborne early warning radar aircraft, two of which were usually forward based in Syria. The Russian radar coverage was further bolstered by the presence of Black Sea Fleet warships in the Eastern Mediterranean.

The presence of Russian ground based radars, A-50 aircraft and warships meant that Moscow's men were able to "see" across huge tracts of the Middle East. It was no surprise that Generals in the Kremlin were able to give a running commentary of allied and Israeli air activity.

While the Russian SAM batteries and Pantsirs were concentrated in Latakia province to defend the Kremlin's main air and naval bases, Moscow's men had clearly been working to bolster the effectiveness of the SyADF main missile engagement zone around Damascus over the previous 18 months. As well as delivering new Pantsirs to the SyADF, the Kremlin revealed it had been running a major re-training effort to re-build the SyADF.

After the 14th April missile strikes, Syria television broadcast a report from Dumayr airbase to the north east of Damascus. This showed new variants of the Pantsir were present in Syria and also went inside a Syrian air-defence command post. The old 1970s-vintage radar scopes associated with Soviet era SAMs were gone and the command team were working on 21st Century computer systems. One radar screen appeared to show aircraft movements across a large swathe of the Middle East, including northern Israel, Jordan and Iraq.

The Russian and SyADF deployment in early 2018 had to be viewed in context of the on-going battles in Syria at the time. The Syrian government was in the final stages of mopping up the last pockets of rebel resistance around Damascus, including the large rebel held East Ghouta pocket. Moscow and Damascus were determined to head off Western interference in this battle.

As well as positioning more Syrian Pantsirs in Damascus and bringing a second Russian S-400 system, known as "double digit SAMs", into Latakia, the Russians had a P-400 Bastion anti-ship missile system based near the Syrian port of Tartus to try to force allied ships far out to sea, extending their missile firing ranges so the land-based air defences had more time to detect and intercept them.

Additional Kalibr missile-equipped Admiral Grigorovich-class and Kilo-class conventional powered submarines were sent to the Mediterranean and two Russian Naval Aviation Il-38 maritime patrol aircraft were sent to Syria to make life more difficult for allied warships and submarines attempting to get into position to fire cruise missiles at Syria.

The newly re-vamped SyADF was put to the test in February 2018 when the Israeli air force launched a major response strike in reaction to an incursion over the Golan Heights by an Iranian Saegheh "stealth" drone. Eight Israeli Lockheed Martin F-16I Sufa fighter jets were launched to strike against 12 targets, including four air defence batteries and the control site for the Iranian drone at T-4 airbase in Homs province. The Israeli jets reportedly flew by the most direct route over Golan Heights before launching stand-off guided weapons at their targets. The SyADF responded with a salvo of 27 SAMs that scored a near hit on one of the Israeli jets, forcing the crew to eject.

This was a major boost to SyADF morale and Syrian media lauded its missile crews for their endeavours.

An Israeli Defence Forces inquiry later blamed the F-16Is crew for being too focused on aiming their weapons and not activating their defensive aid suite when they came under SAM attack. The Israeli defence minister at the time claimed that "nearly half of Syria's air defences" had been destroyed in these strikes.

T-4 airbase came under a new attack on 9th April but there were no reports of a reaction by the SyADF, suggesting that this time the Israeli jets approached from the south or east, away from the Damascus missile engagement zone.

The next big test of the SyADF came on the morning of 14th April when the US, France and UK launched a major cruise missile strike against targets they said were involved in Syria's chemical weapons programme.

US, British and French government leaders threatened to launch strikes in response to an alleged chemical attack on East Ghouta a few days earlier. In response the Russian ambassador in Lebanon, Alexander Zasypkin raised the stakes. He stated that if any Russian military personnel were killed or injured by Western air strikes in Syria, Russia would hit back. "If there is a strike by the Americans, then... the missiles will be downed and even the sources from which the missiles were fired," Zasypkin told Hezbollah's al-Manar TV. (3)

When the Western strikes did occur, they took place far from Russian bases and the US military command in the Middle East warned Moscow beforehand that the strikes were coming. There was no attempt by the US and its allies to interfere with the Syrian forces fighting the remaining rebels in the East Ghouta pocket.

This strike saw 76 of the 105 allied cruise missiles aimed at Syria's main chemical research facility on a hillside above Damascus. The remainder were aimed at two storage sites in the Homs countryside. All the allied missiles were fired from outside Syria's borders.

The Russian Ministry of Defence subsequently claimed 71 of the allied missiles were shot down. This included 20 in Homs province and the remainder around Damascus. The Pentagon vehemently denied that any of its weapons had been hit by Syrian missiles. It also denied Russian claims that several airbases and other targets were struck by allied missiles.

SyADF Surface-to-Air-Missiles fired and kill claims, 14th April 2018

Pantsir (SA-22): 25 missiles and hit 24 targets;
Buk (SA-17): 29 missiles and hit 24 targets;
Osa (SA-8): 11 and hit 5 targets;
2S-125 (SA-3): 13 missiles and hit 5 targets;
Strela-10 (SA-13): 5 missiles and hit 3 targets;
Kvadrat/Kub (SA-6) : 21 and hit 11 targets;
S-200 (SA-5): 8 and hit no targets."
Total 112 SAM fired
Source: Russian MOD

The Kremlin later published a set of photos of missile debris and claimed to have taken possession of two undamaged US Navy Tomahawk Land Attack Missiles (TLAM) that were recovered intact by the Syrian military. One of the images appeared to show the intact warhead of a TLAM. While the debris seemed to include components from all the allied missile types used – TLAM, JASSM and Scalp/Storm Shadow – the wreckage did not appear to represent the remains of 71missiles.

The accounts of the US and Russians appeared irreconcilable. Both sides had the technical means to monitor the missile engagement in real-time, but neither seemed inclined to engage in an open debate about the performance of their weapon systems and radars, for obvious reasons.

One thing seemed clear. Israeli claims to have knocked out half the SyADF in February were exaggerated. Further Israeli air strikes took place on 29th April and 8th May, with the first strikes taking place near the northern cities of Aleppo and Hama. According to local media reports the Aleppo and Hama raids involved Israeli aircraft flying out over Jordan and Iraq to approach their targets from the east in areas where there was limited SyADF and Russian radar coverage. They then fired stand-off missiles at their targets. The 8th May strike appeared to have been carried out with stand-off missiles fired from within Israeli or Lebanese air space. Later in May, the Israeli air force commander revealed that Lockheed Martin F-35I Adirs took part in these raids, in the type's first ever combat missions.

This was only a prelude to a major air strike on 10th May, aimed at targets linked to the Iranian presence in Syria. According to an Israeli Defence Force infographic, around three dozen targets were hit in the strikes. The Russian claimed 28 Israeli aircraft fired 60 stand-off cruise missiles, and further 10 surface-to-surface missiles were fired. The Israeli air force reported that 100 SAMs had been fired in response.

From a variety of sources, including satellite imagery, Syrian news reports and Israeli bomb damage assessment video, around a third of the Israeli targets have since been identified. Only two of them were linked to air defence including one Pantsir system and a radar site for an S-200 battery. The remainder appeared to be storage depots and barracks reportedly used by Iranian forces.

Israeli government ministers on 11th May talked about "devastating" the Syrian air defence network but a few days later the Israeli air force sources briefed the media that only five SAM batteries had been hit in the 10th May raids. Again, reports of knock out blows against the SyADF appeared to have been over hyped.

On 1st May the Russian landing ship Nikolai Filchenkov was photographed sailing through the Bosphorus, heading to Syria. On her deck were around a dozen large vehicles under tarpaulins. Although the vehicles could not be positively identified, they matched the shape of Pantsirs or Buk air defence systems. A replenishment of the SyDAF appeared to be underway.

The common theme running through all the air and missile operations against Syria since 2018 was the reliance of the Israeli, US, British and French air forces on stand-off missiles. The US Navy Raytheon TLAM has range of more than 1,000 kilometres, the US Air Force Lockheed Martin JASSM's range is 370 kilometres and MBDA Scalp/Storm Shadow/MdCN can hit targets 560 kilometres from the launch point. Israeli air force stand-off weapons, including the IMI Delilah missile and Rafael Popoye, have reported ranges from 78 kilometres to 250 kilometres.

Despite the "mission accomplished" rhetoric from US President Donald Trump and Israeli government leaders, the SyADF appeared to be very much in still in business. Two more suspected Israeli air strikes on 24th May and 18th June involved stand-off attacks from outside Syrian air space.

Israeli and US coalition air commanders had little appetite to send manned aircraft downtown over Damascus. Their caution suggests that claims of the SyADF being "devastated" were just meant for public relations purposes, not prudent military planning.

The Il-20M incident in September 2018 took another turn with the Russian government announcing that it was going to supply three S-300 battalions to the Syrian Air Defence Force. Moscow backed this up by declaring large blocks of airspace over the Mediterranean as exercise areas to deter further Israeli incursions. Russian missile crews were sent to train their Syrian counterparts to operate their new equipment and increase the integration of the two country's air defence organisations.

Moscow blamed the loss of the aircraft and its 15 crew on the Israeli Air Force, which was conducting an air strike as the Russian aircraft was returning to its base in Latakia province. Russian political leaders and diplomats made it clear to their Israeli counterparts that they needed to stop their wide-ranging campaign of air strikes across Syria against what the Israelis dubbed "Iranian-linked" bases.

As a result, the Russian military issued a notice to airmen (NOTAMs) on 18th September closing off nine exercise areas of airspace above international waters off Lebanon, Syria, and to the west of Cyprus for rocket firings over eight days. Five of the exercise areas ran in a near-continuous block of airspace from the northern limit of Syrian territorial waters, along the coast of Lebanon, and ending south of the Israeli city of Haifa, according to maps issued by the Cypriot aviation authorities. This in effect created a barrier of Russian warships, as well as Russian-controlled airspace up to 19,000 feet around the Syrian coast, which forced foreign aircraft to fly at high altitudes, making them easier to detect on radar. Eventually, Russian-Israeli relations were returned to something akin to normal, but the incident was an interesting exercise in political-military messaging.

As far as Russian political leadership was concerned, its armed forces had effectively deterred a Western intervention to undo the Syrian victory in East Ghouta. It is a moot point as to whether the Russian A2/AD forces in Syria would have been able to defeat a full-scale Western or Israeli attack, but the risk that this might escalate into an all-out war that would have led to significant casualties appears to have been enough to make Western capitals pull back from the brink.

The positioning of Russian A2/AD systems in Syria was highlighted by the head of the UK's Strategic Command, General Sir Patrick Sanders, at the virtual Air & Space Power Association Conference 2020 on 15th July 2020, as a continuing to challenge to Western military operations in the Eastern Mediterranean region.

General Sanders described Russian A2/AD deployments as an "exemplar of multi-domain integration". "We see this played out in the Eastern Mediterranean right now," he told the conference. "The interplay of Russian systems since 2015 from the use of disinformation to the use of hard power has been continuously developed and has created an "A2/AD bubble" that they can turn on and off at will. To defeat our adversaries in an environment like this we need to operate across all domains and at a high tempo," he said. "Anything else will not work, that is the only way to overmatch [the A2/AD bubble]."

Chapter 11
America's Great Escape

The Mil Mi-8 troop-carrying helicopters created a huge dust cloud as they sat down on the helipad at the former American base south of Kobani. A Mil Mi-35 gunship circled overhead to provide top cover.

On the ground Russian Military Police troops started fanning out into the abandoned airbase that only few hours before had hosted US, British and French special forces. A Russian television crew accompanied the soldiers as they entered empty mess halls, gyms and radio rooms, filming the events. Half eaten meals, dog eared novels and recently delivered sports equipment was strewn everywhere, giving the impression that the base's occupants had left in a hurry.

Only a few days before, the Pentagon had released its own film of its troops leaving the same base. Columns of US Army mine-protected vehicles were lined up beside a rough airstrip waiting to be loaded into the cavernous hold of a USAF Air Mobility Command Boeing C-17 Globemaster airlifter.

Behind the vehicles, a gaggle of forklift trucks could be seen preparing cargo pallets and ISO containers for loading. Overhead a pair of US Army Boeing AH-64D Apache attack helicopters circled the airstrip to monitor the movement of civilian vehicles on the roads that passed south. Operation Break Glass was well underway.

Only days earlier 1,000 US troops had been patrolling north-eastern Syria in alliance with a local militia organisation known as the Syria Democratic Forces (SDF). At the start of 2019 the Kurdish-led SDF, helped by US, British and French special forces advisors and airpower, had overrun the last Islamic State enclave in eastern Syria, bringing to an end the five-year-old Jihadi Caliphate.

In a bizarre and now infamous telephone conversation, US President Donald Trump agreed to a request from his Turkish counterpart, Recep Tayyip Erdoğan, to pull US troops out from Syria to allow Turkish troops to occupy a buffer zone on the Syria side of the border.

President Erdoğan had long viewed the SDF militia as a front for what he called "Kurdish PKK terrorists" and he had repeatedly pressed Trump to allow Turkish troops to enter Syria to hunt them down. When Trump agreed to pull US observation posts back from the Syria-Turkish border at the beginning of October 2019 it set off a chain of events.

Erdoğan's operation kicked off on 9th October with a series of air strikes on Kurdish positions by Turkish Air Force Lockheed F-16C/D Fighting Falcons and armed Bayraktar tactical drones. These strikes concentrated on targets inside the 30-kilometre-deep security zone that the Turks wanted to set up, free of SDF militia fighters.

Turkish tank columns, accompanied by pro-Turkish Syrian militia fighters pushed across the border around the towns of Ras al Ayn and Tell Abyad. Small contingents of US troops had occupied bases near each town but days before the Turkish attack they had been pulled back to large US bases further south.

The US troops simply mounted up in their armoured troop carriers and drove out of their bases but their commanders in the Special Operation Joint Task Force - Operation Inherent Resolve (SOJTF-OIR) headquarters at a US base near Erbil in Iraq arranged for US fighter jets and General Atomics MQ-9 Reaper drones to be overhead to protect their retreat.

The Central Intelligence Agency (CIA) station in Qamishli was caught in the crossfire when Turkish artillery opened fire on the city, prompting one of the agency's Sikorsky S-92 helicopters to make a dash into the danger zone to bring out America's spies. A video clip posted online showed the civilian crewed helicopter flying between buildings to land at the CIA base in a downtown district.

With fighting raging across northern Syria, on 13th October President Trump now ordered all the 1,000 US troops in Syria to be evacuated from the country.

On the same day the Kurdish leadership of the SDF agreed a deal to allow Russian and Syrian troops to enter the territory they controlled to take over from US troops and hopefully block any further Turkish advances. These were desperate times for the Kurdish fighters of the SDF who felt they had been betrayed by Washington.

US commanders had prepared for this eventuality and had a contingency plan, codenamed Operation Break Glass, ready to go to organise the mass evacuation of their troops and equipment from Syria. During 13th October, the plan was activated and US troops began falling back on two of its main operating bases, one in north west Syria, south of the town of Kobani and the other in the east of Syria near Hasakah. Control of the air over northern Syria was an essential component of the plan.

Although the 1,000 US special forces troops in Syria, as well as small contingents of British and French troops, were vastly outnumbered by Syrian, Russian, Turkish and SDF forces, the coalition troops had overwhelming air supremacy. US aerial firepower devastated an attack on a US outpost in February 2018 by a force of Russian mercenaries, inflicting hundreds of casualties. Every US aircraft in the Middle East could potentially be mobilised to protect the American ground troops as they withdrew, including Boeing F-15E Strike Eagles based in Jordan, Lockheed Martin F-22 Raptors and Lockheed Martin F-35A Lightnings in Qatar, as well as Boeing F-18E/F Super Hornets embarked on the USS Abraham Lincoln in the Arabian Sea. MQ-9 Reaper and MQ-1C Grey Eagle drones were on-station at airbases in Kuwait and Iraq.

These fighters and drones were all continuously positioned in combat air patrols over the key US bases, with tankers refuelling the jets to ensure a on-going presence. It is unclear if RAF Eurofighter Typhoon jets based on Cyprus joined in this protection effort but RAF Airbus A330 Voyager tanker aircraft were tracked by their transponder flying over northern Syria on several occasions during the evacuation period. Raytheon Sentinel R1 airborne stand-off radar aircraft from the RAF's V Squadron were also tracked flying around Syria at this time, helping to monitor troop movements across the country.

Based at a specially constructed airbase at Harir near Irbil in northern Iraq, the

160th Special Operations Aviation Regiment (SOAR) had four Boeing MH-47G and eight Sikorsky MH-60M helicopters. It was their job to carry elite troops of the US Joint Special Operations Command, or JSOC, on raids to kill or capture high-value Islamic State personnel.

Within Iraq and Syria a network of more than two dozen helicopter landing sites was operated by the US Army's 244th Combat Aviation Brigade. Its AH-64D attack, Boeing CH-46E Chinook and Sikorsky UH-60 Blackhawk helicopters spent their time moving around the sites depending on the tactical situation. At any point in time eight AH-64Ds and a similar number of UH-60s would be operating from landing zones inside Syria.

The main US Central Command theatre reserve was the Special Purpose Marine Air-Ground Task Force - Crisis Response - Central Command or SP-MAGTF-CC, which was based at Ahmed al Jaber Airbase in Kuwait. This US Marine Corps unit was based around a dozen Boeing MV-22 Osprey tiltrotors from Medium Tiltrotor Squadron 161 and two Lockheed Martin KC-130J Hercules tanker/transports from Marine Aerial Refueler Transport Squadron 252, which were on standby to rapidly move a battalion of marines to emergency situations.

As the withdrawal operation gathered momentum, the US, British and French special forces started pulling out of a string of small forward bases across north-western Syria and falling back on the US airstrip 25 kilometres south of Kobani.

In a race to escape advancing Syrian, Russian and Turkish columns, the allied special forces often only left their bases with a few minutes to spare. At one base near Manbij that was captured intact by Syrian troops on 14th October, Russian journalists filmed half-eaten meals left on the mess-hall tables. This abandoned base has been home to a British SAS contingent since early 2018 and British Special Forces Sergeant Matt Tonroe was based there until he was killed in Manbij town while on an operation to capture an Islamic State sleeper cell in March 2018.

To prevent another US base in north western Syria being captured, the Americans called in two McDonnell Douglas F-15E Strike Eagle jets to mount an air strike to destroy a large ammunition dump. This caused a huge plume of smoke to engulf the base that had been set up in a former cement factory north of Raqqa city.

The American airstrip, dubbed the Kobani Landing Zone or KLZ, was built in a field by US military engineers in 2016 to open the way for giant cargo aircraft to land the heavy arms used by the Kurds to defeat the Islamic State and capture their capital Raqqa. The massive base included helicopter landing pads, fuel dumps, ammo bunkers and prefabricated accommodation for several hundred troops. An RAF Hercules suffered major damage trying to land at the airstrip in 2017 and subsequently crash-landed at an airbase in Iraq.

On 14th October giant USAF C-17 and Hercules transport aircraft started flying into the base to pull out the 600 US and allied troops who were now almost surrounded, after Syrian, Russian and Turkish troops threatened to cut all the road routes to Iraq. A Lockheed L-100-30 Hercules aircraft flown by charter companies linked to the CIA - its modern day Air America - was also tracked landing at the air strip in the days after 14th October. The bulk of these missions were flown by C-17s from the expeditionary airlift squadron assigned to the 379th Expeditionary Wing at Al Udied Air Base in the Gulf state of Qatar. Aircraft were identified in imagery released by the Pentagon as being from the 437th Airlift Wing (437 AW) at Charleston AFB in South Carolina. They shuttled between Kobani and the US airbases at Harir and Ali al Salem in Kuwait, helped by the US Marine Corps KC-130J tanker/transports of the SPMAGTF-CC.

The British contingent of special forces troops and intelligence experts was now concentrating with their American comrades on the air strip to take their turn to be picked up RAF Hercules transport aircraft, flown by pilots of the special forces support unit, 47 Squadron.

Kobani Landing Zone was in a precarious position. Russian, Syrian, Turkish and SDF troops were all within 10 miles of the base and the political situation was evolving by the hour in a very unpredictable way. To secure the site while the lightly armed special forces contingents packed up their equipment, hundreds of US Marines of the SPMAGTF-CC were flown in to beef up its perimeter defence. An added layer of protection was provided by the presence of four AH-64D from the 1st Attack Reconnaissance Battalion of the US Army's 1st Aviation Regiment, flying from KLZ.

The value of the Kobani Landing Zone was dramatically illustrated on 26th October when it provided the launch pad for the raid that led to the death of the Islamic State founder, Abū Bakr al Baghdadi. SDF and US intelligence had tracked the infamous Jihadi to a hideout in Idlib province, some 120 kilometres to the west of KLZ.

Troops from JSOC's strike unit, the famous Delta Force, were given the job of leading the raid and they were to be carried to the target by MH-47Gs from the 160th SOAR. While most media reports claimed that the strike force launched from an airbase near Irbil, subsequent briefings in the Pentagon said the raiders staged through a forward base in Syria, close to Idlib. That base could only have been KLZ.

The raid was a dramatic success. Apaches, from the detachment based at KLZ, machine-gunned several insurgents who tried to fire on the assault force, allowing the raiders to land from the Chinooks and then storm Baghdadi's hideout. The assault team then successfully recovered to Kobani to refuel, en route to its home base at Harir.

President Trump now decided to change his mind about pulling all his troops out of Syria and ordered the US military to remain in the country to secure strategic oil fields close to the border with Iraq. US Central Command wanted to ensure they had enough troops to defend these oil fields so it ordered a contingent from the US Army armoured brigade in Kuwait to move into Syria with Bradley heavy troop carriers. This was easier said than done. There were few roads into this region that were not controlled by hostile forces.

American generals turned to the USAF to move the Bradleys and within days C-17s assigned to the 379th Wing at Al Udeid were back in action. The 62nd Airlift Wing C-17s first flew to Ali al Salem airbase in Kuwait to pick up the Bradleys and then they flew into a desert airstrip to the north of Hasakah. This was a dramatic demonstration of airlift power that few nations could match.

While the Americans were retreating from Syria, Russian and Syrian troops were surging into the region controlled by the SDF, the former ally of the US. This followed on from the 22nd October agreement between Presidents Putin and Erdoğan to allow joint Russian and Turkish military patrols in the border security zone.

Senior Russian, Turkish and US officers now talked daily over what was dubbed the "deconfliction hotline" to choreograph these deployments to prevent any accidents or incidents that might spiral out of control.

Syrian army units rapidly launched a three-pronged move across Kurdish-controlled territory in the north east of the country in a bid to fill a power vacuum left by the surprise withdrawal of US troops.

The Syrian columns were not initially armed with large quantities of artillery or armoured vehicles suggesting they were aiming to first establish a "trip wire" to deter Turkish advances into Kurdish-controlled territory rather than launch an immediate attack on Ankara's forces. Kurdish fighters of the SDF co-ordinated the move after a political deal between Kurdish leaders and the Damascus government was brokered by the Russians on 13th October.

The presence of Russian Military Police with two of the Syrian columns added to the impression that the Syrian deployment was aimed at making a political statement.

In north-western Syria, government troops and Russian Military Police, accompanied by several Syrian T-72 tanks carried on low-loaders, moved quickly on the night of 13th/14th October to drive to the outskirts of Manbij to head off a move by Turkish-backed fighters of the Syrian National Army (SNA) to enter the town. Syrian troops then moved into Kobani on the Turkish border during 16th October after US forces left.

The central Syrian column moved through the town of Tadqa in the early hours of 14th October, with armed SUVs, commercial trucks loaded with several hundred infantry and eight T-55 and T-62 tanks moved north to set up a base at Ayn Issa later that day. They were followed by a column of three BM-21 rocket launchers later in the week. Russian troops in a Gaz Tigr utility vehicle were filmed with this column, apparently co-ordinating air support, on 17th October.

A smaller column of troops from the Syrian garrison at Hasakah, which had been isolated between Kurdish lines since Islamic State took over swathes of eastern Syria in 2013-14, moved to take up positions around the town of Tal Tamr in the north-west of Hasakah town. This column appeared from the available imagery to only comprise armed SUVs and infantry.

Some Syrian troops skirmished with SNA fighters around Manbij on 14th and

15th October but the government forces in the central sector between Ayn Issa and Tal Tamir had not clashed with Ankara's troops or allies. The Syrian force of several hundred troops from the 17th Division that had been isolated by Islamic State and then the SDF in the north-eastern border city of Qamishli since 2014 remained in and around its garrisons. This city had not yet come under direct ground attack but it was inside the proposed Turkish 30 kilometre security zone. At least two Syrian air force Ilyushin Il-76 transport aircraft were tracked by transponder data flying to Qamishli following the start of the Kurdish-Syrian accord.

The Syrian columns pushing into the Kurdish-controlled region appeared to be moving to establish links with the Kurdish-led SDF forces and set up blocking positions to head off Turkish advances towards the cities of Raqqa, Qamishli, Hasaka, Kobani and Manbij.

The exact details of the agreement between Russia, Syria and the Kurds were not made public. It appeared that Damascus and Moscow did not sign up to launch an immediate counter-attack against the Turks alongside the SDF militia. It was also very unclear if or when Syrian troops would move further east past Raqqa and Hasaka into the heartland of the SDF near the Iraqi border but there were reports of Russian officers meeting Arab tribal leaders east of Dier Ez Zor to smooth the way for government troops to enter this region.

Russian political leaders and diplomats stressed that they wanted to head off a direct confrontation between Turkish and Syrian troops, which indicated that the Syrian troops would only establish "backstop" positions along the M4 road to stop Turkish troops moving beyond their initial enclaves around Tell Abyad and Ras Ayn. The Syrians let the SDF take on the brunt of the fighting between the M4 road and north to the Turkish border. The Russians and Syrians wanted to establish facts on the grounds that Ankara and Washington could not wish away.

To support their troops who were now policing the border security zone in co-operation with Turkish units, Moscow dispatched an extra battalion of Military Police to Syria. It arrived at Hmeymim airbase in western Syria on a shuttle of Ilyushin Il-76 airlifters, along with more than 30 armoured vehicles, on 26th October. An RuAF detachment of Mi-35 attack and Mi-8AMTSh transport helicopters was re-positioned from Hmeymim airbase to Kweires airport, east of Aleppo, to begin flying air patrols eastwards over advancing Russian columns. The Russian helicopters then flew to Qamishli airport in the heart of the Kurdish region in north-east Syria to provide air support to Moscow's troops policing the region. The Russian Ministry of Defence's Zvezda television channel posted video imagery online on 11th November showing two Mi-35s and one Mi-8AMTSh landing at Qamishli airport. The helicopters made a low-level approach to Qamishli city before circling and landing at the nearby airport. A ground support element, including at least one fuel tanker and a Pantsir S-1 anti-aircraft gun/missile system, was seen near the airport's aircraft ramp in the video imagery. Another Mi-8 was seen on the ground on the ramp, although it is not clear if it was a Russian or Syrian helicopter.

The opening of Qamishli airport to Russian helicopters made it the second airbase in north-eastern Syria to have a Russian military presence. On 17th October video imagery appeared online showing Russian military vehicles and personnel at Tabqa airport, south of Raqqa city, as an RuAF Mi-8AMTSh landed.

The next phase of US withdraw took place on the night of 13th/14th November when the last US troops flew out of KLZ, as recounted at the start of this chapter. Early the next morning Russian Mi-35s and Mi-8s began landing on the airstrip and Russian Military Police troops started to spread out across the base. A camera crew from the RT television network was with the Russian troops to film scene. It appeared that the US troops had left the site intact including helicopter landing pads, barrack buildings, medical facilities and fuel tanks.

The appearance of Russian helicopters across northern Syria added a new dimension to Moscow's push to project military forces into the heart of the Kurdish region, formerly controlled by the SDF under the protection of US troops.

Qamishli airport was the only airfield to the east of the Euphrates with a hardened runway under Russian and Syrian control and has been a key logistic hub for Syrian troops isolated in the region by Islamic State fighters in 2014. It played an important role in the Syrian government's air bridge to the besieged city of Dier Ez Zor between 2014 and 2017. After the agreement between Damascus and the SDF in October to allow Syrian troops to expand their presence in north-eastern Syria at least two Syrian Il-76 transport aircraft was tracked heading towards Qamishli airport.

The arrival of Russian forces at Kobani Landing Zone was a symbolic event, signalling the most difficult element of the US withdrawal from northern Syria was complete. President Trump partially reversed his pull-out order and several hundred US troops remained based around a couple of oil fields in eastern Syria. The remaining US enclaves were in remote desert regions with poor lines of communications back to supporting US forces in Iraq. Russian and Syrian troops were now positioned in the main population centres in the Kurdish region and control critical transport infrastructure, such as Qamishli airport. US influence in Syria was now well and truly in retreat.

Chapter 13
The Battle for Idlib - Drone Battles with Turkey

High in the spring sky the drone looked serene as it circled over Syria's Idlib province. It was broad daylight and the Syrian troops were taking cover waiting for the Turkish unmanned aerial vehicle to go away before restarting their advance. Two days before the drones had starting attacking the Syrian convoys across the province in retaliation for a suspected Russian air strike on one of their battalions that left dozens of Turkish soldiers dead.

Slowly the missile started to rise towards the drone. It impacted just in front of the drone's tail, sending it spinning to earth. Fire started to spread down the drone's fuselage and large chunks began falling off it as it spun out of control.

The open involvement of Russian and Turkish troops in several days of high intensity fighting around Idlib was the most serious sign of outside involvement in the nine-year-long Syrian conflict. After inflicting heavy blows on each other, Moscow and Ankara called a draw, leaving the fate of Idlib still hanging.

By the end of 2019 Idlib province in north west Syria was the last rebel enclave free from the control of the Damascus government or occupied by militia fighters loyal to Ankara. Some three million people were crammed in to the shrinking enclave, with more than two thirds of them refugees from other parts of Syria. More than 100,000 of these refugees had re-located from other parts Syria under the various reconciliation deals negotiated by the Russians in other enclaves around the country over the previous three years. The population was dependent on international humanitarian aid for its daily survival.

Dozens of rival rebel groups vied for control of the enclave, with the most heavily armed and dominant one being the Hay'at Tahrir al Sham or HTS, which had morphed out of the Syrian branch of al Qaida, the Nusra Front, in 2017. Assassinations and random killing were the normal way for these groups to settle their disputes.

To add to the pervading feeling of despair, the Syrian government had been pursuing a policy of attrition against the enclave over the previous four years, with routine, and very randomly targeted, air strikes, artillery and rocket attacks aimed at making life as unpleasant as possible for Idlib's population. Both sides accused each other of atrocities against civilians and prisoners. Many of the government troops serving in the frontlines around the enclave had been driven from Idlib city and neighbouring towns in a rebel offensive in early 2015. This was war as blood feud.

To free up troops for the 2017 and 2018 offensives elsewhere in Syria, the Russian military had negotiated a ceasefire around Idlib and in partnership with Turkey, had set up a demilitarized zone around the enclave. Russian Military Police and Turkish soldiers policed the zone from a series of observation posts positioned at important points around the confrontation line.

Despite this agreement, the Damascus government was determined to drive the rebels out of Idlib or kill as many of them as possible. An initial attack in

August 2019 made some gains and allowed the Syrians to surround a Turkish observation post at Murak on the southern edge of the enclave.

This set the pattern for Syrian offensives: heavy artillery and air strikes would pound frontline positions, often assisted by Russian jets and attack helicopters. Syrian troops would then try to infiltrate past thinly held sectors, forcing the rebels to retreat when they feared being encircled. Often only a few dozen square miles would be lost but the Damascus government was slowly chipping away. Its summer offensive took some 10% of the enclave. It had planned to launch a sustained offensive in the autumn of 2019 but the crisis in the north-east after the Turkish incursion temporarily derailed this operation.

The offensive resumed in December 2019 and followed a similar pattern, but with more government troops committed along the whole length of the enclaves eastern and southern frontlines. Russian aircraft supported the operation with air strikes and surveillance. This two-pronged offensive aimed at seizing control of the strategic M4 motorway linking Hama city with Aleppo, and bringing the capital of the rebel held enclave into artillery range.

After capturing Ma'arrat al Nu'man, the second city of Idlib province, over 27-28th January, the Syrian force swung northwards to advance up the M4 motorway towards at the town of Saraqib as another column of Syrian troops was moving southwards from the city of Aleppo.

The US special envoy for Syria, James Jeffrey, on 30th January 2020 described the government offensive as a "massive movement of troops" and said it had been backed by 200 Russian and Syrian air strikes over the previous three days. Jeffrey added that the Syrian move had left several Turkish observation posts around Idlib cut off by the government advance and had forced 700,000 refugees - some 25% of the enclave's population - to flee towards the Turkish border.

Syrian forces began their next offensive on 24th January, with news and social media reports from the Idlib region indicating heavy fighting to the north and south of Ma'arrat al Nu'man. Fearing the government troops were about to encircle the town, opposition fighters pulled out leaving it abandoned.

Social-media posts and imagery from the battle zone indicated the Syrian Tiger Force or the 25th Special Forces Division had borne the brunt of operation on the Ma'arrat al Nu'man axis, backed by smaller units of the Republican Guard. On the Aleppo axis, the 30th Republican Guard Division and armoured units of the 4th Division were in the forefront of the attack. The presence of personnel from Lebanese Hizbullah was revealed when tribute pictures of three fighters were posted online on 29th January. The day before imagery was posted online of a Iranian Ababil-3 unmanned aerial vehicle drifting to earth by parachute in south-east Idlib after suffering a mishap.

Opposition forces struck back with two suicide bombs mounted in BMP armoured vehicles, which killed several government troops in Zahraa and Khan al Sabil on 26th and 29th January. The media arm of HTS posted video imagery online of these attacks filmed from a small unmanned aerial vehicle.

The success of the opening moves of the latest government offensive appears to be threatening the viability of the last opposition-held enclave in Syria. After taking Ma'arrat al Nu'man and pushing to within 5 kilometres of Saraqid, the Syrian troops brought Idlib city itself within range of their BM-21 and BM-27 rocket launchers, as well as 152mm artillery, for the first time.

The Syrian revolution was now at a tipping point and the existence of the Iblib enclave appeared to be entering its endgame. In Ankara, this was setting off alarm bells and Recep Tayyip Erdoğan was determined to ensure the enclave did not fall, triggering an exodus of millions of Syrians across the border into Turkey. The Turkish President, however, did not wish to get dragged into a war with Russia and Syria over Idlib. The Syrian offensive also served his purpose because it was aimed at destroying the HTS fighters and its Jihadi government in Idlib. If the offensive led to the destruction of the HTS, then groups loyal to Turkey could be installed to run Idlib in the way pro-Ankara militias ran a Turkish-controlled zone north of Aleppo. As with many Syria battles, it was not immediately apparent who was fighting who, or why.

After their initial success around Ma'arrat al Nu'man, the Syrians pushed forward with the aim of capturing Saraqid and opening the M4 motorway, capturing the town on 7th February. This effectively reduced the size of the Idlib enclave by another 40%.

The first major movement of Turkish troops in response to the Syrian offensive towards Idlib city occurred on 3rd February, and involved a convoy of M60 Sabra and tracked armoured vehicles on low loaders. This force apparently came to grief later that day when it was targeted by Syrian artillery fire as it moved along the M4 road towards Saraqid. Images posted online show at least three low loaders carrying M60 Sabra and M113 armoured personnel carriers burned out next to Saraqid's fun fair.

In response at least four major groups of Turkish troops, with each column containing several dozen armoured and support vehicles were sent to Idlib. One column moved through Idlib city during the night of 7th/8th February, which included at least seven M60 Sabra main battle tanks on low loaders and a mix of wheeled and tracked troop carriers. The next column, containing Leopard 2A4 tanks and ACV-15 infantry fighting vehicles, was filmed travelling to the Syrian border from the Turkish town of Oğulpınar. This column appeared to be heading into the northern part of Idlib province, close to Aleppo city. Imagery appeared on 6th February of more M60 Sabra tanks close to Idlib city.

During 9th February footage of a convoy of T-122 Sakarya multiple launch rocket systems (MLRS) driving through Idlib city was posted online. The same type of weapons were seen firing from positions close to Ma'arat al Na'asan in another video clip posted online on 10th February. A group of more than 30 Turkish infantry soldiers were then photographed by the AFP news agency marching along a road between Idlib and Qaminas.

Earlier on 10th February, the Turkish Ministry of National Defence reported that five of its troops had been killed and a further five wounded by Syrian artillery fire on their positions near Taftanaz. In response, the ministry claimed Turkish forces fired on 115 Syrian government targets and destroyed 101 of them, including three tanks, two mortar positions and one helicopter.

In this escalating conflict neither side seemed to be inclined to back down and the Turks began helping the rebels organise a major counter-attack to re-take Saraqid. They deployed their troops in the block position between Saraqid and Idlib city and began handing over weapons and armoured vehicles to rebel fighters. Images of M113 armoured personnel carriers painted in Turkish Land Forces colour schemes being driven by rebel militia fighters near Idlib were posted online. Turkish soldiers armed with Stinger shoulder-launched surface-to-air missiles started firing at Syria helicopters over Saraqid, downing one on 14th February.

The re-armed rebels were defeated when they attacked the town of Kafr Haleb between 14th and 16th February. Russian and Syrian aircraft destroyed more than 10 vehicles, including three Turkish-supplied ACV-15s, with a combination of artillery fire, air strikes and anti-tank guided missiles. These weapons appeared to have been guided by imagery from unmanned aerial vehicles.

The Russian command in Syria was becoming concerned at the escalating fighting and called up reinforcements. On 18th February open-source tracking of aircraft movements over Iran indicated that the RuAF had deployed additional Su-24s to enhance its air group in Syria from a base in southern Russia.

The Turkish policy of relying on the rebels was not going to drive back the Syrian troops so a larger Turkish-backed operation to retake Saraqid started in earnest on 20th February. The day-long battle saw opposition fighters, operating Turkish-supplied armoured vehicles and backed by Turkish artillery fire, attempt to drive government troops from the town of Nayrab in a bid to reach the strategic junction of the M4 and M5 roads. Two Turkish soldiers were reported killed and five wounded by the Ministry of Defence in Ankara, in what it said were Syrian air strikes. It said that in retaliatory fire "over 50 [Syrian] regime soldiers were killed, five tanks, two armoured vehicles, a self-propelled artillery gun and two military pickups were destroyed."

RuAF Sukhoi Su-24s now intervened to strike at the opposition fighters outside of Nayreb, forcing the assault force to pull back, according to reports from the Syrian government and Russian sources. Russian advisors and forward air controllers close to the frontline directed these airstrikes on the rebel and Turkish positions.

The Russian military issued a statement, via its Centre for the Reconciliation of Opposing Sides in the Syrian Arab Republic, late on 20th February claiming to have driven back the rebel assault. "In order to prevent terrorist groups from advancing deep into the Syrian territory, Su-24 aircraft of RuAF delivered a strike at the request of the Syrian command against the terrorists' armed formations that had penetrated the area," the Russian state news agency TASS reported the Centre as saying. "This helped the Syrian troops to repel all the attacks successfully. They eliminated one tank, six infantry fighting vehicles and five pick-up trucks with the militants' large-calibre guns." Retaliatory shelling by the Turkish army wounded four Syrian soldiers, said the Russian military.

Throughout the day reports from the battlefield indicated that this was an intense period of combat operations involving Russian, Syrian, Turkish and opposition forces using aircraft, artillery, tanks, tactical ballistic missiles and MLRS against each other. Imagery from news organisations and social media posts during the 20th February indicated the battle started with opposition fighters loaded on board Turkish-supplied ACV15 infantry fighting vehicles and M113 armoured personnel carriers assaulting government troops holding Nayreb. Turkish T155 155mm artillery batteries and T-122 Sakarya MLRS were filmed firing at Syrian positions, including images apparently filmed from a Russian Forpost unmanned aerial vehicle. Turkish M60 Sabra tanks and Turkish infantry were photographed manoeuvring in positions to support the offensive by opposition fighters.

Later in the day Russian Su-24s were filmed on several occasions dropping bombs on targets north west of Nayreb around a hill that dominated the approach to the government-held town. The Syrian news agency SANA subsequently released a video of the Russian strikes filmed from a UAV that showed air attacks on nine Turkish vehicles during the battle, including one M60 tank.

During the evening, Turkish Defence Minister Hulusi Akar was reported by CNN's Turkish service as urging the United States to send Patriot missile systems to counter the Russian air supremacy over Idlib province. "There are air missile threats against our country and there are previous events of the sort. In that light, there could be a Patriot system battery support here," Akar said.

The intervention of Russian airpower appears to have turned the battle on 20th February in favour of the Syrian government forces, preventing the Turkish-backed opposition forces from reaching the town of Saraqeb on the M5 road.

Although Turkey had deployed significant additional forces into Idlib province during February these forces did not appear to have made much effort to disguise their presence, often moving in large convoys along major roads in daylight and setting up artillery fire positions in open fields. This made it easy for the Russians and Syrians to monitor their movements, making the Turkish vehicles sitting ducks. No doubt this was behind the Turkish request for the US air defence missiles

Fighting between Syrian and Turkish regular forces dramatically escalated on 27th February when 33 Turkish soldiers were reported killed and another 30 wounded in an air strike in southern Idlib. Some unofficial Turkish media reports suggested nearly 100 soldiers were killed in the air strike. (1)

The incident occurred at Al Barah Balioun in southern Idlib, where government troops had been making rapid advances since 23rd February. A Syrian government offensive into the south flank of the Iblib enclave received Russian surveillance support from Orlan-10 unmanned aerial vehicles.

News footage of artillery strikes in the town of Ehsim, close to the site of 27th

February incident, posted online by the A24 News Agency showed two Orlan-10 UAVs circling over a column of Turkish army armoured vehicles while artillery fire landed around them. The column appeared to halt for the duration of the fire, which coincided with the Syrian offensive to the south of the town. Two days later the local Zaitun news agency posted images of an RuAF Tupolev Tu-214R multi-sensor surveillance aircraft orbiting over central Idlib.

There were several sightings of Russian forces on the ground with Syrian troops operating around Idlib during this period. Images of a four-strong Russian special forces team appeared online on 25th February. It was subsequently geolocated to a position near Ma`arat al Nu`man which was captured by government troops in January. The Russian Ruptly news agency uploaded a video clip on 23rd February of what appeared to be three Russian Ground Forces Kamaz-6350-376 prime movers each pulling 152mm 2A65 Msta-B howitzers moving along the M5 highway.

Russia denied involvement in the 27th February strike and the Turkish government blamed Syrian forces for the biggest loss of life among Ankara's forces since it intervened in Idlib province earlier that month. The Turkish government invoked NATO Article 4 provisions and called an emergency meeting of the North Atlantic Council in Brussels, citing a threat to its territorial integrity, political independence and security.

In a statement on 28th February, the Moscow Ministry of Defence blamed the Turks for putting their troops in danger by not informing the Russian military headquarters in Syria of their location. The Turkish troops then got caught in the Syrian strike which was aimed at opposition fighters in the town, said the Russians. "Turkish military who were in the terrorist units' battle formations came under Syrian troops' fire near the inhabited community of Behun [Al Barah Balioun] on 27th February," the ministry said.

The attack took place up to 10 kilometres behind the frontline and despite the denials from Moscow, only Russian forces had the necessary surveillance assets to find such a target and direct fire on to it away from the frontline zones at night. The Syrian air force also had very limited night-attack capability, which again pointed to Russian involvement.

The 27th February attack highlighted the weakness of Turkish air defences over their forward troops. There had been several reports of man-portable surface-to-air-missiles being fired at Russian and Syrian aircraft during the fighting in February. Although two Syrian helicopters and three poorly protected Syrian jets reportedly fell victim to their missiles, the Turkish-supplied or operated small missiles did not downed any Russian strike jets.

The heavy loss of life among Turkish troops on 27th February resulted in fury in Ankara. Turkey's government communications director Fahrettin Altun, told the state-run Anadolu news agency on 27th February, "all known Syrian government targets are under fire by Turkish air and land support units".

In a wave of UAV attacks in the aftermath of this incident, Turkey claimed dozens of Syrian tanks, armoured vehicles and artillery pieces destroyed, along with hundreds of Syrian soldiers killed and wounded, in missile strikes launched from its UAVs. Subsequently, the Turkish military claimed to have killed 3000 Syrian soldiers, as well destroying 151 tanks, eight helicopters, three drones, three fighter jets, [many] vehicles and trucks, eight aerial defence systems and one headquarters during its UAV offensive. (2)

The Turkish military released several video clips of these attacks on 28th and 29th February and subsequent analysis of the imagery seemed to indicate that these took place in the central Idlib region along the M5 highway. However, Turkish claims were exaggerated. From the Turkish drone footage released immediately after the first wave of attacks around 50 individual strikes could be identified and not all of them involved attacks on armoured vehicles. Few of the clips showed targets after attacks making it difficult to determine their impact.

While the initial round of Turkish UAV attacks appeared to be unopposed, after 1st March Syrian air defence assets started to engage the hostile UAVs. Syrian military sources reported by the Damascus-based al Masdran news agency claimed as many as seven UAVs destroyed by the country's air defences. The Izvestia newspaper in Moscow, citing Russia military sources, claimed on 4th March that five Turkish Aerospace Industries (TAI) Anka UAVs and seven Kale-Baykar Bayraktar TB2 UAVs were lost over Idlib to Syrian Buk and Pantsir air defence systems.

Video and still imagery from several sources in Idlib appeared to confirm four Turkish UAV losses after 25th February when the wreckage of one Anka was photographed spread across a field. Dramatic video imagery shot on 1st March - and recounted at the start of this chapter - showed an Anka falling to earth in flames near the strategic town of Saraqeb, which had been a battleground between government troops and rebel fighters since 25th February. Wreckage of the UAV was also filmed later that day. Imagery of the wreckage of two Bayraktar UAVs appeared online on 2nd and 3rd March.

Video and still images of a 9K317E Buk-M2E missile launcher appeared on line on 4th March showing a missile being fired from a field site that resembled the Idlib countryside, although it was not possible to confirm its exact location. Turkish UAV and Syrian missile activity seemed to pause after a finale attack on 5th March in the hours following a summit in Moscow between the Turkish and Syrian Presidents that resulted in a ceasefire and a disengagement zone being declared along part of the frontlines in Idlib.

Turkish UAV operations from 28th February onwards were described in media reports as "swarm" attacks. The video imagery released by the Turkish military was of a high definition and it had an immediate media impact, being shared repeatedly online and was frequently broadcast in the days after the attacks.

The effect on the ground of the Turkish UAV operation, however, seemed to reduce in the days after its start as the Syrian military started to adapt to the new tactical environment by bringing up air defence systems to challenge the UAVs. The shooting down of the Anka UAV on 1st March seemed to be a turning point. A day later Syrian troops were able to fully recapture Saraqib and make other advances that allowed them to take back control of the M5 highway. The Syrians were unlikely to have been able to do this unless the UAV threat had been neutralised or seriously mitigated.

The Syrian air defence operation, however, did not seem to have completely driven the Turkish UAVs from the skies over Idlib, with the Turks reporting continuing UAV strikes on Syrian troops up to 5th March. That day the Turks, for example, claimed to have destroyed four tanks, five rocket launchers and a dozen military vehicles in artillery and air strikes over the previous 24 hours.

This would indicate that the Turkish UAVs were able to penetrate Syrian airspace but not able to sustain medium altitude orbits over the battle zone for prolonged periods. The Russian sources quoted by Izvestia claimed the Turkish UAVs were forced to fly at night and at low altitude to avoid the Syrian air defences, which limited their ability to detect and strike targets.

Both Moscow and Ankara had their own reasons, linked to wider economic and diplomatic relations between the two countries, for wanting to avoid escalating the crisis into open war. The Turks, for example, never directly blamed Russian forces of involvement in the 27th February attack on the Turkish battalion, giving them a way out of crisis but pinning the blame on Damascus. With both sides able to claim "honours even" in the latest round of the Battle for Idlib, the Russians and Turks patched up their differences and signed a new ceasefire deal on 5th March after Putin and Erdoğan met in Moscow. This re-introduced the demilitarised zone and established a series of joint patrols along the M4 and M5 motorways. These began on 10th March and saw Russian troops, escorted by Turkish vehicles, driving along the M4 motorway to edge of Idlib city.

The Turks were happy to head off the collapse of the pocket, while at the same time making the rebel fighters in the enclave totally dependent. The Russians and Syrians had captured some important pieces of territory and reduced the Idlib pocket by almost half.

The Turkish UAV offensive had been a shock to the Russians and Syrians but three of the armed drones had been shot down between 1st and 3rd March, allowing Syrian troops to retake Saraqid and secure control of the M5 motorway. Russia is yet to field armed UAVs in any significant numbers so it relied on conventional strike aircraft with "dumb" bombs to blunt the Turkish-organised rebel counter-attacks. The Russia's own Forpost and Orlan-10 UAVs provided adequate surveillance of the battlefield to allow relatively accurate strikes on Turkish armour and artillery positions supporting the rebel advance. It was not as hi-tech as the Turkish UAV swarm but it was effective.

By the end of March the world would be engulfed by the COVID-19 pandemic and Moscow's attention shifted from Syria. The next duel with Turkish UAVs would be found further to the west in North Africa.

Russia's Generals

General Valery Gerasimov has been chief of the Russian General Staff since November 2012 and is the public face of the transformation of the country's armed forces in the following decade. (Russian Ministry of Defence)

Sergey Shoigu has been Russia's defence minister since 2012. He is a close confidant of President Putin and played an important role in the Crimea and Syrian campaigns. (Russian Ministry of Defence)

Colonel General Sergey Surovikin was appointed head of the Russian Aerospace Forces in November 2017 after playing a key role in the campaign in Syria. He is the first non-aviator to command the Russian or Soviet air force. (2018) (Russian Ministry of Defence)

Vice Admiral Aleksandr Moiseev was appointed to command the Northern Fleet in May 2019. He commanded the Black Sea Fleet during the November 2018 Kerch Bridge incident, which led to the capture of Ukrainian navy ships attempting to enter the Sea of Azov (Russian Ministry of Defence)

Russian Land Power

The annual Victory Day Parade in Moscow is a major event for the Russian military, allowing many units to exhibit new vehicles and weapons. (Russian Presidential Press and Information Office)

The upgraded T-72B3 is the mainstay of Russian armoured units on accout of its reliability and fire. (Vitaly V. Kuzmin)

The BM-30 Smerch multiple launch rocket system gives Russian artillery brigades the ability to hit targets out to 90 kilometre range. (Digr)

The Russian Airborne Forces have their own specially developed family of airportable armoured vehicles, based on the BMD vehicle, that can be parachuted into combat zones. (Russian Ministry of Defence)

Russian Naval Power

Russia's aircraft carrier Admiral Kuzetsov made a dramatic foray to the Mediterranean Sea to in October 2016 to launch its jets into action over Syria. (UK Ministry of Defence/Crown Copyright)

The Steregushchiy-class corvettes, Boiky, is one of the newest ships in Baltic Fleet, entering service in 2013. (UK Ministry of Defence/Crown Copyright)

The Russian Navy has invested heavily in small but heavily armed warships such as the Vasily Bykov class of corvette, which is equipped with Kalibr land attack cruise missiles. (UK Ministry of Defence/Crown Copyright)

The Yagelnaya Bay naval base is home to the Northern Fleet's main group of attack and ballistic missile firing nuclear submarines. The Akula III boat, the K-335 Gepard, is seen here in front of the base's missile loading gantry. (http://militaryrussia.ru/blog/)

Russian Air Power

A Tupolev Tu-145 maritime patrol craft of Russian Naval Aviation on patrol over the North Atlantic in August 2019 (UK Ministry of Defence/ Crown Copyright)

Tupolev Tu-160 strategic bombers first flew in the 1980s and the production line has since been re-started to bolster Long Range Aviation's strength. (UK Ministry of Defence/ Crown Copyright)

Il-22M surveillance aircraft during a mission over the Baltic Sea during April 2020. (UK Ministry of Defence/Crown Copyright)

Sukhoi Su-27 of the 6th Air and Air Defence Army on patrol over the Baltic Sea in June 2019. The legacy Su-27 is in the process of being phased out in favour of more modern versions of the Flanker. (UK Ministry of Defence/ Crown Copyright)

Watching from Space

Ara Bay naval base in home to the Victor- and Sierra-class boats of the 7th Submarine Division. This image dates from August 2018. (Digital Globe/Maxar Technologies)

Severodvinsk, near Archangel, is at the centre of Russian nuclear submarine operations and is home to the country's only nuclear submarine assembly facility, as well as other facilities dedicated to repair and overhaul of submarines. This image is dated from August 2018 and show more than dozen boats in various states of repair and construction. (Digital Globe/Maxar Technologies)

Boguchar is home to the 3rd Guards Motor Rifle Division, which is assigned to the Western Military District. The division was formed in 2016 as part of a move to establish new units along the border with Ukraine. (Digital Globe/Maxar Technologies)

Strugi Krasnye garrison, west of St Petersburg, is one of the closest Russian military bases to Estonia, where NATO troops are based. The elements of S-400 air defence systems are seen in this image from 2019. (Digital Globe/Maxar Technologies)

War Zones

Sukhoi Su-34 strike jets made their combat debut in Syria in September 2015 at the start of the Russian military intervention. (Russian Today)

The Russian blockade of the base at Perevalne, where the main Ukrainian combat units on Crimea were based, was instrumental in the campaign to undermine the Kiev government's attempts to organise resistance. (Anton Holoborodko)

Aftermath of the Russia multiple rocket attack on 11th July 2014, near Zelenopillya, devastated a Ukrainian brigade, inflicting hundreds of casualties and rendering the unit combat in-effective. (Info Napalm)

The opening of the Kerch bridge in April 2018 has transformed the ability of the Russian military to reinforce the garrison in Crimea and hinder Ukrainian access to the Sea of Azov (https://rosavtodor.gov.ru/)

Chapter 14
Russia in Libya

On the satellite images the distinctive outline of a Sukhoi Su-24 strike jet could be seen next to the hardened aircraft shelter at Libya's al Jufra Airbase. In other satellite images, Mikoyan MiG-29s and newly installed radar stations were visible. A Russian airbase was taking shape in the Libyan desert in May and June 2020.

Days after the arrival of the jets was first spotted by amateur internet military enthusiasts, US Africa Command filled in further details about the latest Russian military deployment. It released a set of air-to-air photographs showing the Russian aircraft flying across the Mediterranean Sea from Moscow's airbase in Syria. They showed a Tupolev Tu-154 flying in formation with the Sukhois and MiGs during the long-distance ferry flight. Other satellite pictures released by the Americans showed the Russian jets on the ground at Hmeinyan airbase in Syria, where US Africa Command said they had been repainted to disguise their identity.

The incident brought back memories of the 2015 deployment of Russia aircraft to Syria, which also caught out Western decision-makers. What was perhaps surprising about the Russian move into Libya was how little of a surprise it was. Intelligence indicators had been building for years and the North African country's chaotic civil war appeared to be an open door that was waiting for Moscow to move through.

Western intervention in Libya in 2011 led to death of the country's strongman, Muammar Gaddafi, commonly known as Colonel Gaddafi in the western media. Almost immediately Libya descended into anarchy as rival factions manoeuvred for control of the country and its large oil and gas reserves. Criminal gangs, Jihadi fighters and people-smugglers seemed to operate with impunity. Neighbour states and other powers started to back rival groups. Intelligence operatives from the US, UK, France, Italy and many Arab nations flocked to the country to find out what was going on and to gain influence. The United Nations launched a reconciliation bid to try to form an effective government but progress was glacial. Air strikes were launched by the US and France against Islamic State enclaves. After migrants started using Libya as a transit route to Europe in 2015, the European Union set up naval patrols off the coast to try to turn back the migrants.

Moscow had been a long time ally of Gaddafi stretching back to Cold War days and during the 2010s it put a lot of effort into trying to regain its lost influence in Libya. The first public sign of these moves emerged in December 2016 when one of Libya's main warlords, the self-declared Field Marshall Khalifa Haftar, visited Moscow for talks with the Russian foreign minister Sergei Lavrov about opening arms sales to his militia force which controlled most of eastern Libya. A few weeks later, Haftar was hosted onboard the Russian aircraft carrier Admiral Kuznetsov as she returned home from her cruise off the coast of Syria.

While onboard Haftar carried out more talks with Russian leaders via a video link to senior officials in the Kremlin. Despite the public wooing of Haftar by Moscow nothing appeared to come from these talks and there was no public or covert opening of arms supplies to Libya by the Kremlin at this point.

A senior political operative in Washington DC told the author soon after these events that Haftar was not impressed by Moscow's offer. "Everything in Libya is driven by oil - who controls it, who can sell it and who gets the money from it," said my source. "Haftar may have been familiar to Moscow because of his links during the Cold War but he drives a hard bargain and is determined to avoid being anyone's puppet."

According to my source, around the same time as the Russians were making their overtures to Haftar, the French, Americans, Turks, Egyptians and Emiratis were all making rival pitches to the Libyan warlord. On the coat tails of these country's diplomats and intelligence operatives came a posse of oil-company executives making offers to boost hydrocarbon exports and hence revenues. "The Russians offered Haftar the full Syria package – air support, special forces and arms sales – but they came with strings attached so Haftar decided not to play along," said the Beltway insider.

Libya's agony continued with fighting raging for the rest of the decade. Haftar decided to make his move in the spring of 2019 to launch a drive to capture Libya's capital, Tripoli, to depose the UN-recognised Government of National Accord (GNA). By early 2020 his Libya National Army (LNA) scored some early successes and approached the outskirts of Tripoli.

Libya's crazy war proved an easy target for open-source intelligence analysts, even if the country's political and military leaders were epitomised by their covert diplomacy and shady business links. The country's desert terrain made it easy to spot military hardware using commercial satellite imagery. Libya's people also regularly post still and video imagery of the various militias that are operating around them, allowing assessments to be made of the weapons in use and who supplied them.

Through the summer and winter of 2019 a steady stream of imagery started to emerge from Libya showing European men in military uniforms, driving vehicles that appeared to be types in use with the Russian armed forces. While much of this materiel, such small arms and trucks, could easily have been bought from third-party or black-market sources, other equipment could only have been supplied with the approval of high-level decision-makers in the Kremlin. Imagery appeared in January 2020 showing the remains of a crashed Orlan-10 unmanned aerial vehicle (UAV), which was then the Russian military's primary tactical drone and had not been recorded as being officially exported.

This was a sign that Russia was now a fully fledged ally of Haftar - alongside the UAE, Jordan and Egypt who had been accused by the UN in December 2019 of breaching the arms embargo against Libya. The UN also accused Turkey of backing the GNA with arms sales. The GNA itself accused the Russia private security company, the Wagner Group, of being on the ground in Libya

helping Haftar's troops advance on Tripoli.
The company has become notorious for its alleged links to the highest level of the Kremlin and participation in covert operations on behalf of the Russian government. Its owner, Yevgeny Prigozhin, is reputed to have close ties to President Putin and several important oligarchs. Wagner operatives appear to be almost exclusively former Russian military and intelligence personnel, according to investigations by Russian and international media organisations.(1) These reports tend to spike after incidents when Wagner personnel are killed in action and their relatives try to secure compensation from the company. Imagery from Ukraine, Syria and Libya of alleged Wagner operatives would appear to support these claims that they are former Russian military personnel.
Open-source tracking of aircraft movements across the Mediterranean in late 2019 added a layer of detail that pointed to high-level Russian involvement to support Haftar's forces as part of a coalition of nations to confront the GNA and its Turkish allies. The ADS-B transponder signals from RuAF transport aircraft showed them heading to Libya from the main Russian airbase in Syria, indicating that the Kremlin had reached an understanding with Haftar and was providing logistic support to Wagner Group staff operating in the country. Even if the infamous private military or mercenary group had decided of its own account to move its personnel to Libya, the participation of RuAF aircraft could only have been authorised by the Kremlin.
Russian military transport aircraft were first identified flying missions to airports in Libya in October 2019. Two missions by RuAF Tu-154M aircraft were detected from their ADS-B transponder signals, taking off from Hmeinyan airbase in Syria's Latakia province.
On both of these missions, the Tu-154M was tracked landing at Al Khadim airbase in Eastern Libya, which was controlled by Haftar. Earlier in October, an RuAF Iluyshin Il-76 cargo transport was also tracked flying westward over the Mediterranean from Hmeinyan airbase towards Libya but its final destination could not be determined.
The spring of 2020 saw the LNA launch a counter-offensive to drive back Haftar's forces from the outskirts of Tripoli, with the strong support of armed Turkish unmanned aerial vehicles or drones. LNA troops captured al Watiya airbase to the south-east of Tripoli after Turkish drones destroyed a number of Russian-made but UAE-supplied Pantsir air defence systems. During April a surge of imagery appeared on line, showing convoys of Russian-made vehicles heading away from al Watiya to escape the LNA advance. One set of images showed an Antonov An-26 landing at the airbase to evacuate European personnel in military uniforms. It appeared as if Haftar's army and their Russian advisors were in serious trouble.
This is when the first satellite imagery started to emerge of the new Su-24s and MiG-29s arriving at al Jufra Airbase, which would block the LNA advance into Haftar's heartland. Soon after the arrival of the jets an early warning radar was identified in overhead reconnaissance imagery released on 18th June by US Af-

rica Command. The US military identified the radar as a Russian-made Spoon Rest mobile system, which is designed to provide tactical support to military activities. "Russia uses this system when deployed to a nation in the conduct of tactical combat operations", said US Africa Command.

In another image released on 18th June, a Sukhoi Su-24 strike aircraft was shown landing on a runway at al Jufra Airbase. Also on 18th June, US Africa Command described the move as part of a concerted Russian drive to expand its influence in Africa. It accused Russia of being the "number-one arms dealer in Africa", saying that Moscow continues to profit from violence and instability across the continent. "Russian government-backed PMCs, such as the Wagner Group, are active in sixteen countries across Africa," it said. "It is estimated that there are about 2,000 Wagner Group personnel in Libya."

"Russia's sustained involvement in Libya increases the violence and delays a political solution," said US Marine Brigadier General Bradford Gering, US Africa Command's director of operations. "Russia continues to push for a strategic foothold on NATO's southern flank and this is at the expense of innocent Libyan lives."

In May, 2020 US Africa Command first reported that "at least 14 MiG-29s and several Su-24s" were flown from Russia to Syria, where their Russian markings were painted over to camouflage their Russian origin. These aircraft were then flown into Libya in direct violation of the United Nations arms embargo, it said. "We know these fighters were now already in Libya and being repaired," said Colonel. Chris Karns, director of US Africa Command public affairs. "Clearly, they came from Russia. They didn't come from any other country. Russia has relentlessly stuck to a narrative of implausible denials in the media. It's difficult to deny facts. Russian interference and masking of activity in Libya is visible."

The Spoon Rest radar, if it was fully operational, could provide early warning of attacks by Turkish armed drones on al Jufra airbase. US did not accuse the new aircraft as being operated by the regular RuAF but it claimed they were part of a mercenary force run by the Wagner Group. Russian private military companies had operated in Ukraine and Syria before but this was the first time one had apparently created its own air force with advanced - if rather old - fast jet combat aircraft. Such a force must have had high-level political support from the top of the Russian government, if only to release aircraft worth several million dollars each from RuAF stocks.

Soon after the arrival of the new Russian fighters, RuAF transport aircraft started flying regular transport missions to Libya. The missions from the Russian-controlled Hmeinyan airbase involved Il-76 cargo aircraft, as well as Tupolev Tu-134 and Tu-154 passenger aircraft.

Open-source tracking of the aircraft's ADS-B transponder data allowed them to be followed flying over the Eastern Mediterranean. They then flew along the Egyptian coast before turning inland at the Libyan border. It is not clear from the tracking data where the aircraft actually landed inside Libya. The aircraft were then tracked returning to Hmeinyan airbase after spending a few hours on the ground, presumably unloading cargo and passengers.

An Il-76 was tracked returning to Syria from Libya on 17th May 2020, which was two days before the first satellite imagery emerged of MiG-29s at al Jufra. Further Russian air movements were then detected on 30th May, 22nd June, 29th June, 30th June and 1st July. In a new development on 29th June and 1st July, flights to Libya by a Syrian Arab Air Force Il-76 were also detected.

The increasing Russian air activity to and from Libya coincided with growing Turkish Air Force air transport missions to airbases in country controlled by the Tripoli government. Through May and into June more than a dozen Turkish Lockheed C-130E Hercules flights were tracked flying from airbases around Istanbul to Misrata airport in eastern Libya. On some occasions formations of two aircraft were tracked heading to Libya. A handful of Turkish Air Force Cessna C650 Citation VII executive jets were also tracked flying into Tripoli's Mitiga airport. The Turkish aircraft usually flew south, to the east of Crete to avoid Greek airspace, before turning westwards to Libya.

Providing logistic support to their deployed forces by both Russia and Turkey is a natural continuation of decisions to insert personnel into Libya. Turkey described is personnel in Libya as "specialist advisors" and Russia did not acknowledged any military deployments on the ground in the country by its regular military.

The Russian move into Libya remains very much a work in progress. On the surface it appears to be a similar environment to Syria but there are different dynamics at play. The Libyans are not as desperate for Russian help as the Syrians were in 2015 and have proved able to drive a very hard bargain with their prospective benefactors.

Chapter 15
Russia's War in Syria Assessed

The satellite pictures of Hmeinyan airbase in Syria say it all. At the start of August 2015 it was a sleepy provincial airport used by members of Syria's elite families to visit the Mediterranean beaches. Barely six weeks later it was a fully functioning Russia military airbase, with rows of fighter jets all around the airport, ammunition dumps built next to the runway and tanks dug into earth ramparts to protect the base from rebel attack.

The audacity of Russia's move to set up the airbase in the midst of Syria's civil war was immediately apparent. Over the following five years, the Russian military made equally audacious moves to help Syria's President Bashar al Assad defeat his opponents - sailing their aircraft carrier Admiral Kuznetsov from the Northern Fleet to bolster the attack on Aleppo, firing cruise missiles from submarines in the Mediterranean, flying in an army field bridge to help the Syrian army cross the Euphrates and surging columns into north eastern Syria to take over US bases.

As well as a willingness to take risks, two other things came to characterise the Russian campaign in Syria. The first was economy of effort and the second was speed of reaction to events.

Despite the huge media coverage the Russian military in Syria received, the deployed force probably never involved more than 5,000 troops at any point in time. The vast majority of them were aircraft mechanics, logistic personnel required to move supplies from the Tartus docks to the airbase and security personnel to patrol its perimeter or crew air defence batteries. Rarely did the number of Russian jets go above 30 and probably only around two thirds of them were actually bombers. Russia advisors and special forces operatives fanned out to train the Syrian army but probably no more than a few hundred soldiers were involved in this effort. Battalions of military police troops patrolled Syria's crisis zones but only four of these units were deployed at peak effort - some 1,200 troops in total.

All of these personnel have been professional officers or contract soldiers so there was little public concern back in Russia at the steady drip of casualties. The deaths of Russian private security operatives generated even less concern among the public back in Moscow.

This modest commitment of personnel was in direct contrast the US interventions in Iraq and Afghanistan which involved more than 100,000 troops in each country at their peak. President Putin's Syria deployment was done on the cheap but his gamble on limiting troop numbers proved a success. The Damascus government was now secured, Russia's prestige restored across the Middle East and Moscow's arms sales are rising across the region. It was a gamble to go in to Syria with such a small force but it paid off and President Putin can now reap the benefits.

Russian military commanders have proved very adept at understanding the

Syrian battlefield and exploiting opportunities for maximum effect when they emerge. Time and again, Russian troops would suddenly appear at places they were least expected. The rapid move into north-east Syria in the autumn of 2019 was perhaps the best example of this and at a stroke US influence across a huge tract of Syria was removed. There were limits to this strategy, as the private contractors of the Wagner Group found out to their cost in 2018 when they tried to advance on US positions in eastern Syria and found themselves under heavy US bombardment. Scores were killed or wounded. This was a rare miscalculation by the Russians.

One of the biggest impacts of the Syria intervention has been the re-establishment of a permanent Russian naval presence in the Eastern Mediterranean, supported by an anti-access, area denial (A2/AD) umbrella. This makes Russia an important player in this key region which is emerging as a major area of exploration for undersea gas and oil.

Russia's incursion into Syria ticked all the boxes from the Kremlin's point of view. President Assad's government, however, remains weak and the country's economy is a basket case, which could lead to the civil war reigniting. For now, though, events have gone Moscow's way.

Chapter 16
Understanding Putin's Military

Every 9th May President Vladimir Putin takes the dais above Red Square in Moscow to watch the annual parade of troops and military hardware. The event is a national holiday across Russia celebrating the victory over Nazi Germany in World War Two - or as it is known to Russians - the Great Patriotic War.

During the Soviet era, many Western observers called the Moscow event the "May Day Parade" and linked it to celebrations of the Communist revolution. They often got it confused with the annual parade to mark the October Revolution that brought the Soviet state into existence, which was celebrated every 7th November. The last of these Soviet parades took place in 1990.

Since Putin's rise to power the October Revolution celebrations have not returned to the Russian national calendar except for a one-off event in 2019 to recreate the iconic 1941 parade when German troops were at the gates of Moscow. The parade's participants famously marched direct to the front to turn back the German spearheads from the Soviet capital. The 2019 event was a celebration of a great Russian military victory, not a Communist one.

After Putin's rise to power, he ordered a major expansion of the Victory Day Parade in May with more military participants, more hardware on show and higher-profile foreign guests. Some Western observers saw this as part of a bid to turn the clock back to the days when the Soviet military was a colossus that aimed at global domination.

At first glance the Victory Day Parade looks very Soviet. It is in the same location as those classic Soviet parades, there are columns of tanks and rocket launchers, and some of the units seem to be marching behind Soviet flags. The men and women on parade, however, are not Soviet soldiers and Putin's Russia is not the Soviet Union.

In the following chapters, the state of the Russian military in the third decade of the 21st century will be profiled, looking at its equipment, key deployments and important units. It is useful first to explain some important context and themes that run through this analysis of the 21st Century Russian military.

Openness

The Victory Day Parade is now broadcast live on the English-language service of the Russia Today or RT television network, with commentary usually provided Rory Suchet, son of the British television news anchor John Suchet and nephew of the actor David Suchet. Western viewers are usually impressed by the production values that involve the positioning of cameras streaming images from multiple vantage points, including on top of tanks driving across Red Square or from the cockpit of fighter jets above the Russian capital. Red Army veterans are the stars of RT's reporting, with dignified old men receiving prominent coverage. The Russian soldiers who have just marched across Red Square are also routinely interviewed to say how proud they are to participate in the event. Units and commanders are openly identified to signify the honour and prestige of the event. Close-up footage of the latest hardware to enter Russian service is also broadcast. This is clearly an example of an organisation that is comfortable being in the public eye, although RT is hardly ever critical of Russia's military.

For better or worse, the Russian military of today has learned to live with the modern media era. It has embraced 24-hour rolling news, social-media channels and online commerce. The Soviet mentality, in which almost all details of the armed forces were classed as state secrets, has gone. While the Russian media landscape is not comparable with Western style openness, it cannot be compared to the Soviet era.

Most importantly, the Russian public have fallen in love with the internet and almost every aspect of national life - including military life - is exposed online. So when the Russian Navy's only aircraft carrier caught fire in a dockyard in the Arctic city of Murmansk in December 2019, images of the incident appeared on line within minutes.

Soldiers in isolated garrisons use the Russian equivalent of Facebook, the VK network, to post images of their girlfriends, to complain to their parents about the water in their barracks not working, and to leak stories to the media. There is even a Trip Advisor-style website that allows soldiers to post reviews of their barracks, rating the food and internet reception. Most of European Russia has also been photographed by Google Street View cameras, which means many military bases can now be easily identified from the signs outside their main gates.

Russia military chiefs have tried to clamp down on social-media use in a bid to avoid Ukrainian internet investigators exposing troop deployments but they have not yet imposed blanket bans or a return to Soviet-era media control. This is because they are now in a competitive market to encourage young men and women to join the military. Russia's armed forces are moving towards being a professional service not a conscript army - so they have become very savvy at projecting a positive, and hopefully convincing, image to the Russian public.

As a result it is now possible to build up a very accurate order of battle of the Russian armed forces from open sources, identifying major bases, important equipment, significant units and their commanders. This was just not possible in the Soviet era except by employing secret intelligence-gathering techniques.

Units and Regalia

Almost all contemporary Russian military units trace their antecedence to their Soviet predecessors that passed into the service of the new Russian Federation after the formal dissolution of the Soviet Union on 26th December 1991. The Russian Federation Armed Forces and Ministry of Defence formally came into existence on 7th May 1992.

The new Russian units took on the titles and battle honours of their Soviet predecessors, as well as inheriting their equipment and barracks. Over the next 30 years there was a determined drive to de-Sovietise the Russian military, with the most obvious aspects being the dispensing with commissars or political officers and the apparatus of Communist Party control. The Russian Navy renamed several ships, dropping overtly Communist-linked names and replacing them with Tsarist names or linking ships to historic cities.

In army and air force units, World War Two-era unit titles and battle honours are given great prominence in a bid to link their modern successors to heroic actions in the Great Patriotic War. Tsarist-era standards and flags were introduced to provide linkage to patriotic battles in the Napoleonic and Catherine the Great eras.

The use of symbols and history by the modern Russian military is a clear sign that it is attempting to position itself as a national institution, not a vehicle of a political party or faction. This messaging has the approval of President Putin because it suits his nationalist agenda - but it also hints that the senior leadership of the Russian military are looking to secure their long term place in Russia's future national order.

Professionalisation

The professionalisation of the Russian military is by far the biggest break from its Soviet heritage. The old Soviet-era Communist Party viewed the country's professional soldiers with great suspicion. Under Stalin, hundreds of thousands of Red Army officers were killed or exiled in the purges. The commissar system, which assigned a political officer to each unit, was brought in to ensure that professional officers were never able to challenge party control. Mass mobilisation via conscription also meant Soviet professional officers were never able to be certain of their soldiers' loyalty.

The conscript system that was the hallmark of the Soviet military was designed for industrial-age warfare. It was structured to ensure a constant flow of low-paid and poorly trained soldiers into the massed ranks of the Red Army. In World War Two these conscripts were cannon fodder and if the Cold War had ever turned hot, the Soviet Army would have repeated these tactics. Under the totalitarian Soviet system, these conscripts were treated with contempt and forced to live in basic barracks, run by brutal officers who had little concern about their troops' welfare.

The treatment of Soviet conscripts in Afghanistan and the indifference of the Soviet state to the parents of soldiers killed in that war played an important role in the demise of the Soviet Union. When the same scenario played out in the Chechen wars of the late 1990s it created a national scandal and undermined the credibility of the post-Soviet military in the new Russia.

With the demise of the Soviet control apparatus that was used to force millions of young men into the ranks of the Red Army, it became impossible for the Russian military to continue to rely on conscription. Putin's move to professionalise the Russian armed forces was perhaps the most significant change in way Moscow organises and uses its military.

In the Soviet era, senior officers and technical experts, such as pilots, aircraft maintenance engineers, air defence missile operators, and some submarine crews, were all long-term professionals. The rank-and-file, as well as junior officers, were all conscripts who served two years in uniform. This was even the case in the supposedly elite units of the Airborne Forces, Naval Infantry and Special Forces or Spetsnaz.

Under Putin, this system was turned on its head. To augment the professional officer corps, professional or contract servicemen were recruited. This allowed whole units up to battalion size to be made up of professional soldiers. In the navy, only professional officers and sailors serve onboard submarines and the air force has been able to professionalise most of its ground maintenance organisation. Hundreds of thousands of conscripts continue to be called into the military every year but the length of time conscripts serve in uniform has been reduced to one year and they are legally banned from serving outside the territory of the Russian Federation, except in time of war.

This, in effect, creates a two-tier military, with the professional elements that are combat-ready all the time and can be sent to serve outside Russia, and the conscript-based units that are at low levels of combat readiness. This situation has been evolving over the past 20 years. Professionalisation started in the Airborne, Spetsnaz and Naval Infantry before being rolled out across the wider Ground Forces.

By the time of the 2008 Georgia war only the Airborne and Spetsnaz boasted all-professional units. At the time of the 2014 conflict with Ukraine, each Ground Force brigade had one battalion out of four manned by contract soldiers. In the air force and navy, conscripts remained in widespread use guarding bases, driving supply trucks and filling bunks on surface ships that have a coastal-defence role.

The exact number of contract soldiers is not clear and the statistics released by the Russian Ministry of Defence are put out in such a way that makes year-on-year comparisons difficult. The trend towards increasing numbers of contract personnel, however, is clearly on a distinct upward trajectory.

The revolutionary nature of this development cannot be stressed too much. For the first time, Russia has ground units that can be held at high readiness for combat operations, manned by professional soldiers.

Organisation

As well as moving to professionalise the Russian armed forces, Putin and his military chiefs re-organised their command structures to make them more usable.

The old Soviet division of the armed forces into its main branches remains but it has been significantly modified. The main branches of the armed services remain the Ground Forces, Navy, Strategic Missile Forces, Aerospace Forces and the Airborne Forces.

Between 2010 and 2015, a re-organisation of the military district structure took place that grouped all conventional forces - with the exception of paratroops, long-range bombers and strategic transport aircraft - under the control of a network of five joint strategic or district commands.

On top of these a new National Defence Command Centre was opened in Moscow in December 2014 to control Russian military forces on operations around the world. This linked all major military command posts by secure data-links and allowed video conferencing with senior commanders. On several occasions Putin was filmed visiting the centre to personally direct operations in Syria or participate in military exercises.

The joint strategic or district commands are a very new feature and see units from different services combined under a single commander. They each boast two or three Ground Force armies containing land combat units, an Air and Air Defence army controlling fast jet, attack helicopter and air defence units, as well as a navy fleet. This template is slightly modified to meet the unique strategic challenges in each region. It makes their commanders very powerful figures and they are all highly capable officers who are earmarked for future advancement.

The Southern Military District covers the southern region of European Russia, including the volatile Caucasus region, Crimea and the Black Sea. Within this district, the Black Sea Fleet is a sub-command controlling all naval, air, air defence and land forces deployed on Crimea. This saw ground force units on Crimea passing into the naval service to ease command and control. Air units and air defence batteries in the command's area of responsibility remained part of the aerospace force but report to the Black Sea Fleet headquarters on day-to-day operational issues. This district manages the ongoing confrontation with Ukraine and is responsible for dealing with incursions by NATO forces into the Black Sea. Since 2018 it has been led by Colonel General Aleksandr Dvornikov, from his headquarters in Rostov-on-Don, who commanded the Russian intervention in Syria in 2015 and is tipped to be a future head of the Russian military. In late 2020 he organised the deployed of Russian peacekeeping troops as a buffer between Armenia and Azerbeijan.

The Western Military District controls forces around Moscow and the west of European Russia. It borders NATO territory in the Baltic States and its Baltic Fleet in turn commands all naval, air, air defence and land forces deployed in the Kaliningrad enclave between Poland and Lithuania. Aerospace force and ground force units in Kaliningrad were transferred into the naval service to ease command and control. Air defence batteries in the command's area of responsibility remained part of the aerospace force but reported to the Baltic Fleet headquarters on day-to-day operational issues.Regular military exercises involving the district's troops take place in the territory of Belarus, which is Russia's key Eastern European ally. Western Military District troops are well known from their participation in the Moscow Victory Day Parades and its units based around Moscow usually receive new tanks and other armoured vehicles for trials. The commander in 2020 was Colonel General Alexander Zhuravlev, another veteran of the Syria campaign who oversaw the capture of Aleppo in 2016.

In Urals and the west of Siberia, the Central Military District is Russia's strategic reserve with its units being readied for deployment to border regions in time of crisis. It also manages day-to-day military relations with former Soviet

Central Asian republics. Another Syrian veteran, Lieutenant-General Aleksandr Lapin, was its commander in 2020 and he oversaw a major exercise involving Chinese troops in 2019.

The Eastern Military District has a massive span of responsibilities from the Chinese and North Korean borders, the Pacific Ocean and the Arctic Far East coast. The Pacific Fleet has its own sub-command on the Kamchatka peninsula, known as the North Eastern Group of Troops and Forces or the Kamchatka Flotilla Coastal Forces, which, like the forces in Kaliningrad and Crimea, controls naval, air, air defence and land forces in the region.

Controlling all Russian forces and operations in the Arctic is the Northern Fleet Military District. It was initially set up in 2014 and expanded into a fully fledged military district in 2021. It brought all the air, land and naval forces on the Kola Peninsula and the string of islands along Russia's northern coastline out towards Siberia under the banner of the Northern Fleet. This saw aerospace force and ground force units in this region transferred into the naval service to ease command and control. Air defence batteries in the command's area of responsibility remained part of the aerospace force but reported to its headquarters on day-to-day operational issues. Vice Admiral Aleksandr Moiseyev runs the command from his headquarters in Severomorsk. He is a submariner of considerable repute and had previously headed up the Black Sea Fleet, masterminding the operation in 2018 that led to the capture of Ukrainian naval craft during the Kerch incident.

There remain several central commands that operate at a strategic level and are directed from the National Defence Command Centre. These include the aerospace force's Long Range Aviation heavy bomber command, which control's Russia's air-delivered nuclear weapons, and its strategic airlift force of transport aircraft.

The Main Intelligence Directorate, or GRU, is the Russian military's own in-house intelligence service. As well as its infamous network of spies working in foreign countries, it also controls the Special Forces or Spetsnaz brigades. These units are controlled centrally but can be allocated to military districts for specific operations. Underwater covert operations are the domain of the Main Directorate of Deep-Sea Research, or GUGI, which operates a fleet of mini-submarines and mother-submarines that deliver them to operational areas. Although drawing crews and resources from the Northern Fleet submarine force, the GUGI is controlled direct from its headquarters in St Petersburg.

Russia's land-based nuclear deterrent remains under the command of Strategic Rocket Forces, which has its own network of hardened underground command posts. It is closely related to the Missile Defence Forces which control the network of early warning radars and the ballistic missile defence shield around Moscow.

The central theme of all these recent reforms of the Russian military command structure is to streamline and improve operational efficiency. Operational command and speed of reaction are to the fore as opposed to bureaucratic single-service or stove-piped chains of command. When President Putin wants to speak to his military commanders it is now very obvious who owns problems and their solutions.

Chapter 17
Russia's Warriors

Russian Generals have a fierce reputation. They are supposed to be big, brash and disinclined to take any criticism. So when I was ushered into the office Major General Anatoly Volchkov, Commander of the Russian Military Contingent in Kosovo at Pristina airport, I was not expecting an easy interview. The British Royal Air Force group captain, who was joint commander of the airport and my host for the day, said the Russian general had not done any media interviews before so he did not really know what to expect.

The Russian general, however, proved to be charming, well-informed and very confident speaking to a representative of the Western media, even via an interpreter. He was not the officer who had led the 200-strong contingent of Russian troops to seize Pristina airport from under the noses of NATO a few months before but he was very proud of the Russian soldiers who had pulled off that manoeuvre.

The 1990s had treated Russia's military very badly. The Warsaw Pact and then the Soviet Union itself had collapsed. A string of Soviet republics had secured their independence from Moscow. The nadir for Russian military men was the December 1994 assault on the Chechen capital, Grozny. Insurgent fighters ambushed the chaotically organised Russian troops, forcing them to flee and leave their dead behind to be eaten by dogs. It was a fiasco that totally destroyed what was left of the reputation of the Russian military's top brass. Not only had they been shown to treat their soldiers' lives with complete disdain but they could not even defeat a rag-tag guerrilla army on Russia's home soil.

So when the Russian column raced to Pristina airport in June 1999 to beat the Americans and British to the draw, Russian army officers had a spring back in their step. General Volchkov trotted out the required politically correct statements about NATO-Russian co-operation to solve Kosovo's problems but I could almost see him winking at the nonsense he was spouting. He was clearly very happy about Russia getting one over on the Americans and the British.

My brief conversation with the Russian General ended amicably enough. He was happy Russia was back on the world stage and wanted people to know it. Back in the centre of Pristina city at the main British Army compound I soon found out that Cold War attitudes were still alive and kicking in the Western military.

One British officer let slip that Ministry of Defence counter-intelligence operatives had recently offered up a warning that Russian soldiers in Kosovo had to be kept away British tanks for fears that they would steal the secrets of their specially reinforced armoured plates.

Since then, Russia's military has undergone a major transformation and a new East-West confrontation has frozen relations with Moscow. So who are the men who serve in the new Russian military? What makes them tick and how do they go about their business?

The Generals and Admirals

A former member of the Soviet Army Spetsnaz once summarised to me the mindset of the current generation of Russian senior military officers. "They still enjoy their work," he said. My friend is now a citizen of a former Soviet republic but still travels extensively around Russia meeting representatives of its government and military while working for an international non-governmental organisation. He described the bulk of Russia's senior military commanders as "professionals to their core" who relish military service, the history of their units and the prospect of seeing action. "The soldiers in most of Europe's armies don't really have it in their hearts to kill people any more – they have gone soft," said my friend. "Russian officers are different. They are still ready to start killing whenever they get the order. They are psychologically ready for action. They are still a proper army."

In September 2017, remarkable video footage emerged of a Russian general on the banks of the River Euphrates near to the south of the city of Dier Ez Zor. He was in full combat gear, directing the construction of a pontoon ferry over the river to allow Syrian troops to continue their advance against Islamic State fighters. Russian army engineers and Syrian troops were unloading the pontoons from trucks, dropping them in the river and lashing them together to form a ferry. Every so often Lieutenant General Valery Asapov could be seen joining in to pull the pontoons together. Asapov was an Airborne Forces officer had been seriously injured in the fighting in Grozny in 1995, enduring four major operations before returning to command a battalion of paratroopers, even though he walked with a limp. (1)

Days after he was filmed helping the Syrian army to cross the Euphrates the Russian military announced that Asapov had been killed in action when the bridging site had come under attack by Islamic State armed drones. These were modified to drop hand grenades and mortar bombs on their targets. It was a very 21st Century weapon and the incident epitomised the transformation of warfare. When Asapov was commissioned into the Soviet Airborne Forces in 1987 it would have been beyond his wildest imagination to think that he would be killed in action in such circumstances. Russia's soldiers, sailors and airmen have had to ride a wave of change.

The most famous modern Russia general is Valery Gerasimov, who, since 2012, has been Chief of the Russian General Staff or Moscow's most senior military officer. He is credited with being the mastermind of Russia's military renaissance, largely because of his supposed authorship of the so-called "Garasimov Doctrine". This is seen by many Western observers as the blueprint for Russia's hybrid-warfare strategy, that relies on cyber warfare, disinformation, special forces and precision-guided weapons to confuse and defeat opponents.

Garasimov's role in the creation of the current Russian armed forces is perhaps over hyped. The key building blocks of the transformation were put in place by Russia's first civilian defence minister, Anatoliy Serdyukov, who was ousted in 2012 as a result of a bout of Kremlin in-fighting. His successor, Sergey Shoigu, picked Garasimov for the top military job and the two men then oversaw the execution of Serdyukov's reforms.

Since 2012 Garasimov has been the public and international face of the Russian military. He was always at Putin's side during Victory Day Parades in Moscow, representing Russia at international conferences or meetings with foreign military chiefs. In effect, Garasimov is the front man of the Russian armed forces. The real work was done by the younger generation of senior officers.

The men who actually led Russia's troops into action over the past decade are a generation behind Garasimov and several of them are already being tipped to take over as head of Moscow's military in near future. The top two contenders for the top job are Andrey Serdyukov and Aleksandr Dvornikov and they were intimately involved in Russia's recent wars.

Serdyukov was deputy commander of the Southern Military District during the Crimea crisis and the Donbass war in 2014 and 2015. He is credited with helping to organise the rapid and bloodless operation to disarm Ukrainian troops on Crimea. In 2020 the paratrooper was head of the prestigious Airborne Forces.

His rival, Dvornikov, was instrumental in setting up the Syria campaign in 2015, including working in great secrecy in Moscow with the famous Iranian Revolutionary Guards Corps commander Qasem Soleimani to develop the successful plan to bolster Syrian government forces. Dvornikov then moved to Damascus to oversee the Russian deployment and the first months of the campaign. The Russian move caught the Americans by surprise and was seen as a major success. Dvornikov was picked for the Syrian command because he became known to Putin in the old East Germany and gained his trust then.

The successful launching of the Syria campaign was a major boost for the morale of the Russian military and its generals. It was akin to the experience of the 1991 Gulf War in exorcising the ghosts of defeat in Vietnam for the US military or the 1982 Falklands War that ended Britain's retreat from empire. For Russia's generals, Syria showed they could actually win a shooting war again. Even though they had scored a major success against the Ukrainians in the Donbass, the Kremlin's desire to keep a political distance from that operation meant the Russian military could not boast about its performance. In Syria there were no such restrictions, with medals, promotions and other honours flowing thick and fast. Dvornikov rode this wave with some success, even leading a contingent of Syria veterans to a glitzy ceremony in the Kremlin's St George Hall to receive medals from Putin. After returning from Syria he was made a Hero of the Russian Federation and eventually took command of the Southern Military District so was involved in managing the on-going crisis with Ukraine, as well as the tense Caucasus region.

Russia's Navy also has its share of rising stars who have earned plaudits in conflicts of the past decade. The commander of the Black Sea Fleet in 2014, Vice Admiral Aleksandr Vitko, is credited with organising and starting the psychological-warfare campaign that ultimately led to the Ukrainian forces on Crimea surrendering without firing a shot. In a matter of days he had mobilised his outnumbered troops and sailors to blockade their Ukrainian counterparts in their barracks and on their ships. Just over a year later, his sailors launched the Syria Express to move the Russian military contingent to Syria. He has since been promoted to the number-two job in the Russian navy.

Under Putin the status and prestige of Russia's military top brass has risen. It is not quite at Soviet-era levels but the humiliations of the 1990s are thing of the past. Russia's President, however, is a hard task master and failure is never rewarded. Public failures are particularly unwelcome in the Kremlin. Successful officers, however, can be rewarded, protected and their past misdemeanours over looked.

The career of Sergei Surovikin, who in 2017 led the final phase of the Syria campaign that drove Islamic State fighters from the centre and east of the country, provides some examples of the darker side of the Russian officer corps. He was on the losing side in the August 1991 Moscow coup and spent several months under investigation for his role in plot. On his return to the duty he went out of his way to prove his loyalty to the new order. When he was a divisional commander in 2004 he was accused of beating up a colonel after he learnt the officer had voted for the wrong candidate in a local election. A month later while Surovikin was berating a subordinate for his failings, the unfortunate officer drew his pistol and shot himself dead in full view of the staff in the divisional command post. (2) This does not seem to have harmed Surovikin's career prospects, and on his return from Syria he was appointed commander of the Russian Aerospace Force, despite not being a pilot. His success in Syria was judged enough to justify his promotion and being the first commander of the Russian or Soviet air force to have not been a career aviator.

The main career danger for senior officers in modern Russia comes from scandals involving corruption or the abuse of conscripts. It is part of President Putin's carefully crafted public image that corruption and abuse by high officials are never tolerated and the military top brass are not exempt from this. There is a steady stream of cases of officers, some involving generals and admirals, being sacked and jailed. The Kremlin makes sure these get extensive coverage in the media. The crimes range from unauthorised selling of equipment or buildings to illegal hunting on military property, and the most common is using conscripts to build senior officer's private homes. The reality, of course, is that crimes of high-flying or well-connected officers are often overlooked.

Major General Andrei Gurulev was accused in 2013 of diverting two of his conscript soldiers to repair his apartment in Moscow and guard his country house. A year later he played a prominent role in the Donbass war, successfully commanding the intervention of Russian combat troops. By December 2014 all the charges had been dropped and Gurulev was promoted to lieutenant general and rewarded with a top job in the Southern Military District headquarters. (3)

The Colonels

It is often stated that sergeant majors are the back bone of the British and US armies. They enforce discipline amongst soldiers, boost morale at time of crisis and advice senior officers on the mood of the troops. The Soviet military never had a corps of senior non-commissioned officers. With the demise of the old Soviet-era commissars, 21st Century Russian officers have far greater power and control over their troops. The Russian military is held together by its colonels in the ground and air forces and ship's captains in the navy. These officers have immense power over their personnel during both peace and wartime.

The professional officer corps of the Russian armed forces is around 220,000 strong – just under a quarter of the total strength - and unless they get caught in a corruption scandal can expect to serve in uniform until their retire. (4) There are some 30,000 cadets or officers under training at Russia's prestigious military schools. The cadets undergo between four and five years military of education, including studying for degrees, before they serve in frontline units. Towards the end of their cadet service they undergo professional training in their career branch before arriving at their units as young lieutenants in their early to mid 20s. Many of today's officers are the sons of Soviet-era soldiers and there is great resistance to changing the system of military education, which is seen by traditionalists as a way of maintaining the skill and expertise of the Russian officer corps.

A Russian newspaper recorded a meeting between the then President Dmitry Medvedev and a group of senior officers just after he assumed the head-of-state job in 2008. Russian military chiefs wanted to expose the new President to some of their rising stars, who could lobby for a bigger defence budget and the ending of the conscript system. According to one of the participants, the officers tried to explain to the President that some 18 years of neglect of the country's military had left it barely functioning as a fighting organisation. "Much of the dialogue depends on an artificial dichotomy between combat (combat training) and noncombat (housekeeping) officers, and on the need to shed the latter," recorded one participant in the meeting. "It is easy now, of course, to belittle officers in the 1990s, and much of the 2000s, who tried to keep their subordinates paid and housed, and conscripts from beating or killing each other, at a time when there was not enough money, fuel, equipment, or even troops for training. A lot of officers neglected those housekeeping duties and turned to private schemes, crime, or corruption in those days. The two naval officers practically begged Medvedev for contractees [professional personnel] because their conscripts can't learn their jobs in one year." (5)

More than a decade on from then, the reforms the officers requested have largely come to pass. Russian officers can now concentrate on preparing for combat and events since 2010 have given them plenty of opportunity to put their skills to use around the world.

This would first come in the spring of 2014 with the operation to seize Crimea and a few months later during the war in the Donbass. For the commanders of Russian Ground Force units, these operations were like nothing they had faced before in their careers. Crimea was a highly politically sensitive mission that was being carried out on home territory in the full view of the international media. Strong discipline was required to ensure that there were no accidents that led to the situation escalating into an all-out shooting war. There was also immense political pressure from Moscow to ensure the Ukrainian troops surrounded in their bases quickly surrendered so President Putin could declare victory. During the month long operation, international journalists watched as Russian commanders negotiated and bullied demoralised Ukrainian contingents into surrendering.

While the Crimea operation was unfolding, a large force was being mobilised to concentrate around the borders of Ukraine. This saw several brigades deploying battalion tactical groups of contract or professional soldiers to the Rostov-on-Don region. By August 2014 these battalions were in action inside the Donbass. This proved to be the most intense conventional combat in Europe since the Second World War. As the war continued into 2015, the weather worsened and the Russian military had to keep their troops fighting in sub-zero temperatures. Russian battalion commanders led their men into action for sustained periods, involving almost every weapon and type of equipment in their military's inventory. The only capabilities not employed by Moscow were air strikes, naval gunfire and nuclear weapons.

The Donbass war went well for the Russian regular military and in almost every engagement they out-fought and overwhelmed their opponents.

Twenty-year-old Dorzhi Batomunkuev was a T-72 tank gunner in the 5th Separate Tank Brigade from Ulan-Ude. In late 2014 his battalion of contract soldiers was sent to the Rostov-on-Don region to act as a reserve force. They were called into the Donbass in February 2015 and they were soon locked in combat with Ukrainian tanks during the Battle of Debaltseve.

Batomunkuev's tank was hit and caught fire. He suffered severe burns and was evacuated to a field hospital in Donetsk, where he was interviewed by a reporter from the Novaya Gazeta newspaper. Despite his wounds, the soldier was keen to praise his officers for their leadership and combat skills.

"They [the Ukrainians] pounded us," he said. "The battalion commander responded by jumping into his tank and was off, destroying first one tank, then another." (6)

"Our commanders are all great," he added. "There was no commander who was scared and was afraid of something. We were all on a par, regardless, [of whether] you are a colonel or an ordinary [soldier]. Because we fight side by side. The commander of my battalion ... He is now in Rostov, just as burned in the tank as I [was].

The Syrian war proved a different test for Moscow's military with the Russian Aerospace Force (RuAF) in the lead. Never before had the RuAF or its Soviet predecessor been entrusted with such a strategic mission. This would put the RuAF's officers to the test. Not only were they sent to fight in a new theatre, against a new enemy, but they were employing many new aircraft and weapons for the first time.

The death of Colonel Ryafagat Khabibulin and his co-pilot Yevgeny Dolgin after their helicopter was shot down in Syria in July 2016 generated extensive coverage in military and local-media outlets. The two helicopter pilots were hailed as heroes but their obituaries revealed a lot about the career progression of RuAF officers. Khabibulin was the commander of the 55th Helicopter Regiment, based at Korenovsk in southern Russia, so was leading from the front by taking to the air in a Mil Mi-25 attack helicopter in Syria. (7) The 55 -year-old veteran had graduated from flight school in 1988 so missed the chance to fly in Afghanistan. Throughout the 1990s he flew Mi-8 and Mi-24 helicopters from the 55th Regiment in action across the Caucasus as the region was engulfed in multiple wars. In 1994 he survived his helicopter being riddled with 98 bullets and spent several months in hospital recovering from his injuries. Fourteen years later he was in the thick of the Georgian war flying casualty evacuation missions to frontline positions to rescue 40 wounded soldiers.

Eventually rising to command his regiment, Khabibulin deployed to Syria in 2015. His 24-year-old co-pilot, was a graduate of the Syzran Higher Military Aviation School and was on his second posting. The two were flying a Syrian helicopter that they had volunteered to fly to deliver ammunition to an isolated frontline position when they were shot down and killed.

Even allowing for the concentration of the heroic deeds of Khabibulin and Dolgin, their obituaries highlighted that Russian officers spend long periods of their careers serving in the same unit or branch to build technical expertise and local knowledge. This cadre of professional officers is the bedrock of the Russian military.

In 21st Century Russia, the Colonels realise there is a limit to their power, even if for ones who are officially Heroes of the Russian Federation, the country's highest decoration for valour. Russian paratroopers are famous for their battlefield bravery and heavy drinking when back in barracks. Hero of Russia Colonel Vladimir Seliverstov, commander of the 331st Guards Airborne Regiment, led his men across Red Square in the May 2018 Victory Day Parade but by the end of the year he had been relieved of his command. The Colonel and some his senior officers visited a local bar and indulged in too much vodka. When he questioned the military experience of a group of civilians a fight broke out. The bar owner called his bouncers to eject the paratroopers. The Colonel retaliated by calling his 40-strong-quick-reaction squad from his barracks. The arrival of civilian police settled the matter and the paratroopers retreated, carrying their unfortunate Colonel back to base. The next day after mobile phone footage of the incident appeared in the local media, the Colonel tendered his resignation to the head of the Airborne Forces. The way the incident ended is a sign of how the modern Russian military, even its supposedly elite forces, realise that their place in society is not what it was in Soviet times. (8)

The Contractors

The Soviet- and Yeltsin-era armies were notorious for their disgruntled, drunken and bullied conscript soldiers. Hazing or bullying of young soldiers was rife, mothers protested outside army barracks to get their sons back, and Russian generals found themselves portrayed as national pariahs in the media.

Today almost three quarters of Russian soldiers, sailors and airmen are professional officers or contract servicemen. Just over 200,000 conscripts are called up to serve in the military every year, the smallest number since conscription was started by Tsar Peter the Great in 1699. More than 400,000 young contract soldiers, airmen and sailors are now paid salaries to fill the ranks of the 21st Century Russian military. (9) They lead very different lives to their conscript predecessors and a lot is known about their lives and military careers thanks to their love of the internet and social media. Just like other young men around the world, they live their lives' online, posting images or video clips of important and unimportant events, their families, as well as where and when they go to war.

Monitoring the online social media profiles of Russian servicemen has now become a well-trodden path for a number of groups of Ukrainian cyber warriors who specialise in building up large databases of Moscow's military men. The Inform Napalm and Censor.Net groups tracked Russian servicemen deploying to Crimea, Donbass and Syria from their social-media profiles on the VK network.

By distilling this mass of information it is possible to build up a good picture of the typical experience of modern Russian soldiers. The vast majority of contract servicemen start out their careers as conscripts, doing their one-year-long period of military duty. Given that only a small percentage of Russian 18-year-olds are called up, and that any young man with a university place or a job in the defence industry can get an exemption, a disproportionate number of contractors come from country areas or working class districts of urban areas.

Volunteers are offered three year-long contracts to serve as professionals. The wages are on a par with the Russian national average for industrial or agricultural workers. They join up for many of the same reasons other young men join the military in Western countries – they want to escape from left-behind communities where there are few job opportunities, or to gain work skills that might help them in future. There is also good number who want to prove their machismo in elite units, such as the Airborne Forces or Spetsnaz.

Advertising and promotional material for contract service includes plenty of imagery of derring-do by macho-looking soldiers. In a documentary about the Northern Fleet's submarine force in 2019, the then head of the Russian Navy, Admiral Vladimir Korolyov, said, "only a real man can be a submariner". (10) The politically correct diversity and gender-equality agendas that are now common in Western armed forces are conspicuously absent from the Russian military.

In the Ground and Airborne Forces, contract soldiers are now prevalent in every brigade with at least one out of every four battalions being composed entirely of contractors. All but one of the Airborne Forces four divisions are entirely comprised of contract solders, and the remaining division has some 50% of conscripts in its ranks.

In the navy, contractor sailors are concentrated in the crews of submarines and the larger warships that sail outside of Russia's territorial waters. Navy officers say it is not possible to develop the right level of skills to operate complex warships in just a year's conscript service. This results in conscripts being relegated to crewing smaller coastal vessels, working in naval bases or the Coastal Force combat and missile units.

A similar system is employed by the RuAF, Space Forces, Strategic Missile Forces and Missile Defence Forces, with conscripts standing guard at bases, loading supplies in depots or driving trucks. Any job that requires any technical skill has been taken over by contract servicemen.

Social-media profiles of contract soldiers shows that they are now pervasive across all branches of the Russian military. As the numbers of conscripts called for service each year continues to drop, the professional soldier, sailor and airman is becoming the norm in Moscow's military.

Chapter 18
Russian Land Power

The phrase "Russian steamroller" was coined to describe the massed attacks by waves of Red Army troops on the Eastern Front in World War Two. The Soviet military build-up during the Cold War - to create overwhelming massed tank divisions in central Europe to confront NATO - added to the impression that this was Russia's traditional way of war.

With the collapse of the Soviet Union in 1991, the new Russia found itself still a nuclear superpower but without the money or people to sustain the old Soviet military. When Vladimir Putin launched his drive to rebuild Russia's armed forces after he came to power in 2000 many Western observers assumed the Russian military leadership would return to their tried-and-tested model of building up forces to outnumber those of any of the country's potential opponents. When Putin enhanced the prestige of the Victory Day parades in Moscow and increased the number of tanks and other items of military hardware on parade, he further added to the impression that a new Cold War- style arms race was underway.

For Russia's land forces the 21st Century was seen them go through a dramatic transformation. However, there has not been a significant expansion of Russia's land forces or even a huge spree of purchases of new equipment: rather, there has been a process of professionalisation and other measures to improve their readiness and quality. This process first gained momentum after the 2008 Georgia war, and a new series of reforms were started in the wake of the 2014 Ukrainian crisis.

President Putin's political and media image revolves around him being seen as a "tough guy" or a "man of action" who has restored Russia's status as a great power that is respected around the world. Disasters such as the sinking of the Kursk nuclear submarine in 2000 and the high casualties during the Georgia war in 2008 dented his image of competence. This made the Russian President determined to overhaul his armed forces and bring them into the 21st Century. The top brass still contained Soviet-era generals who were not up to the job and they were destined to be cleared out. However, the biggest impediment to reforming the Russian military was the conscript system. This was a hangover from the Soviet era and it meant that the bulk of Russian land units were engaged in little more than basic training of recruits for most of their time. Hundreds of thousands of soldiers would be trained up during their period of military service and just at the point where they were ready for action, they would be released from service and go back to their civilian lives.

On top of this, the unpopularity of heavy casualties in Afghanistan in the 1980s and then in the Chechen war in the 1990s meant that Russian conscripts were legally barred from service outside the country, except in time of war. The poor conditions in most military bases and continuing reports of bullying meant draft-dodging - both by legal and illegal means - was endemic. While many

Russian's were proud of their armed forces' record in World War Two, few were happy to let their children serve in its ranks.

So when Putin came into office one of his first acts was to announce his intention to reduce dependence of the military on conscripts. In 2008 the length of military service was limited to one year in a bid to accelerate the push to expand the number of professional or contract soldiers. The Soviet and later Russian officer corps had long been made up of professionals but never before had the majority of the rank-and-file of the country's armed forces been made up of professionals. The aim was not to totally professionalise the armed forces but to make a critical mass in each major unit, such as brigades and divisions, professional so that significant operations could be undertaken without involving conscripts.

This was a slow and expensive activity that only really gained traction in the so-called elite units, such as the Airborne Forces, Naval Infantry and Spetsnaz, during the first decade of the 21st Century. It was not until 2008 when the newly appointed defence minister, Anatoliy Serdyukov, put in place the plans and funding to allow professionalisation of land forces to take place on a significant scale. As Russia's first true "civilian" defence minister who had not been a Soviet-era general, Serdyukov, was instrumental in shaking up the old hierarchy of the military. He sacked thousands of generals and colonels, scrapped outdated equipment, closed hundreds of military bases and downsized most land forces units. A significant chunk of money saved was ploughed into recruiting more than 100,000 contract soldiers who were to be posted across the land forces.

By the early years of this century's second decade, most Russian brigades had enough contract soldiers to put at least one battalion-sized unit on the field for combat operations.

This also had a major impact on the officer corps of Russian land forces units. No longer were they preoccupied with running repetitive training for a conveyor belt of conscripts but could run more complex and demanding tactical training. Russian military equipment also could be more complex and did not have to be designed to be operated by conscripts with limited training. This allowed the fielding of increasing quantities of information-era systems such as electronic warfare systems and unmanned aerial vehicles.

There was a downside to not having to rely on conscripts who had no say in whether or not they were in military. Russian officers had to start being concerned about their soldiers' living conditions and whether their families were happy. They also had to get involved in recruiting drives to fill the ranks in their units. This was new territory for many Russian officers.

As part of Serdyukov's reforms the Russian land forces underwent significant re-organisation to streamline their organisation. The over-arching organisation of Russia's land forces did not change much. Although Russians refer to their military as the "army", there is not a single Russian Army. Russian land forces are divided into the Ground Forces, Airborne Forces, Coastal Forces of the Navy and special forces units of the Main Intelligence Directorate of the General Staff, or GRU. They each have separate commands, training organisations, recruiting systems, administrative organisations and equipment procurement processes. For operations their personnel and units are assigned to the command of military districts or the National Defence Command Centre in Moscow.

The Ground Forces are still the largest branch of the Russian armed forces and they are estimated to have between 200,000 and 250,000 personnel. The exact strength is not published by the Russian Ministry of Defence and some estimates lump all land units together, including the personnel of the Airborne and Coastal Forces. (1) The next strongest service branch with land units is the Coastal Forces, which probably boasts some 50,000 personnel - but this figure is usually included in the strength of the Russian Navy. Then the Airborne Forces are estimated to have some 45,000 to 50,000 paratroopers in its ranks. Ambitious plans were announced in 2016 to expand the Airborne Forces but they are progressing slowly.

Thanks to Serdyukov's reforms the main type of Russian land formation is the independent or separate motor rifle or tank brigade and they can be found in both the Ground and Coastal Forces. Russian brigades usually boast around 4,000 troops and they are grouped into four all-arms battalion tactical groups. In motor rifle brigades, there are three infantry or motor rifle battalions and one tank battalion, backed by supporting artillery, air defence, reconnaissance, electronic warfare logistics and in many cases unmanned aerial vehicle sub-units. In tank brigades the mix of infantry and tank units are reversed, with a similar mix of supporting elements.

Three or four Ground Force brigades are then grouped into a combined arms army, which is supported by independent artillery, rocket, tactical ballistic missile, air defence, electronic warfare, transport and chemical warfare brigades. A Russian army usually has some 15,000 to 20,000 troops so is akin to a US or NATO division.

The Coastal Forces are part of Russian Navy fleets and are concentrated in strategic locations, where a combined arms corps headquarters controls a mix of motor rifle brigades, artillery, air defence, Naval Infantry and coastal defence missile brigades. Naval Infantry brigades are unique organisations trained in amphibious assault operations and to be embarked on navy warships for expeditionary missions. The Coastal Forces corps headquarters are in Crimea, Kaliningrad and the Kola Peninsula, as well as the Kamchataka Flotilla Coast Forces, which each control between 10,000 to 12,000 personnel. As part of Russia's renewed interest in the Arctic region, the Coastal Forces have formed what are termed tactical groups to garrison a series of bases stretched across the far north in purpose-built bases that are designed to survive the Arctic winter. These groups are equipped with snow vehicles, anti-ship and anti-aircraft weapons. It is believed they are drawn on a rotational basis from the Coastal Forces motor rifle units.

The Airborne Forces have their own distinct chain of command for operations and report directly to the National Defence Command Centre for missions of strategic importance, although they can also be placed under military district control for specific operations. Despite the Serdyukov reforms, the Airborne Forces retained their divisional and regimental structure.

Each airborne or air assault division comprises two or three regiments, which in turn each have two battalion tactical groups. Unlike in the Ground Forces, the majority of airborne personnel are professional soldiers, which makes them some of the first units to be mobilised for overseas operations. Airborne regiments boast around 2,000 personnel. There are several independent airborne or assault brigades that each have some 2,000 to 3,000 troops. All Airborne Forces regiments are equipped with light air-dropable BMD series armoured vehicles and light self-propelled artillery systems. All the airborne units are closely linked with Russian Aerospace Force airlift and helicopter regiments to enable their strategic and tactical air movement.

The GRU Spetsnaz brigades are considered to be military district-level assets and are assigned for strategic level activity. Each Spetsnaz brigade is some 1,200 personnel strong and they are in effect highly trained light infantry formations, which can also be broken down to carry out raids behind enemy lines, advising foreign military units during combat or running training activity for allied forces.

A handful of reconnaissance brigades are being formed by the GRU to provide specialist technical reconnaissance and target-acquisition support to armies and military districts. These units appear to be equipped with ground-surveillance radar, unmanned aerial vehicles and electronic warfare capabilities.

The main Ground Forces units are assigned under the day-to-day operational command of Russia's five military districts or joint strategic commands, which each have deal with unique strategic circumstances. The Western Military District covers the northern half of European Russia, including the capital, Moscow and St Petersburg. It has three armies; The 6th Army based in St Petersburg, the 1st Guards Tank in Moscow and the 20th Guards to the south.

The Southern Military District has responsibility for the Caucasus, Crimea and the border with Ukraine. It has one army in the eastern Caucasus, one in western Caucasus and the newly formed 8th Army is close to the Ukrainian border. The Central Military District in the Urals and western Siberia has two armies and is in effect Russia's strategic reserve. Out on the Pacific coast, the Eastern Military District has a defensive role with five small armies. These formations often do not have their full complement of supporting units and equipment.

As a result of the 2014 Crimea crisis, the Russian Ground Forces looked again at its force structure and deployment. In 2016 it re-introduced the division level of command and positioned them in strategically important locations. Four of these new divisions were formed in the Western Military District close to the border of Ukraine and new garrisons were required to house them. The Southern Military District received three of the new divisions, with one requiring a new garrison close to Rostov-on-Don on the Ukrainian border. The other division was based in existing garrisons in the southern Caucasus. Two final two divisions were formed in existing garrisons in the Central Military District. These 8,000, strong divisions were formed by amalgamating two motor rifle brigades so did not actually increase the size of the Russian Ground Forces.

The equipment used by the Russian land force units is a mix of legacy and new, which is unlikely to change for several years despite much-publicised procurement projects for exotic weapons such as the Armata tank with its revolutionary fully automated turret.

The majority of Russian tank battalions are equipped with upgraded versions of the classic T-72 tank. Only a handful of units have the T-90 tank with its hard-kill defensive aid system and only a dozen or so brigades have the T-80 tank. Upgraded versions of these later two tanks are starting to be fielded, with the T-80 going to Arctic-roled units of the Coastal Forces because their power system performs well in cold climates.

A majority of motor rifle battalions have the BMP-2 or 3 infantry fighting vehicles but a sizable number still have the wheeled BTR or tracked MTLB armoured personnel carriers. These later vehicles are rugged, easy to maintain and operate.

The Airborne Forces have their own specialist air-droppable vehicles and a re-equipment programme is underway to replace their older BMD-2s with the new BMD-4 variant.

The Spetsnaz brigades are equipped with a mix of BTR-82 wheeled armoured personnel carriers, Tigr tactical vehicles, Typhoon mine- protected vehicles and D-30 122mm towed howitzers.

Tube, rocket artillery and tactical ballistic missiles are the Russian land forces' undoubted strengths and modernisation programmes are underway to sustain and enhance these capabilities. Its best systems - the self-propelled 2S19 Mista-S 152mm and the towed 2A65 Mista-B - entered service in the final years of the Soviet Union and the Russian Ground Forces kept buying them throughout the 1990s and 2000s to re-equip all their independent artillery brigades and a significant number of the artillery battalions within tank and motor rifle brigades.

Rocket brigades also started receiving the new 9K51M Tornado in 2014 and all the ballistic missile brigades have received the Iskanker-M to replace the old Tochka weapon.

During the 2010s, the T-14 Armata and its sister family of infantry fighting vehicles have been under trial but despite several announcements of its imminent delivery to tank battalions, the production-standard vehicles have still not materialised. While the revolutionary qualities of this system are much publicised, the Russian Ground Force so far have not been persuaded that they work or are worth paying for. New orders for the upgrading of further batches of T-72, T-80 and T-90 tanks continue to be placed.

The Russian land forces have amassed considerable combat experience over the past decade in Crimea, the Donbass and Syria and the lessons from these conflicts are starting to be reflected in new organisations, tactics and procurement programmes. All Russian land forces training exercises now incorporate some lessons from these conflicts, including counter-UAV tactics, air-land integration and advisor work with indigenous forces. This combat experience spans air-land integration in Syria, training/advisor operations in Syria and the Donbass and full-on conventional combat against the Ukrainian army in 2014. The Syria experience has seen Russian special forces operatives, artillery and air assets all have to combine to execute missions in congested and confined battlespaces. This was a very new experience for Russian air and ground commanders and taught them many important lessons.

The Donbass conflict from the summer of 2014 through to the spring of 2015 saw extensive use of artillery and rockets to dominate the battlefield. These battles saw the Russians make extensive use of UAVs and signals intelligence to locate Ukrainian battalion-sized units. Rockets and artillery were then used to devastate these targets, with whole battalions being wiped out in single fire missions. The devastating firepower of Russian artillery shaped the battlefield and ultimately forced the Ukrainians to accept a ceasefire on Moscow's terms. The ability of the Russian artillery and rockets units to rapidly find targets and then devastate them greatly impression senior US and NATO commanders. One British Army officer commented that if a major British formation was engaged against a Russian land force in the Baltic region there was "a danger that the British Army could be lost in an afternoon". (2)

In both the Donbass and Syria, the Russian military have found themselves running "train and assist" missions for local forces. This has heavily involved middle-ranking and senior officers but also lightly armed Military Police battalions. These professional units have been used to monitor ceasefires, deliver humanitarian aid and co-ordinate refugee movements.

Although much publicity was given to Moscow's mastery of the dark arts of what is termed "hybrid warfare" in Crimea and the Donbass, Russian success in these conflicts had much to do with local knowledge, language skills and the divided loyalties of their populations.

Russian land power in the third decade of the 21st Century has come a long way from the hard days of the 1990s when a lack of political leadership and economic collapse threatened the very existence of Russia as a viable state. The economy has turned around and Russia's current President sees the country's armed forces as an important national asset.

Over the past two decades Russian land forces have undergone professionalisation, modernisation and been involved in significant combat operations. The end result of this process is that Russia's land forces are significantly smaller than they were in 1991 but boast far better trained, equipped and motivated units. Out has gone the reliance on overwhelming mass and a drive to field quality units has taken its place.

Russia's land forces still place artillery and rocket firepower at the heart of their way of war, even if the manoeuvre forces need to exploit any success created by artillery and rocket bombardments are smaller in size.

The professionalisation drive was instrumental in building the forces that succeeded in Crimea and Donbass. However, the professional Russian land forces units probably don't have more than 150,000 contract soldiers in their ranks. This is little bigger than number of professional soldiers in the British or French armies. Around 150,000 conscript soldiers serve in the Russian Ground, Airborne and Coastal Forces but at any point in time probably less than half of them can be considered fully trained to be involved in complex combat operations.

The implications of the downsizing of Russia's land forces are significant and often little understood by outside observers. They suggest that Moscow only has enough trained and effective land units to conduct one major operation, in a single theatre, at a time. Some 10,000 Russian troops were massed for the Donbass operation in August 2014 but battalions had to be drawn in from several brigades and regiments, which meant they had to be formed into combat brigades on the battlefield or just before they went into action. This was a far from ideal situation and meant it took several months for the Russians to mass and prepare their forces for action.

Russian land forces are also spread thinly around the country's borders and lack overwhelming strength except in very small areas, unless troops are moved from other deployments. The most likely regions where Russian land forces could be drawn into conflict - the Baltic States, Belarus, Ukraine, Georgia and the Nordic region - all hold very distinct challenges for Moscow.

Western fears that the Russian Western Military District (WMD) would be able to launch overwhelming force against Estonia, Latvia and Estonia prompted the deployment in early 2017 of three NATO Enhanced Forward Presence battle groups to the Baltic States. These units each only contain around 1,000 troops, causing some NATO soldiers on duty in the Baltic States to jokingly refer to themselves as being "speed bumps" for mass Russian tank attacks. Concerns persist among some NATO politicians and media commentators that a mismatch remains between NATO's forward units and any Russian attack force, leading to the scenario of a re-run of a World War Two-style Soviet offensive with massed ranks of tanks rapidly over-running outnumbered NATO troops across a wide front.

Although the WMD has considerable forces at its disposal and could be reinforced rapidly with airborne units, it suffers from the wide geographical dispersion of its major units. Many of the WMD's high readiness units containing a large number of professional soldiers are based far from the Baltic States.

As a result, the Russian military lacks sufficient forward-deployed and high-readiness ground units to mount an overwhelming surprise attack, from a standing start, against the Baltic States, particularly Estonia and Latvia that share a border with Russia. The 800 kilometres plus distance from the Moscow or Voronezh regions - where the bulk of the WMD's armoured forces are based - to the Estonian and Latvian borders means that it could require several weeks to mobilise and deploy these forces to any potential combat zone in strength, giving NATO time to react.

Fully professional airborne regiments are based at Pskov close to the Estonian and Latvian borders, but with a combined strength of 6,000 troops they are not strong enough to overwhelm NATO forces in the Baltic States on their own without reinforcements. Even with reinforcements, the WMD ground forces lack the manpower to secure and fully occupy all of Estonia and Latvia in the face of active or "stay behind" resistance from local defence units and civil disobedience from the approximately 3.3 million people in the two most exposed Baltic States.

The balance of professional and contract manpower in the major ground combat units of the WMD is offset to a significant degree by the long-range artillery and rocket systems, ground attack and strike aircraft, tactical air defence systems, and attack helicopters deployed near Estonia and Latvia. This gives these forces the potential to inflict heavy casualties on NATO forces, dealing a sudden shock that would temporarily unbalance allied forces.

From tracking the posting of commanders to key positions in the WMD, it is possible to identify several senior officers - including WMD commander Colonel General Zhuravlev - who have held key combat commands in Donbass and Syria. The fast-moving and violent tactics employed by Russian or Russia-advised forces in these two theatres involved decisive manoeuvre operations to isolate, surround, and then force the surrender or withdrawal of opposing forces.

This all points to any Russian offensive against Estonia and Latvia being similar in its kinetic violence and rapidity, and at its heart it would be an attempt to psychologically shock NATO forces rather than physically destroy them. The high concentration of long-range strike weapons - artillery, rockets, attack helicopters, and fast jets - on the Latvian and Estonian borders, rather than traditional metrics of land power such as infantry and tank numbers, are more pertinent to the capabilities of the WMD. Thanks to its firepower, the WMD has the potential to inflict a significant shock to NATO forces in the Baltic States.

This "shock" might not actually involve the occupation of all three Baltic States but would involve inflicting heavy loss of life and substantial damage to the military equipment of NATO forces, and could likely precipitate the retreat or surrender of a major fighting formation. Such an incident would be enough to make NATO sue for peace on Moscow's terms without necessitating a long and costly occupation. This would be a break with the old-fashioned Soviet-style "steamroller" warfare of massed-armoured operations.

Russian military intervention in Belarus poses many different challenges because of the complex internal political situation in the country. The Belarus armed forces have a long-established and close relationship with their Russian counterparts so an open military conflict between Moscow and Minsk is unlikely. A situation where the Belarus military fracture is more realistic but Minsk's troops are heavily outnumbered and outgunned by troops from the Western Military District's two motor rifle divisions based near the Belarus border. Any conflict in Belarus would look a bit like the Crimea and Donbass operation but happening simultaneously. It would be messy but Russian force would easily prevail.

The frozen conflict with Ukraine poses very different challenges for Moscow than in 2014-15. In mid 2020 two new Russian divisions were based on the Ukrainian border and they provide a well placed first echelon force to move to support locally recruited militia forces in the Donbass. The Black Sea Fleet's army corps on Crimea also provides a third manoeuvre grouping that could strike at Ukrainian forces.

While Russian forces have been built up the Ukrainian army has also enhanced its capabilities since 2014, including taking delivery of US-made Javelin anti-tank missiles.

Just as in the Baltic States the options for a military assault and occupation are challenging. A full-on Russian invasion and occupation of Ukraine - a country of more than 41 million people - would require a huge land force of hundreds of thousands of troops. The 215,000 strong Ukrainian military although outgunned by Russian land forces would still require at least a comparable sized force - which Moscow does not have - to defeat it in detail.

This suggests that the object of any Russian land operation would be inflict a decisive battlefield shock that prompts political concessions from Kiev.

If armed conflict were to break out between Russia and Georgia, the restructuring of ground forces units in the North Caucasus over the past decade into the 49th and 58th Armies considerably enhances the flexibility of Russian attack options, enabling more co-ordinated operations on both the Abhkazia and South Ossetia fronts.

Although modernisation efforts have dramatically enhanced the Southern Military District's firepower and other capabilities, the number of soldiers that can be committed to any action against Georgia remains relatively modest: the 49th and 58th Armies could theoretically field 35,000 troops, of which only 15,000 would be contract soldiers, reinforced by approximately 10,000 contract troops from the airborne and naval infantry units based in the district.

Nevertheless, Russia maintains a military advantage by having deployed forces on the ground since 2008 that include the integrated elements from South Ossetia and the Russia-financed and modernised Abkhazian Armed Forces. Any military advance by Russia could theoretically happen within hours, and carry the benefit of strategic surprise, whereas any reaction by the West would take substantially longer to mobilise. Unlike in 2008, the Russian military now has to sustain considerable forces in Crimea and along the Ukrainian border, so the SMD would not be able to give Georgia its undivided attention in any future crisis on multiple fronts. This suggests that any future Russian operation would aim to inflict a 'short, sharp shock' against Georgia to impose terms, rather than an attempt to occupy all of the country for a sustained period.

Russia's current armed forces in the Nordic region are a shadow of those deployed during the Soviet era, consisting of at most seven brigades or about

30,000 troops. They are also geographically split into three smaller groups with limited ability to mutually reinforce each other. The Kaliningrad exclave is home to the Baltic Fleet's land, naval, and air forces but they have little chance of operating against Finland or northern Norway, for example.

The collective Russian forces positioned around the Nordic region could not stage a theatre-level war to overwhelm and occupy a single Nordic state without major reinforcements from strategic reserves. However, a surprise Russian attack could lead to limited territorial gains, such as the seizure of Arctic or Baltic islands or border regions in Finland and Norway.

If Russia chose to divert its strategic reserves to attack an individual Nordic state it would have a better chance of success but this would take time to organise and might be counteracted by reinforcements from NATO or other allies.

More realistic scenarios for confrontation with Russia involve the threat of force or the imposition of naval and air blockades to secure political or economic concessions. Potential targets for such a coercive strategy include Norway's offshore oil and gas infrastructure, Sweden and Finland's Baltic islands, or early warning radar installations in the far north of Finland, Norway, and Sweden. Russian options include the physical occupation of these locations through surprise raids by helicopter-borne or amphibious forces.

The days of Soviet army groups being poised to simultaneously sweep across Scandinavia, the inner German border, European Turkey and into Iran are long gone. Russian land power still packs a powerful punch but the steamroller has been replaced by a stiletto.

Chapter 19
Russia's Surface Fleets

In December 2019 the Russian Navy's only aircraft carrier, the Admiral Kuznetsov caught fire while she was being overhauled in a dockyard in the northern city of Murmask on the Kola Peninsula. Within a matter of minutes video images of the blaze were posted on social media and started to be watched around the world. The fire was soon extinguished but the incident illustrated that in the 21st Century it is very difficult to keep much about the Russian Navy surface fleet secret. In the days of the Soviet Union such things would have been kept under wraps for months or years.

Today the Russian Navy is one of the most open of Moscow's armed services. As a result of the Kursk disaster in August 2000, the Russian Navy has mounted a major drive to turn around its public image in a bid to attract professional or contract sailors. The navy has mounted outreach activities, such as Navy Day parades every July, open days for school and college students and regularly invites the local and international media on board its ships and into its bases.

All the major Russian naval bases and shipyards are in or very near large civilian port cities so naval vessels are routinely observed and photographed by local civilians and foreign tourists, with the results posted online. Russia's ship-building industry is desperate to win export orders so routinely invites the international media to visit their facilities. These yards are now owned by private or semi-private companies that have to report their financial status to shareholders, both in Russia and overseas, so their order books are widely discussed in the Russian and international media.

Commercial satellite imagery has also transformed the monitoring of Russian naval activity, making it very easy to account for every warship in Moscow's fleet. The quality of this imagery is often far superior to that available to US or NATO analysts for much of the Cold War so it provides a real window on the state of Russian Navy. Large warships are intrinsically difficult to hide and the Russian Navy does not waste its time trying to do so.

When looking at the Russian Navy it has to be remembered that it is in effect four distinct fleets which rarely operate together as a concentrated force. Each is configured and equipped to operate to in its own unique geographic and strategic circumstances. The Northern Fleet is the largest force and it contains the navy's only aircraft carrier, along with the bulk of its ocean-going large warships. Its main role is to patrol Russia's northern coast and protect its nuclear ballistic missile firing submarines. The Baltic and Black Sea Fleets are so-called "inland navies" that are designed to operate in the confined waters of their respective home regions. This means they have smaller warships and are supported by strong land-based anti-ship missile and naval aviation assets. There is also a smaller Caspian Sea Flotilla that operates in that inland sea. Out in Russia's Far East, the Pacific Fleet has the primary task of protecting the small contingent of nuclear missile submarines based in the region, as well as defending the region's long coastline.

Each fleet has a spread of capabilities from submarines, cruisers, large frigates and destroyers, to mine-sweepers, fast attack missile boats to amphibious landing ships, as well as shore-based naval aviation fighters, anti-submarine helicopters and maritime patrol aircraft or seaplanes. For defence of naval bases and strategic terrain, motorised rifle and missile units of the navy's Coastal Forces are assigned to each fleet, as well as brigades of Naval Infantry, who are trained and equipped for amphibious warfare.

From the collapse of the Berlin Wall in 1989 up to March 2014 Russia's Northern Fleet was considered by many western politicians and senior military commanders as being little more than a quaint operator of vintage Soviet-era ships and submarines. For much of this time countries neighbouring the Kola Peninsula were more concerned about the environmental impact of abandoned reactors from disused Soviet submarines than with any specific military threat from Russia, which was beset by internal political crisis and economic stagnation for much of the post-Cold War period.

The Crimea crisis in 2014 made many of those perceptions obsolete overnight. The Northern Fleet now has had to be considered a strategic competitor. In the immediate aftermath of the Russian Crimea operation in February-March 2014 the Northern Fleet did not have a high profile but this changed in October 2016 when the carrier Admiral Kuznetsov led a battlegroup out from its home base at Severomorsk and into the Norwegian Sea. Russia's only aircraft carrier then kept on heading south through the English Channel with fighter jets and attack helicopters on display on her flight deck.

Tourists flocked to the White Cliffs of Dover to watch as the carrier, soon dubbed the "ship of shame" by the then UK defence secretary, Michael Fallon, headed west into the Atlantic. Less than a month later, the carrier's jets were in action over the Syrian city of Aleppo and had flown the first-ever combat missions by Soviet or Russian embarked carrier aviation.

While the Admiral Kuznetsov's Mediterranean deployment attracted considerable media attention, it has since emerged that the carrier was plagued by serious technical problems during the cruise. Arrestor wire problems led to the loss of two jets in the Mediterranean and temporarily meant its air group had to move ashore to the Russian airbase in Syria to continue operations. Subsequently, the Admiral Kuznetsov has been beset by further technical problems and a major accident in October 2018 which epitomised the Northern Fleet's legacy of two decades of budget cuts and under-investment.

These problems aside, Moscow still has ambitions for the Northern Fleet and it continues to receive significant investment to fund the procurement of new submarines and warships. Increasing interest in the High Arctic region means the Northern Fleet's importance can only grow. Unique among Russian Navy fleets, the Northern Fleet is a Joint Strategic Command in its own right putting it on a par with Russia's other four military district headquarters. As such it controls all air, land and naval forces on the Kola Peninsula, most of Russia's

Arctic islands, a large stretch of the northern Russia coast stretching eastwards towards Siberia and all air, land and naval operations in Arctic up to and over the North Pole.

From his headquarters on the hill about Severomorsk's harbour the Northern Fleet's commander, Vice-Admiral Aleksandr Moiseyev, can usually see the bulk of his fleet's surface combatants tied up at their moorings. The large capital ships of the 43rd Missile Division dominate Severomorsk and citizens can watch their comings and goings from the promenade around the famous Defenders of the Arctic statue. These Soviet era ships include the nuclear powered Kirov-class cruisers Pyotr Velikiy and Admiral Nakhimov, the Slava-class cruiser Marshal Ustinov, the Sovremennyy-class destroyer Admiral Ushakov and four Udaloy-class destroyers. They were joined in December 2018 by the first of the modern Admiral Gorshkov-class frigates and second of this class joined the fleet in 2020. Before her refit began in 2017, the Admiral Kuztensov, could also be regularly seen anchored off Severomorsk prior to deploying on operations or training exercises.

Further along the Severomorsk promenade are the piers where its Ropucha-class ships of the 121st Brigade of Landing Ships, as well as the two newly arrived Ivan Gren-class amphibious ships, are birthed. Around the bay are the piers used by the fleet's five auxiliary intelligence-gathering (AGI) ships – which are usually called spy ships by the Western media - of the 159th Independent Battalion of Reconnaissance Ships.

Up the coast at Polyarny is the headquarters of the Kola Mixed Force Flotilla, which is tasked with the coastal defence of the region. This includes six Gisha-class missile boats, three Nanuchka- and Tarantula-class anti-submarine corvettes, nine Sonya-, Natya- and Rubin-class minesweepers. This flotilla also controls the five Kilo-class and one new Lada-class conventional attack submarines which are based at Polyarny. The Kilos are old Soviet-era boats and they rarely go to sea.

Supporting the Northern Fleet's warships and submarines are several specialist shore-based units of the Coastal Forces' 14th Army Corps. These include the 61st Naval Infantry Brigade, 80th and 200th Separate Motor Rifle Brigades, 536th Coastal Missile Brigade, which is equipped with P-300 Bastion-P long range anti-ship missiles, and signals-intelligence detachments. In total these Coastal Force units probably muster around 12,000 personnel in total.

The Northern Fleet Naval Aviation component is based at four airfields around Severomorsk. This includes the Admiral Kuznetsov's air group of just over 30 Sukhoi Su-33 and Mikoyan MiG-29KR combat aircraft is based. Shore-based Su-24 bombers and MiG-31 fighters are also based south of the port city. A dozen or so Kamov Ka-27PL/PS anti-submarine, Ka-29 assault and Ka-31 early warning helicopters are available to deploy on Northern Fleet ships. To provide anti-submarine cover there are 10 classic configuration Iluyshin Il-38 maritime patrol aircraft and two Il-20T instrumented trial aircraft to support missile firings at test ranges around the Barents and White Seas. Logistic support is provided by a fleet of 10 Antonov An-26, Tupolov Tu-134 and Mil Mi-8. Long-range maritime patrol support for the Northern Fleet is also provided by the 19 Tupolov Tu-142 turbo-prop maritime patrol aircraft based at Kipelovo airbase to the east of St Petersburg. Since 2017, the Northern Fleet has fielded its own regiment of Israeli-designed but Russian- assembled IAI Forpost tactical unmanned aerial vehicles to support land and maritime operations.

The Northern Fleet has a number of core missions that drive its operational activity. It has to provide nuclear power ballistic missile firing submarines (SSBNs) to carry out at-sea-deterrent patrols armed with nuclear weapons, under the direction of the national command authority in Moscow. Protecting these SSBN patrols is the responsibility of the Northern Fleet's submarine and surface forces. These deterrence patrols in the Barents Sea and High Arctic regions have long been the staple of the Northern Fleet stretching back to the Soviet era and they take up a significant amount of resources, particularly its nuclear powered attack submarine (SSNs) fleet.

Its next strategic mission is to provide naval forces for power-projection missions around the world, either providing independent naval battlegroups based around the Admiral Kuznetsov and Kirov-class cruisers or dispatching individual vessels on global flag-waving missions to support Russian diplomacy. Balancing the requirements for power-projection with protecting its strategic deterrent has long been challenge for the Northern Fleet. The later task seems to take priority with on average only two or three warships a year are dispatched by the Northern Fleet on global missions, with the remainder of activity being in regions closer to the fleet's home bases.

Russia's ship- and submarine-building industry suffered grievously during the 1990s from privatisations, asset-stripping, budget cuts and a loss of expertise. This downsizing hit the shipyards of Murmansk, Olenya and Severodvinsk hard as they were sold off to private operators or transferred to state-controlled commercial enterprises. Many of these shipyards only stayed in business because they secured funding, including from Western governments to dismantle former Soviet nuclear submarines and dispose of their redundant reactors.

The Northern Fleet suffered heavily in the 1990s as the overhaul and modernisation of its warships was repeatedly delayed and the purchase of replacement ships failed to get approval from the government of President Boris Yeltsin. Putting off the recapitalisation of the Northern Fleet's capital ships for two decades by delaying the building of a new aircraft carrier came back to bite Moscow in October 2018 when the PD-50 floating dock at No 82 Ship Repair Yard at Roslyakovo, near Murmansk, sank as the Admiral Kuznetsov, was being manoeuvred out after a refit period. As the 330-metre-long dock sank underneath the carrier, one of the PD-50's cranes toppled onto the deck of the Admiral Kuznetsov. Although the damage to the carrier appeared to be only superficial the loss of the PD-50 created a major headache for the Northern Russian Navy. The dock was the only one in northern Russia that could take Admiral Kuznetsov out of the water to carry out work on her hull, throwing into doubt whether the carrier will be ready to return to service by 2022. A plan was hatched to extend an existing dry dock at No 35 Shipyard in Murmansk to take the carrier. Further delay has been caused because of a dispute with contractors.

For the leaders of Russia in the 21st Century, their armed forces are instruments designed to achieve political, diplomatic and economic advantage. The Northern Fleet is no different. Its operations and re-equipment programme gives important indications of how Moscow sees its utility in the future. The lack of investment in new aircraft carriers and other new capital ships in favour of Kalibr cruise missile-firing submarines and frigates, as well unmanned aerial vehicles, coastal defence missiles and mini-submarines, shows that the Kremlin is aiming to enhance the Northern Fleet anti-area, access denial (A2/AD) capabilities rather than boosting its blue-water power-projection capability. The deployment of new S-400 air defence systems to the Kola Peninsula and elsewhere along Russia's northern coast over the past decade adds to this impression.

By creating an A2/AD "umbrella", or what Russian officers call an "anti-air dome", stretching out from the Kola Peninsuala, Moscow wants to ensure than Western forces will not be able to launch any kind of incursion into the Northern Fleet's area of responsibility in a crisis or conflict. Kalibr cruise missiles have a range of 1,500 kilometres or 810 nautical miles so the Northern Fleet has the potential to threaten precision strikes across Scandinavia, Iceland, the United Kingdom and the Arctic region.

Forpost unmanned aerial vehicles have been active on the Kola Peninsula since 2017 and they are a critical element in establishing a precision strike "kill chain" or command-and-control structure. Russian Aerospace Force Long Range Aviation heavy bombers, Tupolev Tu-95s and Tu-160s, equipped with air launched Kh-55 and Kh-101 precision-guided munitions have also staged through airbases on the Kola Peninsula adding to the inventory of smart weapons that can be brought to bear.

Before 2014 Western governments, naval commands and intelligence agencies paid little attention to Russia's Black Sea Fleet. The region was considered by many to be a strategic backwater in which little of consequence happened. This all changed during the course of one week in February 2014 when the fleet's ships, aircraft and naval infantry were mobilised to spearhead the Russian military campaign to drive Ukrainian forces from the Crimea peninsula. A year later the fleet's amphibious vessels transported the bulk of Russia's military contingent to Syria to begin Moscow's intervention to protect President Bashar al Assad's government in Damascus. A re-equipment programme is now well underway to enhance the capability of the Black Sea Fleet's seven warships, seven submarines, 10 corvettes, seven landing ships, nine mine counter-measures vessels, four intelligence-gathering ships, 33 assorted missile and patrol boats, amphibious forces, land-based anti-ship missiles and land-based airpower.

Russia's Black Sea Fleet is one of the country's most historic and iconic military formations traces its history back to 1783 when Queen Catherine the Great's military strongman, Prince Potemkin, set up the first naval force in Crimea after he led the campaign to capture the peninsula from the Turkish Ottoman empire. The fleet's history has been inextricably intertwined with Crimea and its home port Sevastopol. Dramatic sieges during World War Two saw the Soviet-era Black Sea Fleet in the thick of the action. During the Cold War period, the fleet projected Soviet naval power into the Mediterranean and further afield.

The collapse of the Soviet Union led to the independence of Ukraine and division of the fleet and its assets between Moscow and Kiev. This left the Russian Black Sea fleet headquarters inside Ukrainian-controlled Sevastopol and much of the fleet also remained based there, alongside their Ukrainian counterparts.

The post-1991 new Black Sea Fleet saw itself spread across two countries and two main operating bases. The parts of the fleet that were not based in Crimea were home-ported at Novorossiysk, across the Kerch Straits. Smaller patrol ships were based Tuapse, Temryuk and Taganrog along the coast of the Sea of Azov and Black Sea.

Until 1998 the two countries maintained what was called the Russo-Ukrainian Black Sea Fleet under bilateral command. There then followed a formal partition and Russia signed the first of a series of leases for their bases in Crimea from Ukraine. This was an uneasy relationship with repeated arguments over unpaid electricity bills, the presence of Russian intelligence operatives in Crimea and Ukrainian searches of Russian supply trucks and vessels.

The disputes over the status of the Crimea bases also impacted on the Russian navy's modernisation plans and it was not until 2010 that any plans to re-capitalise the Black Sea Fleet could be confirmed. It was announced that Novorossiysk would be the home of new frigates, destroyers and submarines, along with major investment in new facilities.

Despite the uncertainty caused by the disagreements with Ukraine, the Russian Navy command and the government in Moscow continued to see the Black Sea Fleet as a strategically important command. It remained in control of the only warm water-ports in mainland European Russia, which had 365/24/7 access and played an important role in the 2008 war with Georgia.

The fleet continued to follow the Soviet and Russian tradition of being responsible not only for naval operations by warships and submarines but also retained its own amphibious brigade of naval infantry and supporting landing ships, shore-based anti-ship missile batteries and land-based fighter, strike and maritime patrol aircraft. In essence, it remained a balanced force that retained the potential for power projection operations. Although Russia's global ambitions and military resources were significantly diminished during the 1990s, Moscow strenuously opposed several efforts to modify the 1936 Montreux Convention Regarding the Regime of the Bosphorus Straits. This guaranteed Soviet and then Russian warships - within agreed parameters - the right of passage from the Black Sea into the Mediterranean and Moscow was not going to give this up. These convention rights would make it possible for the Black Sea Fleet to transport and sustain the Russian military contingent in Syria from 2015.

The overthrow of the Ukrainian President, Viktor Yanukovych, by pro-European Union protestors in Kiev in February 2014 set in train the events that led to the Russian seizure of Crimea. In the space of a week, the political decision to strike was taken by President Vladimir Putin, and then the planning and preparation for the operation was rapidly put in the train by the Black Sea Fleet headquarters in Sevastapol under its dynamic commander, Admiral Aleksandr Vitko. He emerged as a pivotal figure in the operation, with a reputation for being an aggressive and tactically innovative naval officer.

To achieve tactical and strategic surprise, only units already on Crimea could be used to lead the operation. This meant Vitko's 810th Naval Infantry Brigade and its supporting units, including a detachment of naval Spetsnaz, would have a prominent part in the Russian operation. Vitko then masterminded the deployment of his Naval Infantry, eventually backed by army reinforcements, to blockade Ukrainian troops inside their bases. The success of the Black Sea Fleet's operation - which captured Crimea almost without a shot being fired in anger - led to growing Western concern about the effectiveness of what became known as hybrid warfare tactics.

The seizure of Crimea in 2014 prompted a response from NATO to reassure Ukraine and other NATO allies in the Black Sea region. This involved the stepping up of naval patrols in the Black Sea and the flights around the Crimea by allied intelligence gathering aircraft. To counter this Black Sea Fleet warships and aircraft have been involved in several close encounters with NATO vessels and aircraft, including low-level passes over US and British warships by Su-24 strike jets.

The Russians also routinely staged high-profile missile-firing exercises in the Black Sea by both surface-to-air and anti-ship weapons. These were aimed at demonstrating capability and reinforcing sovereignty over the sea and air space around Crimea.

In May 2018, the bridge over the Kerch Straits opened and effectively ended Crimea's physical isolation from the Russian mainland. The strategic implications of this land link to Crimea are immense, easing reinforcement options for the Russian military and reducing reliance on sea traffic to re-supply the Black Sea Fleet's bases. However, this strategic link has to be protected from sea-borne threats.

The 18 kilometres long Crimea Bridge, which opened after three years of construction at a cost of $3.7 billion, is a vital artery connecting Crimea with the Russian mainland and a powerful means of controlling the Sea of Azov and shipping to the Ukrainian ports of Mariupol and Berdiansk. Any damage to the bridge would limit Moscow's capacity to reinforce Crimea and support its economy, and would also have a serious political impact given its prominence.

The Black Sea Fleet had suffered from under investment and constraints on its future development because of disputes between Kiev and Moscow before 2014. The vast majority of the surface fleet ships, weapons and aircraft date from the Soviet era. It currently boasts seven major surface combat vessels and four of them - a Slava -class guided missile cruiser, a Kashin-class guided missile destroyer and two Krivak-class guided missile frigates - are all ex-Soviet navy ships. As a result of the 2010 State Armaments Programme three Admiral Grigorovich-class guided missile frigates equipped to fire Kalibr cruise missiles were built for the Black Sea Fleet. A further three were to be built for the fleet for delivering from 2016 but two were sold to India instead and the third delayed. To provide additional surface capabilities, the fleet was augmented during 2018 by three Buyan-M corvettes - one new build and two transferred from the Caspian Sea Flotilla - which are equipped to fire Kalibr cruise missiles. Additional anti-submarine frigates have also occasionally been deployed to the eastern Mediterranean from the Baltic Fleet. Northern and Baltic Fleet landing ships have also been dispatched to assist the Syria Express.

Efforts to rebuild the Black Sea Fleet's submarine forces have been more successful, with six new-build Improved Kilo-class/Project 636.3 diesel attack submarines entering service from 2014. Two or three were routinely forward based at Tartus in Syria to allow them to operate continuously in the eastern Mediterranean. They are all equipped to fire Kalibr missiles and they routinely fired them at targets in Syria.

The coastal defence capability of the fleet's 11th Independent Coastal Missile Brigade was enhanced in 2010 when the first Bastion P-300 anti-ship missile entered service. After 2014, the 15th Independent Coastal Missile Brigade was formed in Crimea with Bastion P-300 and Bal anti-ship missiles. The presence of Bastion P-300 missile launchers in Syria was only revealed in November 2016 when a video clip was released by the Russian military showing one of the missile launchers firing land-attack variants of the P-800 Onik missiles at a target near Aleppo.

Post 2014 the Black Sea Fleet's naval aviation component was boosted by the arrival of the first of a dozen Sukhoi Su-30M fighter aircraft in Crimea. These jets significantly enhanced their air-to-air capabilities and the regiment's pilots took their jets to Syria in early 2018 to fly combat missions. A dozen Su-24s are also operated by naval aviators on Crimea.

The tempo of the Black Sea Fleet's operations has massively escalated since 2014. It has participated in two major operations that have had geopolitical effects. To date the Kremlin has been happy with the outcome of these operations, which have expanded Moscow's power and influence in strategic regions. The impact on the morale of the Russian armed forces of these successful campaigns has been immense. The Syrian intervention showed that the Black Sea Fleet possessed considerable expertise in expeditionary operations and that its personnel could adapt to complex and rapidly changing environments. For the Black Sea Fleet, the prestige of being involved in these operations has been significant and its sailors, naval aviators and naval infantrymen have had pride of place in the annual Moscow Victory Day parades since then.

On 26th June 2018 it was announced that the architect of the Black Sea Fleet renaissance, Admiral Aleksandr Vitko, was being assigned "a new place of military service in the Navy High Command". Vitko proved to be an aggressive and effective commander during the Crimea operation and he showed considerable flair for tactical innovation during the Syria campaign. It is likely that the world has not heard the last of Admiral Vitko.

Like its Black Sea Fleet counterpart, the Baltic Fleet is one of Russia's oldest military units tracing its lineage back to 1703 when Tsar Peter the Great ordered the building of the first Russian fleet to fight for supremacy against Swedish dominance of Central and Eastern Europe.

It played an important role during World War Two, supporting Soviet advances through the Baltic States, and then was a significant part of Warsaw Pact forces in the Baltic region. The loss of the three Baltic Republics and Belarus after dissolution of the Soviet Union left the Baltic Fleet split between its historic base at Kronstadt Island, near St Petersburg, and at Baltiysk in the Kaliningrad enclave, wedged between Poland and the newly independent Lithuania.

This accident of history means that the Baltic Fleet's main mission is maintaining sea lines of communications between Baltiysk and Kronstadt, as well as the air, land and sea defence of the Kaliningrad enclave. The fleet command in Baltiysk incorporates all the air, land and sea units based in the enclave and controls the RuAF air defence based there as well. This combined force of comprises 25,000 military personnel, including a naval infantry brigade and a motor rifle brigade, air defence regiments with the S-400 surface-to-air missiles, as well as a coast defence brigade with Bastion-P and Bal anti-ship missiles. Air assets include naval aviation regiments, with around 50 Sukhoi Su-27, Su-30SM and Su-24 combat aircraft and some 30 Mil Mi-24, Mil Mi-8 and Kamov Ka-27 and Ka-29 helicopters, as well as Forpost tactical unmanned aerial vehicles (UAV). Iskander-M tactical ballistic missiles based in Kaliningrad have the potential to hit Berlin, Copenhagen and Warsaw.

Baltiysk port is the home to bulk of the fleet, which is based around one Sovremenny-class destroyer, two Neustrashimyy-class frigates, four Steregushchy-class corvettes, two Buyan-M-class missile ships and a single Karakurt-class missile corvette. There are also nearly 20 smaller missile boats and five minesweepers. Supporting the Baltic Fleet's Naval Infantry Brigade are four Ropucha class landing ships and two Zubr-class large hovercraft. While the Neustrashimyy-class frigates, Steregushchy-class corvettes, Buyan-M class missile ships and Karakurt corvettes all date from the post-Soviet era, these are not big warships and they are not designed for sustained blue-water operations. With only one old-model Kilo submarines, the Baltic Fleet has limited undersea warfare capabilities.

The Kronstadt base is home to the Baltic Fleet Soviet-era Kilo class submarines and around half a dozen small corvettes and patrol craft, as well as several training schools and officer academies. In the nearby city of St Petersburg is the headquarters of the Russian Navy.

Out of all of the former Soviet naval groups, the Pacific Fleet is the one that has suffered the most since the demise of the Soviet Union. At the height of the Cold War it boasted more than 85 major warships, 88 nuclear and conventional

attack submarines and 32 SSBNs, as well as two aircraft carriers. (1)
The collapse of the Berlin Wall in 1989 put an end to Moscow's attempt's to challenge the US Navy in the Pacific. During the 1990s dozens of its warships and submarines were destined for scrap yards and one its the aircraft carriers ended up in a Chinese theme park as a tourist attraction.
Twenty-first Century Russia has shown little interest in a new arms race in the Pacific and has provided limited investment to sustain or modernise the Pacific Fleet. Its main focus is to provide an alternative at-sea deterrent force of SS-BNs to complicate the US ballistic missile defence shield. Even this activity is done with minimum resources - only four SSBNs are in service with the Pacific Fleet, protected by five Akula-class attack and five Oscar II-class cruise missile-firing submarines. Two of the old Delta III SSBNs have been replaced by new Borei-class submarines but the Akulas and Oscar IIs are plagued by maintenance problems with only two or three able to put to sea at any point in time, according to satellite imagery of main Pacific Fleet submarine base at Vilyuchinsk over the five years up to 2020.Two of the Alukas are in long term maintenance or storage with little prospect of returning to the fleet in the near future. The conventional Kilo-class submarines are little better with only three out of the seven on the Pacific Fleet's books appearing to be in working order at any point in time.
The 36th Division of Surface Ships is built around 1980s warships, including the Slava-class cruiser Varyag, four Udaloy I-class destroyers and two Sovremennyy-class destroyers. Between 2015 and 2020 it has received two Steregushchy-clsss corvettes. It is supported by four or five Ropucha- and Alligator-class landing ships, as well as nearly 30 assorted patrol and missile boats.
Warships regularly sail from Vladivistock on goodwill cruises around the Pacific and Indian Ocean regions. However, the ability of the Russian Pacific Fleet to project power in time of conflict is a moot point. Moscow appears more interested in using its Pacific Fleet, particularly its submarines, aircraft and amphibious forces, to operate along Russia's northern coast and into the Arctic Circle.
The Pacific Fleet's naval aviation component has a strong emphasis on long-range maritime patrol with a mix of 18 Tu-142s and 14 Il-38s. These later aircraft are some of the first to be upgraded to the new N configuration. Some 16 Ka-27 helicopters are available to be embarked on warships.
Three Naval Infantry Brigades serve in the Fleet's Coastal Forces, as well as two missile brigades equipped with the Bastion-P weapon systems.
How does Russia's naval power line up against its potential opponents at the start of the third decade of the 21st Century? When Russia's warships are added up, on paper it boasts an aircraft carrier, three large cruisers and more than 30 frigates and destroyers, as well as more than 50 nuclear and conventionally powered submarines. This is bigger than any other European navy, bigger than the Japanese navy but behind the Chinese and US fleets.
This tally, however, does not convey the true nature of Russian naval power because it does not take into account its geographical distribution. Russia's

four surface fleets and one major flotilla lack the ability to operate together as a single fleet or mutually reinforce each other in time of conflict. The Black Sea and Baltic Fleets, as well as the Caspian Flotilla, are effectively bottled into their respective home waters and the Pacific Fleet's surface ships are literally on the other side of the world to the bulk of the Russian Navy. While it would be possible for Russia's nuclear submarine's to roam the globe, the bulk of them are concentrated in the Northern Fleet. This is the age old dilemma of Russian naval power that was cruelly exposed at the Battle of Tsushima in 1905 when the Imperial Russia Baltic Fleet sailed to Pacific at the height of the Russo-Japanese war. The subsequent decisive defeat of the Russian naval force led it being dubbed the "Fleet that had to Die". (2)

When the component Russian fleets are compared to their near neighbours, Russian naval power can be put in its true perspective. The fleets of Russia neighbours are well documented in open sources, including the websites of their navies and ministries of defence.

Out in the Pacific, the Japanese fleet alone outnumbers the Russian Pacific Fleet by five to one, without taking into account the US Pacific Fleet. The 17 submarines of the Russian Pacific Fleet are also outgunned by the US and Japanese submarine forces in the Pacific, which respectively boast 22 and 20 submarines each. This disparity is made worse by the poor serviceability of the Russian submarines, with less than half of them usually being in working order. Except for its ballistic missile-firing submarines, the Russian Pacific Fleet is not a major player in Far East naval line-up against the US, Japanese or Chinese navies.

The Baltic Sea force ratios are also not in Russia's favour, with the seven major surface combatants, 18 minor combatants and one submarine of the Baltic Sea Fleet outnumbered by a coalition of NATO and allied forces. The Finnish, Swedish, Danish, Polish and German navies could potentially mobilise 28 frigates, 23 corvettes and 14 submarines in a major confrontation with Russia. Modern Swedish, Finnish, Danish and German naval forces could be expected to give Moscow's warships a run for their money in any open conflict.

However, the concentration of Russian warships, anti-ship missiles, long-range surface-to-air missiles, tactical ballistic missiles and top-of-the-line fighters and bombers deployed to Kaliningrad means that the enclave would be a major thorn in the side of NATO and European Union forces operating in the Baltic region in any crisis or open conflict. But the Russian Navy would have little opportunity to reinforce or support its isolated Baltic Fleet in a sustained conflict.

In the Black Sea, the Russian Navy faces better odds with its nine major ships, 25 corvettes and six submarines up against a force of 16 major warships, 23 corvettes and 7 submarines drawn from the combined Turkish, Bulgarian, Ukrainian and Romanian navies. However, the Russian warships all tend to be newer and have more long-range weapons, and they are support by land-based missiles and aircraft.

If the Russian Northern Fleet ever came out fighting into the North Atlantic it would face a far stronger NATO force. The combined British, Canadian, Dutch

French, Norwegian, Portuguese and Spanish navies, backed up by the US Navy's forward-deployed warships in European waters, boasts more than 40 frigates and destroyers but the Northern Fleet currently has only 11 major surface combatants. If British, French and Norwegian submarines are combined with the US Atlantic Fleet's nuclear sybmarines then some 37 boats will be available to take on the Northern Fleet's 17 nuclear attack submarines. Not all of the NATO and Russian submarine forces are always available for operations due to regular maintenance requirements but this is most likely to work in NATO's favour. On top of the mismatch between the surface and submarine fleets, the Northern Fleet is totally outmatched in maritime airpower with the British and French having three very modern aircraft carriers compared to the Russian Navy's single ageing and very unreliable carrier. NATO nations also have strong maritime patrol aircraft forces that can operate across North Atlantic region.

A key indicator of the Russian Navy's power-projection capabilities is the state of its amphibious shipping. The current amphibious fleet has just 22 major landing ships, spread between the Baltic, Black Sea, Northern and Pacific Fleet. The Black Sea Fleet has eight, which are heavily committed to re-supplying the Russian contingent in Syria. The other fleets have four or five landing ships each. This means that each fleet has the capacity to move around a battalion's worth of Naval Infantry or 500 troops and their equipment in one lift, which is not a very significant force. It is not really enough make an opposed landing on NATO territory and sustain a bridgehead over an extended period.

With Russia's naval forces at a disadvantage compared to its near neighbours and the United States, what are the Kremlin's plans to bolster its naval power? The Russian shipbuilding programme is largely an open book due to the need for its shipyards to notify their future workload to their shareholders. It is also good politics for the Moscow government to boast about how it is handing out state shipbuilding orders.

It is also possible to verify the progress of much of this work from assessing commercial satellite imagery of Russian shipyards. Building complex warships and submarines is a massive industrial endeavour so it very unlikely that Russia has a secret shipbuilding programme that is had managed to keep hidden from foreign observers.

Overhead imagery of these shipyards can be compared with the news imagery from launch and naming events to build up a reasonably accurate picture of the scale, scope and progress of efforts to build new vessels for the Russian Navy. Even at the sole nuclear submarine construction yard at Severodvinsk it is relatively easy to work out the progress of work by measuring the dimensions of the main assembly hall. The number of submarines under construction inside can then be worked out. The same process yields similar insights into the conventional submarine assembly yard at the Admiralty Shipyards in St Petersburg.

Major Russian warships are assembled largely outdoors at the main shipyards so satellite imagery can provide a great deal of detail. The Pella, Severnaya Verf and Sredne-Nevsky shipyards in St Petersburg appear to have plenty of work, as does the Yantar yard in Kaliningrad. On Crimea, the Zelenodolsk shipyard at Kerch and the More shipyard at Feodosiya started to receive Russian Navy work after 2014. The Amur Shipyard in Komsomolsk-on-Amur is the most active naval yard in the Far East but its work load is nowhere near as active as the yards in St Petersburg. Pork-barrel politics appears to play a role in the Russian shipbuilding industry in just the same way as for its Western counterpart.

The bulk of the Northern Fleet ships, submarines and aircraft date from the Soviet era or are legacy Soviet designs that were manufactured in the early days of the Russian Federation. However, the 2010s, has seen the Northern Fleet begin to take delivery of newly designed ships, submarines and aircraft to begin a re-capitalisation of its fleet.

Putin says he is determined to rebuild Russian naval power and he has set in train a naval modernisation programme. Many of the Russian Navy's large warships and conventionally powered submarines are built at yards in St Petersburg, which just by coincidence is the Russian President's home town. Stop-start funding during the early years of this century was replaced in 2010 by a new State Armaments Programme, or GPV, that set out a 10-year programme to purchase modern military hardware. The Russian Navy received 26% of funding in the GPV, which was the largest allocation of any of the Russian armed services. It proved far from easy for the Russian Navy and the country's shipbuilding industry to deliver on the ambitions of the 2010 GPV. The first of the new ships and nuclear submarines only started to be handed over to the Northern Fleet in 2018.

Over the coming decade the Northern Fleet is to receive four Borei nuclear missile submarines, four Yasen M-class attack submarines, two more Gorshkov- class general-purpose frigates, a Gremyashchy-class corvette, a second Ivan Gren-class amphibious landing ship. The fleet is also expected to receive at least one of the two new 25,000-ton universal helicopter carriers. The addition of the extra submarines will dramatically reduce the average age of the Northern Fleet's submarine force but will not move the dial much in term of hull numbers. The surface force is also not to grow substantially.

The Baltic Fleet's surface fleet is only slated to receive modest reinforcements in the shape of a Steregushchy-class corvette, three Karakurt-class corvettes and one Buyan-M-class missile corvette. A bigger boost is on the way to the Black Sea Fleet in the shape of two Kalibr-capable Buyan-M-class missile corvettes, possibly one Kalibr-capable Admiral Grigorovich-class frigate, eight Karakurt-class corvettes, a Steregushchy-class corvette and six Project 22160 Vasiliy Bykov-class patrol vessels.

The Pacific Fleet has ambitious plans to replace its Soviet era-vessels. These include 10 Karakurt-class corvettes, six Gremyashchy-class corvettes, two Steregushchy-class corvettes and possibly six Kalibr cruise missile-armed Improved Kilo conventional submarines. In the longer term, the Pacific Fleet is destined to get two new Yasem-M nuclear attack boats and two more new Borei SSBNs. The ambitions of the famous Soviet naval leader, Admiral Sergey Gorshkov, to build a ocean-going fleet to rival the power of the United States Navy has long been dropped by the leaders of 21st Century Russia. This despite the modern Russian Navy naming its newest class of frigate after the man who created the Soviet Union's so-called "blue-water" navy. Moscow's naval ship building plans make it clear that there Russian Navy is not investing in the near term in large fleet of blue-water surface vessels. The lack of progress on building a replacement for the Admiral Kuznetsov is very telling.

Preventing Western interference in the sea zones around Russia's coasts is now the priority of the admirals in St Petersburg. The adoption of so-called anti-A2/AD strategies by the Kremlin does not mean that the Russian Navy is retreating into a coastal defence force patrolling the country's 12-mile territorial waters. Russia's new navy is armed with 1,500 kilometre-range cruise missiles and anti-ship missiles that can hit targets some 350 kilometre from shore, while at the same time, 4th generation fighters, maritime patrol aircraft, missile-armed long-range bombers and tactical unmanned aerial vehicles will win air supremacy over Russia's fleets and hunt for enemy warships. These powerful capabilities mean that most of the Baltic, Barents and Black Seas, as well large parts of the Arctic and Sea of Japan are not safe for Western warships to venture into. Moscow has exported an A2/AD umbrella to the Eastern Mediterranean to protect its forces in Syria.

Moscow's naval power now make it very difficult for the United States and its allies operate warships near to Russia's coast in time of conflict. President Putin wants to keep it that way for many years to come and is investing heavily ensure his navy can continue to keep Washington's navy at arm's length.

Chapter 20
The Submarines of the Northern Fleet

"The Russian undersea threat is real". Vice Admiral Andrew Lewis, the head of the US Navy's 2nd Fleet, told an event hosted by the Centre for Strategic and International Studies on 28th November 2019. (1) Other senior officers across Western military, government, and private-sector organisations have made similar claims, describing the Russian Northern Fleet's submarines, or boats as they are know, as an increasing threat to NATO naval operations in the North Atlantic and Western economic interests in the High Arctic.

In May 2018, the then UK defence secretary Gavin Williamson, warned the Royal United Services Institute (RUSI) think-tank in London that to "look at Russia's resurgence under President Putin, its submarine activity has increased 10-fold in the North Atlantic." (2)

The head of the Royal Navy, First Sea Lord Admiral Tony Radakin, told an audience of defence contractors in Portsmouth n March 2020 that, "in 2019 we saw the highest Russian activity in the North Atlantic for over 30 years. Submarines are getting quieter, more capable and harder to detect." (3)

One of the most intriguing aspects of Russian Northern Fleet operations has been allegations from senior Western political and military leaders that Russian mini submarines have been reported near fibre-optic cables under the Atlantic that carry high volumes of internet traffic between Europe and North America. The fear is that these mini submarines have been carrying out bulk harvesting of internet traffic for use in Russian information operations. It has also been suggested that the mini-submarine force is contributing to the building of a fixed sonar network, similar to the old US SOSUS system, under the Arctic ice pack.

In a speech at RUSI in December 2017, the outgoing UK Chief of the Defence Staff, Air Chief Marshal Sir Stu Peach, said that the NATO had sought to protect the undersea communications cables that carry the bulk of the world's internet communications "in response to the threat posed by the modernisation of the Russian Navy." (4)

Rear Admiral Andrew Lennon, NATO's submarine force commander, was quoted in media reports in December 2017, as saying "We are now seeing Russian underwater activity in the vicinity of undersea cables that I don't believe we have ever seen. Russia is clearly taking an interest in NATO and NATO nations' undersea infrastructure." (5)

What is reality of these claims? When pressed to provide any details to support them senior US and UK naval officers all claim the intelligence is highly classified and can't be exposed to the public because of the risk of comprising their sources. In this information void is it possible to gain any independent assessment of Russia's submarine force from non-secret or open intelligence sources? Intelligence-collection techniques have evolved since the Cold War, and the scope of open-source intelligence has broadened dramatically. Moreover, mod-

ern Russia is a much more open society than the Soviet Union, which again shapes the intelligence collection environment. However, other aspects of the environment, such as the geography and climate of the Kola Peninsula have not changed appreciably since the Cold War.
During the Cold War, the Soviet military declared whole regions and cities as closed to foreigners and many Soviet citizens to prevent any unauthorised people observing the activities of military units or what was happening inside strategic defence factories, such as submarine-building yards. The Kola Peninsula and most of its major urban areas, including Severomorsk - where the Northern Fleet was headquartered - and the fleet's main submarine bases, were designated closed cities. Foreigners were banned from visiting, except with special permissions. This meant that it was virtually impossible for foreigners to obtain the kind of physical access to the Kola Peninsula that would permit the collection of intelligence on the Northern Fleet through visual observation or through cultivating human sources.
During this period the primary sources of intelligence provided to Western policymakers on the Soviet submarine force were overhead imagery, signals intelligence, or SIGINT, and "contact reports" from Western submarines that managed to track their Soviet counterparts in the Barents Sea.
During the 1950s some of the first covert overflights over the Soviet Union took place over the Kola Peninsula. SIGINT gathering by aircraft also played an important part in detecting activity during the build-up to Soviet submarines sailing. Satellite surveillance took over this mission in the 1960s and satellite imagery of Soviet submarine-building yards gave analysts an insight into key components, such as nuclear reactors, missile launch tubes and propellers, before they were installed on submarines. However, early Cold War-era satellite images were of low resolution and this often made it difficult for analysts to come to definitive conclusions. Overhead imagery was heavily dependent on good weather, which is often in short supply over the Kola.
The launch of the first Lacrosse radar surveillance satellite in the late 1960s gave the US the ability to "look" through clouds. However, the radar satellites were mounted in low Earth orbits, giving the satellite limited time over the target area, which meant that there remained problems of achieving persistent or sustained coverage. This meant manned aircraft were still needed to fly photo reconnaissance missions around the fringes of Soviet airspace during the 1970s and 1980s in a bid fill gaps by taking sideways-looking still photographs and early generation synthetic-aperture radar images of submarine bases on the Kola.
NATO intelligence agencies sought early warning of submarine sailings so that they could cue anti-submarine assets to track them as they moved out to sea and into the North Atlantic. The US and UK navies conducted regular nuclear submarine patrols in the Barents Sea, with the aim of detecting Soviet submarines putting to sea, as well as gaining insights into their technical capabilities by covertly tracking them. A Royal Navy veteran from the 1980s told the author

that if Soviet submarines were able to get out of their home bases undetected then chances of allied maritime patrol aircraft or anti-submarines warships the picking them up out at sea dropped dramatically, even with the help of SOSUS underwater listening networks. (6) These so-called "un-alerted detections" by maritime patrol aircraft or surface ships were very rare, according to the Royal Navy veteran. The North Atlantic was just too big for NATO's maritime patrol aircraft or surface ships to hunt down every Soviet submarine,

In the 21st Century the intelligence gathering challenge is very different. Although nominally the neighbourhoods of some Northern Fleet's bases are still classed as closed to foreigners, many of the towns in the region have been re-classified as open to allow foreigners to participate in oil exploration and support activities. The region also has a vibrant civilian news media. Internet and social media usage is widespread. Unlike in the Soviet period, the Russian Navy's submarine force is now fully professionalised and its boats are manned by contract sailors. To attract recruits and to reassure the public that sailors are being looked after, the Russian Navy opens much of its activity to the Russian news media and runs extensive publicity campaigns for major exercise and foreign deployments.

Senior officers of the Northern Fleet routinely appear in the media and school children make visits to its bases and vessels. Sailors use social media to keep in touch with relatives, using the Russian VK social network. There are also several online groups of Soviet and Russian submarine veterans who share imagery of the contemporary fleet, historical accounts, and debates about related issues. These forums often include accounts of previously unknown incidents, such as accidents, names of current and former personnel, and other detailed information. This has resulted in the availability of a torrent of imagery and information about the Northern Fleet's submarine force that was inaccessible during the Cold War. This allows assessments to be made of the material state of the Northern Fleet's submarines and base infrastructure.

One of the biggest changes since the Cold War has been the transfer of the Russian shipbuilding industry to the private sector in the shape of the United Shipbuilding Corporation and the oil company Rosneft. Although these organisations have sizeable state shareholdings, they operate as pseudo-private sector organisations and, as such, have to keep their current and potential shareholders informed about their order books, cash flow, and future potential orders.

This means that the Russian Navy's current and future procurement plans are now discussed by the companies and the Ministry of Defence. The Russian government, for example, operates a procurement process that involves online tendering websites and it routinely announces defence equipment orders, including plans to scrap redundant submarines and their nuclear reactors.

The main Russian submarine production and support facilities now hold open launch events for submarines and allow the media to tour their sites, providing insights into Russian submarine designs and construction techniques. The submarine facilities in the port city of Severodvinsk - the Sevmash assembly yard and the Zvezdochka repair centre - have invited the media inside their submarine assembly halls, something that was unheard of during the Cold War. Both companies have launched recruitment drives to attract skilled workers, and as such routinely conduct news media and social-media engagement campaigns.

Sevmash is Russia's only nuclear submarine assembly facility. The assembly and launch of the Russian Navy's latest Borei nuclear power ballistic missile firing submarines (SSBN) and Yasen-M nuclear powered attack submarines (SSNs) has been documented in film footage taken inside the assembly hall. Although key components, such as propellers, are obscured for the filming, few Western submarine yards would provide a similar level of exposure.

The Severodvinsk harbour basin is central to the Northern Fleet submarine operations, with many of the fleet's submarines - often more than 10 boats at time being tied up there awaiting repair and overhaul. Citizens routinely film the activities inside the harbour basin and post the imagery online.

The biggest aid to open-source assessments of the Northern Fleet's submarine force is the availability of sub-one-metre resolution commercial satellite imagery. This make it possible to identify specific submarines and even to determine the type of individual weapons being loaded. When they are in port submarines are very difficult to hide from satellite imagery, which offers many opportunities to count, track and assess the fleet's submarines. When combined with ground-level imagery from other sources, this allows for more detailed assessments to be produced. With sufficient batches of high-resolution imagery it is possible to determine how many submarines are in port, and hence to assess how many submarines may be at sea.

Although the Russian Navy now operates in a very different media and social environment to during the Soviet era, it appears to recognise that it needs to maintain operational security, or OPSEC, of specific submarine movements and operations and has put in place several measures to protect its secrets. These are similar to measures adopted by NATO navies. There is no discussion or pre-announcement in the Russian media of submarine deployments prior to the boats leaving their home bases. This is a critical OPSEC measure to prevent alerting NATO intelligence.

The Northern Fleet has sought to-shield some submarines from overhead surveillance. Satellite and social-media imagery has revealed the construction of a floating hanger at the Olenya Bay submarine base, to conceal work on submarines. This base is also home to Russia's mini-submarine unit, the 29th Division. At the Bolshaya Lopatka Naval Base, submarines have been photographed draped in camouflage netting suggesting this is being used to shield the loading of sensitive equipment or weapons.

The Russian military has also introduced strict measures in an attempt to control the use of social media by its personnel. Online investigation and campaigning groups, such as the UK-based Bellingcat and the Ukraine-based Inform Napalm, have revealed compromising details of Moscow's involvement in downing of the MH17 airliner and the Skripal poisoning case. In response, the Russian military restricted social media use by its uniformed personnel. An information campaign was launched to warn troops about the danger of giving away sensitive information. In September 2018 the Russian government moved to introduce legislation to ban troops posting information about themselves, their comrades or the country's armed forces, but this has so far only had limited impact.

Open-source monitoring of the Russian armed forces and units, such as the Northern Fleet, can therefore provide more information about their capabilities and activities than would have been possible during the Cold War, and even at the turn of this century. However, these tools have their limitations. Commercial satellite imagery can be heavily impacted by bad weather, reducing the level of coverage. Social-media feeds have their biases and limitations, and the Russian armed forces are displaying an increasing level of awareness of the OPSEC challenges that they present. Commercial imagery, both electro-optical and radar, offers plenty of potential to monitor the Northern Fleet, particularly if refreshed images are available on an hourly or daily basis. Although commercial organisations will struggle to reach the levels of coverage of the US military, the quality of their product has improved dramatically over the past decade and future developments, as well as cost reductions, can be expected to continue at a similar rate. This OSINT information makes it possible to form assessments of the Northern Fleet submarine force in 2021.

The formal demise of the Soviet Union in December 1991 led to the formation of the Russian Federation. This was followed by the formal transformation of the Soviet Navy into the Russian Navy in January 1992. For the Soviet Red Banner Northern Fleet this was the start of the rapid process of change that has continued to this day. The size of the fleet's submarine force was dramatically reduced, there were significant manpower cuts and base closures followed close behind. A major preoccupation became the dismantling of redundant Soviet submarines and their surplus nuclear reactor cores.

At its height in the mid-1980s the Northern Fleet had 176 submarines in service, including 45 SSBNs, 68 SSN and cruise missile firing nuclear powered submarines (SSGNs), and 63 conventional attack submarines (SSKs). (7) By late 2020, the Northern Fleet had been reduced to just 34 frontline submarines and six mini-submarines. The reliance on conscript sailors was reduced with them being allocated to shore roles or work on surface war ships, making the submarine force the domain of professional or contract sailors.

But many things remained the same. The Northern Fleet remained in the forefront of Russian nuclear submarine development, with the organisation being responsible for the entry to service of new classes of boats, new weapons or systems. Nuclear deterrent submarine operations remained centred on the Northern Fleet and the Barents Sea. Thanks to its prestigious and high-profile role, the Soviet Northern Fleet saw many of its officers rising to high rank in the Soviet Navy. This remained the same in the Russian Navy, with ex Northern Fleet submariners being positioned in key posts across the service. The Russian

Northern Fleet, its subordinate units and vessels retained many of the traditions and honours of their Soviet predecessors. For example, it still retained the formal Red Banner honour bestowed on its Soviet predecessor in 1965.The nadir of the post-Soviet Northern Fleet was the sinking of the submarine Kursk in 2000 with the loss of 118 sailors. The incident was a major embarrassment for the Russian Navy and the newly appointed Russian President Vladimir Putin. This incident led to a significant boost in the funding to the Russian Navy and its submarine arm. These measures were part of a programme of modernisation across the Russian armed forces aimed at improving its readiness, capabilities and effectiveness to enable them to enhance Russia's geo-political position.
The Northern Fleet currently boasts a mixed flotilla of submarine types. It also contains a mix of ex-Soviet and new build submarines. Western observers have long used the NATO code names for the various classes of Soviet-era submarines still in use and for ease of understanding I followed this practice, but provided both for clarity. New Russian submarines are beginning to be referred to by the product names used by the manufacturers.

- The Project 941 Akula (shark) SSBN is the "classic" Cold War submarine made famous in the Hollywood movie, Hunt for Red October, and was dubbed Typhoon by NATO. Only one of these giant SSBNs, the Dmitriy Donskoy (TK-208), now remains in service and it is used for testing and trials work linked to the troubled Bulava ballistic missile. The entry to service of this missile in 2018 suggested that the final Typhoon could be soon destined for scrap. Its Russian name Akula, is rather confusing because NATO used the same name to designate a different class of attack submarines.
- Project 667DRM Delfin (NATO: Delta IV) is a Soviet-era submarine that now bears the brunt of nuclear deterrent patrol duty. All the six remaining Delta IV boats were built during the 1980s and early 1990s. They have all been refurbished since 2010 and this suggests they could be in service until well into the 2020s.
- The Project 9551 Borei (NATO: Dolgoruky) is the new generation of Russian SSBNs. The first of the class entered service with the Northern Fleet in 2013. This process was considerably delayed by technical issues with the Bulava ballistic missiles which were not fully resolved until 2018. The first improved variant, the Project 9552 Borei A, which incorporates changes to its internal design, finally entered Northern Fleet service in May 2020.
- Project 945A Kondor (NATO Sierra II) Soviet-era SSNs were built in the late 1980s and early 1990s. They have Titanium hulls and were considered the quietest Soviet-era boats. They are still considered useful by the Russian Navy. Two of the boats have been overhauled over the past decade but decisions to overhaul the remaining two boats have still not been made.
- The Project 671RTM/RTMK Shchuka or Pike (NATO: Victor-III) submarines were the workhorses of the Soviet attack submarine fleet in the 1980s but only three remain in service. These all entered service between 1990 and 1992 so they are some of the newest boats in the Northern Fleet. One has been

recently overhauled and modernised. It is unclear if the remaining two will modernised.

- The Project 949A Antey (NATO: Oscar II) are the last of the Soviet-era SSGNs and boast a huge weapon fits, including 24 P-700 Granit (SS-N-19) nuclear or conventionally armed cruise missiles and 24 torpedoes. Two of the Northern Fleet's three submarines has been overhauled. It has been suggested that these submarines will eventually be fitted with the Kalibr 1,500 kilometre-range precision-guided conventionally armed cruise missile. This weapon is the Russian equivalent of the US Tomahawk land-attack missile and its employment in Syria in 2015 transformed the strike capabilities of the Russian Navy. The ill-fated Kursk was a Oscar-II.
- Project 971 Shchuka-B (Pike) is the most numerous SSN in the Northern Fleet. They are dubbed Akula by NATO. These submarines were completed in the 1990s so are some of the most modern and quiet in the Northern Fleet. Three versions are in service, which are designated the 971I (Akula I), 971U (Akuka II) and 971M (Akula III). It is the intention to keep them in service for some time and a major overhaul and upgrade programme is underway, with at least two of the Northern Fleet's six boats currently in dock in 2020 being worked on or awaiting modernisation. They are reportedly to being equipped with Kalibr cruise missiles during the modernisation programme.
- The Project 885 Yasen or Ash Tree and Yasen-M (NATO: Yasen) are the newest - and most expensive - attack boats in the Russian Navy service. The cost and complexity of the project has meant it took five years from the first boat entering service in 2013 to the second boat beginning sea trials in September 2018. Its formal entry into service has been delayed by technical problems in the Sevmash shipyard until late 2020 at the earliest. As standard, they are fitted to fire Kalibr cruise missiles. The next four submarines to be built are destined for the Northern Fleet but it is unclear which fleets will operate the next six submarines of the class that are proposed to be built. The second boat is of the enhanced Yasen-M configuration.

The Northern Fleet has a small conventional attack submarines force based around the Project 877-class (NATO: Kilo) and the new Project 677 or Lada-class (NATO: St Petersburg). Its five Kilos are some of the oldest Kilo-class submarines still in service and are not fitted with Kalibr cruise missiles. Only the Improved Kilo or Project 636.3 boats have this weapon but none are in service with the Northern Fleet. Two Northern Fleet Kilos were withdrawn from service and scrapped in 2018 and 2019. The lead boat in the Project 677-class is in service with the Northern Fleet but its entry to service has been delayed by technical issues. Subsequent boats in the class have been allocated to the Baltic and Pacific Fleets but production is running several years behind schedule at the Admiralty yard in St Petersburg. The boats are fitted with Kalibr missiles as standard.

Several submarines and mini-subs configured for unconventional operations are based with the Northern Fleet. The Project 09786 and Project 09787 Nuclear Auxiliary Submarines (SSAN) (NATO: Delta III/Delta IV) are converted SSBNs that are configured to act as "mother-ships" for mini-submarines. Their ballistic missile tubes have been removed and a mini-sub dock built under the submarine's hull. Docking stations for unmanned underwater systems (UUS) have also been seen on the upper rear decks of these submarines. This allows them to transport mini-submarines or UUS far out into the North Atlantic or under the Arctic ice cap.

Six Soviet-era mini-submarines are designed to operate in conjunction with a SSAN, including the Project 1851-class Nelma (NATO: X-Ray) and two Project 1910or Kashalot-class (NATO: Uniform). The latter is a nuclear-powered submarine with titanium hull to allow it to operate at deep depths.

The Project 10831 (NATO: NORSUB-5) Losharik is the most modern mini-sub and it only entered service in 2003, despite being laid down in 1988. It is nuclear powered and designed to operate down to 2500-metre depths under the Arctic ice cap. A mysterious fire on board in July 2019 left 14 crew dead and the submarine badly damaged, resulting in it being tied up in the Severodvinsk basin awaiting repairs. These mini-submarines are complemented by several unmanned underwater system or robots, including Harpsichord-2R-PM, which has been seen in satellite imagery being loaded on the two SSANs.

Since 1991 the order of battle of the Northern Fleet has shrunk dramatically in a bid to try to match its force structure, manpower and infrastructure to its reduced budget in the post-Soviet era.

Its operational nuclear submarines are now concentrated in four divisions, reporting to a rear admiral who is head of the Submarine Forces of the Northern Fleet. The conventional submarines operate under a separate chain of command and report to a flotilla tasked with the coastal defence of the Kola Peninsula.

The mini-sub force is assigned to the 29th Submarine Division, which has its own distinct chain of command although it shares facilities and personnel with the Northern Fleet. It is perhaps the most enigmatic unit of that operates from the Kola Peninsula and its base at Olenya Bay contains the unique infrastructure needed to support mini-submarine operations, including a floating hangar to conceal maintenance and modernisation work. It reports to the Russian Ministry of Defence's Main Directorate of Deep Sea Research, also known as GUGI, which is based in the city of Peterhof, to the west of St Petersburg. This organisation has been portrayed in the Western media as a "naval Spetsnaz" force that is configured for underwater covert missions.

The centre of nuclear submarine operations on the Kola Peninsula is Yagelnaya Bay off the Sayda Inlet. This is home to the Submarine Force Headquarters at the nearby Gadzhiyevo Naval Garrison, as well as two divisions of submarines. These include the 31st Submarine Division, which controls all the Northern Fleet's SSBNs, and the all the Akula-class attack boats are concentrated in the 24th Submarine Division.

Spread in the hills around Yagelnaya Bay is all the infrastructure needed to support SSBN operations including a missile loading dock and crane, submarine docking piers and administration facilities. A large missile and warhead storage and maintenance facility is partly buried underground near the base. This base acted as the model for the Russian facility portrayed in the 2018 Hollywood movie, Hunter Killer, with its facilities recreated in CGI.

There are other satellite nuclear submarine bases currently in operation. The 7th Submarine Division has its headquarters at Vidyaevo on the northern coast of the Kola up a long fjord. Its five Sierra- and Victor-class submarines are birthed by piers in Ara Bay, near to accommodation and administrative facilities.

Further to the west in the Litsa Fjord is the 11th Submarine Division. From its headquarters at Zaozyorsk naval garrison it controls the Bolshaya Lopatka and Nerpichya Bay naval bases. Bolshaya Lopatka is the most active of the 11th Division's bases, being home to a mix of four Victor- and Oscar II-class submarines. This division currently operates the Northern Fleet's first Yasen-class attack boat from Nerpichya Bay and further submarines of this class are expected to join it when they enter service. Nerpichya Bay, rather than Polyarny as mentioned in the movie Hunt for Red October, used to be home to the famous Typhoon-class SSBNs so it has extensive facilities, including a floating dock.

There a number of abandoned Soviet submarine bases round the Kola Peninsula but there does not seem to any sign of recent activity to reactivate them.

The Kola Mixed Force Flotilla has its headquarters at Polyarny and it controls all the minesweepers, corvettes, missile boats and other surface combatants assigned to defend the Kola region. It also has responsibility for the 161st Submarine Brigade, also based at Polyarny, which operates all the Northern Fleet's conventionally powered submarines.

The Northern Fleet Submarine Force is currently commanded by Rear Admiral Arkady Yurevich Romanov, who was appointed to his post in September 2018. His career as an officer in the Typhoon-class of SSBNs provides some insights into the focus of Northern Fleet over the coming years.

He commanded the Dmitry Donskoy during the troubled but ultimately successful test programme for the Bulava sea-based intercontinental ballistic missile. Prior to that he was head of a nuclear submarine compound, chief of the organisational-mobilisation department of the fleet headquarters and commander of the White Sea naval base at Severodvinsk. This latter job included responsibility for bringing new submarines into service and major overhauls at Severodvinsk's two nuclear submarine-building and repair yards. Romanov could be considered an expert at bringing new submarines and equipment into service. As the Northern Fleet is on the cusp of receiving several new submarines this will be an important skill set.

The Northern Fleet's submarine bases are all clearly identifiable in commercial satellite imagery and this allows assessments to be made about the operational tempo of its submarines. It has been possible to compile reasonably complete sets of satellite imagery for all these bases, which indicate which boats were alongside and which ones were undergoing maintenance in shipyards and floating docks. This is very difficult to achieve because the extreme weather over the Kola often obscures Russian submarine bases in cloud for several days at a time. The periods in question cover 29th August to 1st September 2018, 11th to 15th October 2018, 8th to 22nd July 2019, 21st June 2020 and 30th August 2020 . Those boats that could not be accounted for in the imagery were assumed to be underway on operations or training. Some can be confirmed as being out of the water in repair halls. Concurrent with the period of this imagery, the Russian Ministry of Defence made several announcements about submarine movements and Russian media also reported several naval exercises or parades involving submarines. Combining these sources it is possible to build up a picture of the Northern Fleet's recent activities.

These data sets suggests that on average between four or ten of the 34 submarines of the Northern Fleet are at sea on a daily basis. The breakdown of the data by submarine type provides some important insights.

The SSBN force appears to be usually able to sustain at least one Delta IV and Borei- class submarine at sea on deterrent patrols at a point in time but at the end of August 2018 all the Northern Fleet's SSBNs were in port, with one loading missiles. In October 2018 one of these was revealed by the Russian Ministry of Defence to have taken part in a test firing of a Bulava missile. This is likely the boat that loaded missiles at the end of August.

SSN activity averages at between one and eight boats at sea at any point in time out of a total force of 17 submarines. Every class of submarine is active over the periods that were assessed, with at least one boat of each type going to sea, except for the Oscar IIs which were not at sea in August and October 2018.

The conventional submarine force does not appear to be very active with, on one occasion, all the five boats being seen tied up alongside their home piers in Polyarny. Except for the new Lada-class boat, the St Petersburg, all the 161st Brigade's submarines are of the old Project 877 variant so it would not surprising that these boats are suffering from technical and availability issues.

It is harder to make assessments of the activity levels within the 29th Division because its floating hanger allows its mini-submarines to be hidden from view. Its two mother-ship Delta III and IV submarines both were in port during most of the monitoring periods.

A very important unit of the Northern Fleet, which controls just under 10 submarines, is the 16th Brigade of Ships under Construction and Repair. This unit is based in the Severodvinsk harbour basin and it is responsible for new submarines in the process of being accepted into service or old vessels undergoing repairs and overhaul. Imagery of the Severodvinsk basin shows that several of these submarines are in a very poor condition after being tied up there for a number of years. These include two Typhoon SSBNs in the process of being dismantled, a number of mini-subs and Akulas. New Borei- and Yasen-class submarines also operate from the basin during the acceptance trials.

The Northern Fleet's submarine force is inextricably linked to the Russian shipbuilding industry, relying on it for routine maintenance, overhaul and logistic support. These relationships are strong and date back to Soviet times but they have undergone considerable evolution over the past 20 years as many enterprises and organisations have been transferred to private ownership or into state-owned commercial entities.

The commercial relationships between the Technical Department of the Northern Fleet and these commercial entities are complex. Some facilities, such as the PD-50 floating dock within Shipyard No. 82 at Roslyakovo, to the west of Severomorsk Naval Base, remained under state ownership but were operated by commercial entities controlled by the oil and gas giant Rosneft. The United Shipbuilding Corporation subsidiary, the Zvezdochka shipyard in Severodvinsk, has the lead on the modernisation of most of the Northern Fleet submarines and then contracts other entities and shipyards, in the Kola region to actually carry out the work.

Shipyard No 10 Shkval at Oleyna Bay and Shipyard No 35 at Sevmorput continue to play an important part in repairing and overhauling older Victor-, Akula- and Sierra- class submarines. Once these submarines go out of service then the role of these yards will most likely change. Shipyard No 10 is currently working to transform the Soviet Navy's first nuclear-powered submarine, the K-3 Leninsky Komsomol, into a museum display.

The crown jewel of the Russian submarine industry is Shipyard No. 402, the Sevmashpredpriyatie Northern Mashinebuilding Enterprise at Severodvinsk, which is widely known by its nickname, Sevmash. This facility is now the sole nuclear submarine-building yard in Russia and plays a central role in generating new capabilities for the Northern Fleet. It now has an order book that runs well into the 2020s to build several new Yasen-class SSNs and Borei-class SSBNs. The yard completed the conversion of an Oscar II, the Belgorod, into a launch vessel for the new Poseidon nuclear-tipped underwater weapon during 2019 and is soon to start sea trials.

Sevmash has suffered from a shortage of skilled manpower during 2010s, which is often blamed for delays in the delivery of the first Yasen- and Borei-class submarines. Stop-start state funding for the projects on the early 2000s also contributed to the delays. This led to cost the overruns and delays that are familiar to many observers of Western defence-procurement programmes. The shipyard launched recruitment and training drives to address its shortage of staff. Resolving these problems is essential if Sevmash is to deliver all the submarines that are required by the Northern Fleet over the next decade.

The Russian government allocates funding to its navy through a process known as the State Armaments Programme, or GPV. The GPV 2020, which covered the period 2011-2017, set in train a strategic shift away from land forces to naval and air forces, with 26% of total funding going to the navy. This has since been succeeded by GPV 2027, which covers the period 2018-2027.

Although the full details have not been formally released by the Kremlin, Russian media reports and announcements of contract awards by the shipbuilding industry have provided some useful insights. GPV 2027 continued the commitment for the existing Yasen and Borei programes over the next decade, with six more Yasen-Ms set to be completed by 2023 and four more Boreis to be completed by 2021. These submarines have all been laid down and work is underway within Sevmash. There is a commitment to the building of a further two Borei-As by 2027 and four more Yasen-Ms but the completion dates have not yet been revealed. Four of the new Yasem-Ms have been allocated to the Northern Fleet and two are destined for the Pacific Fleet, while five of the new Borei SSBNs are to be assigned to the Northern Fleet and two are to go to the Pacific Fleet.

Conventional submarine production is to continue with six Improved Kilo/Project 636.3s being built for the Pacific Fleet but none are earmarked for the Northern Fleet in the public plans.

GPV2027 committed to modernising the Oscar IIs and 10 Akulas by 2020, including the fitting of Kalibr cruise missiles to both types of submarines, but there is little indication on the progress of this activity. To date there have been no announced firings of these weapons from Oscar II or Akula boats suggesting this work is behind schedule.

Interestingly, GPV 2020 committed to the development of a new version of the Kalibr missile with a range of 4,500 kilometres which would dramatically enhance its effectiveness. Work is also expected to start on a number of future submarine projects, including a successor to the Borei, a fifth-generation conventional submarine dubbed the Kalina, and, a new generation of nuclear attack submarine dubbed the Husky. None of these projects are expected to enter production until the latter half of the 2020s at the earliest due to capacity issues at the Sevmash and Admiralty yards.

GPV2027 left question marks over several projects. So far there has been no indication of any plans for the full modernising of the final Victor- and Sierra-class boats. In January 2019, Russian media reports suggested that 30 Poseidon under water weapons were going to be purchased as part of GPV 2027 and operated by two submarines each in the Pacific and Northern Fleets. Little is known about the Poseidon's capabilities or the doctrine for its use.

The implications of the GPV 2020 and 2027 for the Northern Fleet's submarine force are considerable. The build plan for Borei-class SSBNs means it is likely that all the Delta IV SSBNs will be replaced by the end of the 2020s, by which time they will have served more than 30 years in the fleet.

Plans to replace the Northern Fleet's 16 Sierra-, Victor-, Oscar- and Akula-class submarines are less clear. There are six Yasen-Ms in various stages of production out to 2023 but there is no publicly confirmed commitment when any more will enter service. The fleet's six Akulas and three Oscar IIs are scheduled to be modernised to extend them in service, possibly in the case of the Akulas out to 2050-55. There, is, however, no clarity over the fate of the last of the Sierra and Victors. This would suggest that the Yasen-Ms are replacing these boats and a new class of attack boat will come online around the 2025-2030 period to eventually replace some of the Akulas and Oscar IIs. This is only an assessment of publicly declared plans rather than a firm announcement by the Russian Navy.

Few navies have operated nuclear submarines beyond the 30-35 year mark, so without a successor attack boat programme to follow on behind the Yasen-M the Northern Fleet's frontline strength could start to reduce after 2025 as the older classes of boats reach the end of their operational lives.

The lack of commitment to provide the Northern Fleet with new conventional submarines or even to modernise its existing Kilo-class boats indicates that the 161st Submarine Brigade is likely to suffer from a decline in capability as its submarines get older and more unreliable. It appears that the Northern Fleet will have to wait until the new Kalima-class submarines enter service before it can begin replacing the old Kilos, unless an upgrade project can be funded.

Public-domain commentary on the GPV 2020 and 2027 concentrates on procurement of large platforms and little has emerged in about future plans for new mini-subs and UUS for the 29th Submarine Division. The Russian Navy has shown considerable interest in these systems. Satellite imagery shows what appears to be an unidentified UUS being loaded on Delta III and IV mother-ships at the piers in Olenya Bay.

The role of the Northern Fleet Submarine Force in Russian defence strategy and foreign policy is a mix of continuity and change. This can be determined by looking at the declared Russian policies and doctrine, exercises and training, equipment procurement plans and recent combat operations.

The Russian Ministry of Defence states that the role of its submarine forces is as follows:

"Defeating important enemy ground facilities, searching and destroying enemy submarines, aircraft carriers and other surface ships, landing units, convoys, single transports (vessels) at sea; reconnaissance, the strike force's targeting and target data transmission to it, destroying off-shore oil and gas facilities, landing special reconnaissance groups (units) on the coast of the enemy, mine laying and others."

"The submarine force is an integral part of the Navy and also operate a number of important tasks to ensure the national interests of the Russian Federation in the oceans: preservation of sovereignty in internal sea waters, territorial sea, on the bottom and in the interior, implementation of the jurisdiction and protection of sovereign rights in the exclusive economic zone for exploration, exploitation and conservation of natural resources, whether living or inanimate, located at the seabed, in the interior and the superjacent waters, protection of sovereign rights over the continental shelf of the Russian Federation for exploration and exploitation of its resources, protection of freedom of the high seas, including freedom of navigation, flights, fishing, scientific research, protection of the territories of the Russian Federation from the sea, protection and security of the State Sea Border of the Russian Federation."(8)

These are traditional missions that would be familiar to most navies. The Northern Fleet also retains the important nuclear deterrent-mission that it is a legacy its old Soviet mission. Deterring nuclear attacks on the Russian motherland is carried out by ensuring that its SSBNs can escape detection and attack by foreign navies by disappearing into the depths of the Barents Sea and Pacific Ocean or under the Arctic Ice Cap. A Royal Navy anti-submarine sonar operator told the author that in the Cold War they could detect some submerged Soviet submarines are ranges in excess of 150 nautical miles which show the importance of securing the Barents Sea "SSBN bastion". (9) This must involve not only its SSBNs but also a sizeable element of the Northern Fleet's SSN force to protect its missile-firing boats by shielding them from pursuit by hostile SSNs. In operations other than all out nuclear war, the Russian military envisage using the Northern Fleet's submarines in very distinct ways. The involvement of the Russian Navy in major exercises has revealed some interesting indications of how it envisages employing its submarine forces in a range of combat operations and geopolitical scenarios.

The Russian military has conducted three large-scale or theatre-level exercises since 2017 and all saw significant submarine and naval activity. The first, Zapad 2017, was carried out in the Western Military District and Belarus. Vostok 2018 took place in the sea zone off the Far East of Russia and on land in Siberia. The first thing of note from these exercises was that submarine forces were integrated at theatre level as part of a combined operation. In these exercises, submarine and naval forces were used to defeat opposing naval vessels and also carry out strategic missile strikes with conventionally armed weapons. A major focus of the Zapad 2017 exercise was the testing of anti-area/access denial or A2/AD concepts and tactics to deter or fight off intervention by US-led forces. The exercise scenario envisaged that Russian ground forces were invited to help a friendly nation defeat an uprising supported by hostile foreign powers. Russian air and naval forces were then deployed to deter and defeat foreign military intervention in support of the insurgents. Vostok 2018 involved a more conventional war scenario with two equal sized and equipped forces going toe-to-toe. Exercise Ocean Shield 18 took place in the eastern Mediterranean in September 2018 and saw the first large-scale practice of power-projection by the Russian Navy. In the scenario, a large force of warships and submarines, backed by long range aviation, defeated a defending foreign naval force to allow a naval infantry brigade to carry out an amphibious landing to assist a friendly ally under attack by insurgents.

Russia's intervention in Syria saw Russian submarines used as part of Moscow's military campaign to support the Damascus government defeat rebel forces across the Middle Eastern country. This involved the first ever employment of Kalibr cruise missiles fired in the land-attack role from Improved Kilo-class submarines. These strikes were carried out in co-ordination with air launched cruise missiles and tactical air strikes. Targets were identified by satellite surveillance, signals intelligence and special forces operatives on the ground. In a major innovation for the Russian military, targets were also identified by Forpost unmanned aerial vehicles and these drones then were used to monitor the Kalibr strikes in real-time, with the video imagery being used for bomb-damage assessment. This imagery was also released by the Russian Ministry of Defence as part of its information-operations campaign aimed at undermining support for the rebels. These strikes required considerable co-ordination at a tactical/ operational level in Syria and at a strategic level, involving the National Defence Command Centre, in Moscow.

As far as the Northern Fleet is concerned its equipment programme is clearly aimed at giving it extensive A2/AD capabilities. Its submarine force, is the forefront of these efforts, including the fielding of new attack submarines equipped to fire Kalibr cruise missiles and the retrofitting of these weapons into older Oscar II and Akula submarines.

The Northern Fleet is also receiving surface vessels equipped with Kalibr missiles and during the latter half of 2018 a series of exercises were carried out involving live firings of the missiles from frigates and submarines. In 2018 it established its own Forpost drone regiment on the Kola Peninsula to give the Northern Fleet real-time remote surveillance capabilities for the first time.

Currently, the Northern Fleet only boasts a handful of submarines and warships equipped with Kalibr missiles but this is planned to expand dramatically after 2020.

From the perspective of senior Kremlin political leaders, the development of the Northern Fleet's A2/AD capabilities has many attractions. These capabilities, particularly its submarines and drones, have the potential to be used in expeditionary scenarios similar to the April 2018 scenario in Syria. They also offer the potential in a major crisis or conflict to establish an A2/AD umbrella around the Kola Peninsula, the Arctic region, the Baltic Sea and large areas of Scandinavia and the United Kingdom.

By fielding usable and credible capabilities, the Russian armed forces are offering their political masters options. Not surprisingly, the Kremlin appears to be backing continued investment in Northern Fleet submarine forces and its future development.

The projected expansion of the Northern Fleet's A2/AD capabilities has prompted the US and NATO governments consider investing in forces that could counter them. The US, UK and Norway are procuring additional maritime patrol aircraft and enhancing their own submarine forces. These new anti-submarine warfare (ASW) forces are directly aimed at enabling better surveillance of Russian submarine activity. They are intended to make it more difficult for Russian submarines to launch surprise cruise missile attacks on land targets or attack allied warships, submarines and merchant shipping.

In themselves, additional Western ASW capabilities are not enough to prevent the establishment of a Russian A2/AD umbrella over Northern Europe. Integrated airborne surveillance, air defence, air supremacy and land-attack capabilities would be needed to form a coherent campaign to deter and defeat the Northern Fleet submarines and their supporting forces in the unlikely event of conflict or a major crisis in Europe.

In situations, short of all-out war the Northern Fleet's Submarine Forces potentially pose several challenges for Western countries. The intelligence-gathering potential of Russian submarines, supported by underwater drones, operating in the North Atlantic and Arctic regions is immense, putting at risk key communications and economic infrastructure such as oil and gas production facilities. Nuclear submarines are a key component in Russian operations under the Arctic ice pack giving Moscow the ability to create "facts on the ground" (or the ice) and frustrate Western moves in this strategic region. The 1960 Hollywood movie Ice Station Zebra correctly predicted that nuclear submarines were the most reliable and effective way to move troops and equipment under the Arctic Ice Cap because of the region's extreme climate.

Nuclear submarines, because of their range and endurance, are some of the most globally deployable Russian naval assets. They give the Kremlin the potential to establish A2/AD umbrellas around the world similar to the one set up in Syria to cover the Eastern Mediterranean. When nuclear submarines are combined with land-based air defence, tactical ballistic and anti-ship missiles delivered by Russian Aerospace Force transport aircraft, this gives Russia the potential to rapidly create fait accompli A2AD umbrellas in new operational theatres.

President Putin is determined to restore Russia's great-power status and ensure that the West cannot act with impunity to undermine Moscow's interests. The continued investment in the Northern Fleet is a sign that Moscow is determined to build up forces that give it the ability to change the rules of the game.

While some Western countries have launched efforts to build up their ASW forces to counter the Northern Fleet's submarines, these in themselves do not mean that the political calculations of Western governments in a crisis involving an area covered by a future Russian A2/AD umbrella in Northern Europe or elsewhere will turn out different from those during the April 2018 East Ghouta crisis.

The prospect of Russian submarines firing cruise missiles at targets across Western Europe and sinking even a few Western warships is likely to make NATO political leaders very cautious about risking an open conflict with Moscow over issues that don't impact on the obvious territorial integrity of alliance members or really obvious issues of national importance. Even if Western ASW forces are built up to such a scale that they can overmatch the Russian Northern Fleet's submarines, there must be doubt that a clean sweep operation to sink all Russia's nuclear boats in one go could be realistically carried out. As the US, UK and other NATO nations are not yet contemplating a return to Cold War levels of expenditure on submarines and ASW forces it would appear the current force ratios between Russia and NATO will not dramatically shift. So even without firing shot, the Northern Fleet's submarines have had a political effect. For this reason Moscow is likely to continue to invest in sustaining this force.

While the ambitions of the Northern Fleet to expand its submarine forces are causing concern in Western capitals, the reality of Russian submarine availability and reliability is its Achilles' heel. Out of its fleet of around 40 submarines at any point in time around eight boats are undergoing repairs or overhaul.

The building of new submarines and overhaul of in-service submarines is also plagued by delays and technical problems, preventing the replacement of older boats.

From the evidence of satellite imagery, the operational Northern Fleet submarines also do not appear to be very active, with an average of between four and eleven SSN and SSBN at sea at any point in time. Crucially, the Northern Fleet does not appear to have been able to maintain continuous-at-sea deterrent patrols by its missile armed SSBNs, with all its Delta IV- and Borei-class submarines being spotted in port on at least one occasion. Only between four or eight of the 17 nuclear attack boats appear to be regularly at sea and the vintage Kilo conventional submarines do not put to sea very often.

The two mother-ship submarines of the 29th Division also do not make regular forays into the North Atlantic to launch mini-submarines. Since the Losharik was struck by a serious fire in July 2019 it has been out of action and for most of 2020 was in dock in Severodvinsk basin undergoing repairs, according to satellite imagery of the site. This indicates that the Russia's mini-submarine fleet is not as active as some Western military figures suggest.

Pulling together all the open-source information about Northern Fleet submarine operations suggests that Western media reports of flotillas of up to 10 Russian submarines making forays into the North Atlantic are not credible. Such a surge operation would require almost every active SSN in the Northern Fleet to be up and running at the same time, which seems beyond its current technical capacity. Interestingly, senior Western politicians and military figures never put actual numbers of Russian submarine deployments into the public domain suggesting they are not confident to put their evidence under scrutiny. Many Western naval officers also make claims that Moscow's submarines appear to be quieter and more effective, which is a credible position, but the current underwater duels between Russian and Western submarines appear to only involve a handful of vessels on either side. The days of the Cold War, when the Northern Fleet could field 176 submarines, including 68 attack boats, and threaten to overwhelm NATO navies in the North Atlantic are very much in the past. (10)

Chapter 21
Russia's Airpower

High over the North Atlantic the silver-painted Russian bomber was easy to spot against the blue sky. The two British Eurofighter Typhoon jets pulled up alongside the Tupolev Tu-95, famously known as the Bear by NATO during the Cold War, and their pilots started to photograph the Russian plane. The three aircraft remained in formation for a good half hour before the British planes turned for home. The Russian crew continued heading south west out over the Atlantic until they too eventually turned around and headed back to their base.

These incidents now follow a ritual. A few hours after each aerial incident the Ministry of Defence in London issues a press release announcing yet another successful intercept of Russian aircraft in the UK flight information region or FIR, which is managed by the UK civilian air traffic control organisation. In turn, the Fleet Street media would regularly report this as Russian planes being prevented from entered British air space by RAF fighters. British government ministers would then complained about a rising number of "incursions" Russian bombers or spy planes.

During a visit to RAF Lossiemouth in Scotland in 2016 to talk to the Royal Air Force Typhoon quick reaction alert (QRA) pilots it became very obvious that these intercept incidents are far less dramatic that many media reports and politicians would like them to be. The UK FIR covers 700,000 square miles over the north-east Atlantic, stretching from hundreds of miles north of Shetland down to the Bay of Biscay. This is not UK sovereign airspace which mirrors territorial waters and only reaches 12 miles out from the British coastline.

The Russian aircraft usually head out from bases on the Kola Peninsula and then hooked around the top of Norway, where Norwegian fighters would escort them southwards. Alerted by their Norwegian allies, RAF jets were able to launch with plenty of notice as the Russian aircraft passed into the UK FIR. The RAF pilots and their commanders said their main job was to achieve visual identification of the Russian aircraft because they do not use transponders to broadcast identification information. "We want to make sure they don't stray into the trans-Atlantic air routes and put civilian airliners at risk," said one of the pilots. According to senior RAF officers, at no point had the Russian aircraft actually entered UK sovereign airspace over the past decade, and they nearly always stay hundreds of miles from the UK coastline.

Russian Long Range Aviation (LRA) flights over the North Atlantic, Baltic Sea, Northern Pacific, and Sea of Japan are regularly cited by Western politicians and senior military commanders as a sign of "Russian aggressive intent". But why are the Russians sending their aircraft out on these missions and what do they say about the state of Russian airpower in the second decade of the 21st Century?

The long-range missions are intended, firstly, to boost the navigation skills of LRA aircrew and, secondly, they provide political messaging to internal and foreign audiences. They were a regular feature of old Soviet bomber operations but Western observers often confused missions by Naval Aviation Tupolev Tu-22M3 and Tu-142s with LRA bomber activity. The two organisations had very different reasons for carrying out long-range missions close to NATO territory or Western naval forces. Naval Aviation flights were often co-ordinated with Soviet naval forces and the Soviet LRA was practicing its long-range nuclear strike role. All these missions ceased in 1991 with the end of the Cold War but the Russian government announced their resumption in 2007.

Although this new wave of flights has garnered considerable media attention in the West, the number of incidents has been modest and it is difficult to identify a trend of growing Russian activity. UK Ministry of Defence data shows the RAF launched its quick reaction alert fighters to intercept Russian aircraft in the UK FIR on seven days in 2010, 11 in 2011, nine in 2012, eight each in 2013 and 2014, eight in 2015, five times in 2016, three times in 2017, seven times in 2018, eight times in 2019 and on five occasions in the first seven months of 2020. (1)

On all the occasions that Russian aircraft were intercepted over the North Atlantic they went off without incident, unlike in the Black Sea and Mediterranean where there have been a number of "close encounters". These incidents involve Russian aircraft making high-speed passes in close proximity to US ships and aircraft, resulting in the Pentagon accusing Moscow's pilots of "unprofessional" behaviour. A typical incident occurred in August 2020 when a Russian fighter flew within 100 feet of the nose of a US Air Force Boeing B-52H Stratofortress bomber flying over the Black Sea. The motivation of these close encounters seems to be timed to coincide with a need for the Russian government to high light Western incursions and threats to their borders and airspace. The August 2020 encounter over the Black Sea, for example, occurred at the height of a crisis involving Belarus.

The two sides in this new Cold War appear to be providing mirror images of their rationales for the intercepts. While providing the opportunity for Russian pilots to prove skills in front of their Western counterparts, the close encounters and more benign intercepts have little read-across into future large-scale aerial combat operations in time of war beyond providing some real-world training and experience to air defence command post staffs. The RAF fighter pilots who fly the QRA missions say they in no way replicate the interception of an enemy aircraft in time of war. Russian bombers are not expected to fly straight and level at high altitude, in broad daylight during a real attack on the UK.

To understand modern Russian airpower it is necessary to draw upon a range of sources to first build up a accurate picture of the order of battle of the Russian Aerospace Force, or RuAF, inventory of aircraft, their deployment and capabilities. If the intercepts are the public face of modern Russian air power, what is the reality behind the mask?

The RuAF's airfields are relatively easily monitored using commercial satellite imagery that allows individual aircraft to be identified and counted. By an accident of history few Russian airbases have large hangars or individual hardened aircraft shelters to hide their aircraft in. The RuAF now operates from airbases that were well inside the old Soviet Union so were not on the frontline during the Cold War. As a result they were not provided with hardened shelters back in the 1970s and 1980s and the RuAF has since then not started to build new ones. As a result the vast majority of RuAF fighter jets are parked out in the open come rain or shine, so can be easily counted in satellite images. These numbers are very similar to the publicly announced figures for aircraft delivered by Russian aircraft industry to the RuAF over the past two decades.

One-metre resolution satellite images allow specific models of aircraft to be identified, as well as paint schemes and in some cases serial numbers. Many of these bases are also routinely visited by the Russian and international media to cover high-profile events involving senior Russian and political leaders. This means there is a large amount of still and video imagery in the public domain to aid to understanding of the status of RuAF units and their equipment. Many Russian airbases can also be examined in some detail on Google's Street View application. An added level of understanding can be gained from open-source tracking of Russian aircraft's ADS-B transponders, which allow individual RuAF aircraft to be tracked as they fly around the world.

The 21st Century RuAF is a very different organisation from its Soviet predecessor, which was structured and equipped to fight a high-tempo offensive against NATO forces across the length and breadth of Europe and the Middle East, possibly involving the widespread use of chemical and nuclear weapons. As with its naval and ground force counterparts the RuAF is a shadow of the old Soviet force.

Today's RuAF is configured to fight local wars on Russia's borders rather than stage global offensives but some of its elements have strategic roles. The LRA still has the mission to deliver strategic nuclear strikes with long range cruise missiles but it has also been adapted to carry out conventional strikes in support of ground forces, in co-ordination with unmanned aerial vehicles. Russia's airlift force is also controlled centrally for strategic effect.

The RuAF is also responsible for the Space Force, which controls Russia's reconnaissance and communications satellite constellations, and the Missile Defence Force, which oversees the country's network of early warning radars and the strategic missile defence system positioned around Moscow. The Space and Missile Defence Forces are huge organisations with some 150,000 and 135,000 personnel each, respectively. (2) A high percentage of these are conscripts who stand guard for months on end at remote radar sites, air defence batteries and nuclear missile silos. The military aviation branch which controls RuAF conventional aircraft and air defence units in border regions, has some 145,000 personnel. All its aircrew and technical personnel are professional officers or contract soldiers, with conscripts restricted to non-technical jobs guarding airbases, driving fuel tankers or cooking meals. In these highly technical armed services, conscripts are little more than a source of cheap labour.

Russia's conventional airpower is controlled by five air and air defence armies, which correspond to each tri-service military district or joint strategic command. The heads of these air armies are in effect the air component commanders for their respective districts. Since 2015 these air armies have also incorporated Naval Aviation units to ensure unity of command of all Russian air power in key strategic zones, such as Kaliningrad, Crimea and the Arctic. These air armies have a combined strength of some 800 tactical jets and 650 combat helicopters but individually the strongest air army, which covers the Southern Military District, boasts some 300 jets and 250 helicopters. The smallest one, based in the Urals and western Siberia, only has around 100 jets and 60 helicopters.

Each of these air armies bring together fighter regiments with Sukhoi Su-27, Su-30SM, Su-35 and Mikoyan MiG-31 aircraft. Except for the MiG-31, these are all variants of the iconic two-engine super manoeuvrable Sukhoi fighters which are known in the West as the Flanker. These jets made a big splash at the Farnborough and Paris airshows with their dramatic flying displays - and on a couple of occasions crashes - during the 1990s. Although the legacy Flanker variants entered service during the Cold War the versions in service today were all built over the past 15 years. The MiG-31 is a Cold War veteran but it also has been upgraded with a powerful new radar to support long range engagements with beyond-visual-range missiles.

These fighter regiments each have between 30 and 40 jets and are assigned a specific geographical zone to patrol and protect in co-ordination with ground based S-300 or S-400 long-range surface-to-air missile batteries. These in turn work close with the navy's coastal defence missile batteries to form key components of anti access, area denial (A2/AD) "umbrellas" or "anti missile domes".

Offensive action is the responsibility of bomber regiments equipped with the Su-24 and the Su-34. The 1970s and 1980s vintage swing-wing Su-24s have been upgraded with new electronics to improve the accuracy of their bombing. They are being progressively replaced by the Su-34, which is a dedicated strike variant of the Flanker family, and are able to employ precision-strike munitions, but the Su-24 is still in the majority. One Cold War platform that still has a central place in the RuAF is the Su-25 Rook. Its role is to support ground troops with close air support, to attack enemy troops in frontline positions. The remaining Su-25s have all been upgraded with new electronics to enhance the accuracy of their weapons.

Support for the land forces is the primary job of RuAF army aviation brigades and helicopter regiments, and over the past decade they have all be re-equipped with new machines. The 1970s and 1980s vintage Mil Mi-24s gunships and Mil Mi-87/17 transport helicopters have all been replaced with new-build variants, new Mil Mi-28N gunship and the new Kamov Ka-52 Alligator. Each Russian military district now has at least one army aviation brigade, which usually has squadrons of each of these helicopters as well as half a dozen Mi-26 heavy lift helicopters, and one or two helicopter regiments, which have a combination of Mi-8s and one type of gunship.

North west part of European Russia, including the capital Moscow, falls under the control of the Western Military District and its aviation units are controlled by the 6th Air and Air Defence Army from its headquarters in St Petersburg.

Two major fighter regiments – the 159th Fighter Aviation Regiment and the 790th Fighter Aviation Regiment – are based near St Petersburg flying a mix of Su-27s, Su-35Ss and MiG-31BMs. These units' aircraft are routinely intercepted by NATO aircraft over the Baltic Sea. A regiment of Su-24 reconnaissance variants is based to the south of the city and a regiment of Su-30SMs is based in the south of the district near Voronezh, close to the Ukraine's eastern border. Its Su-24 regiment is in the process of receiving replacement Su-34s.

Two army aviation units with attack helicopters are positioned around St Petersburg and a further two army aviation units are based further south near the Estonian border: the 15th Army Aviation Brigade, near Latvia, and the 440th Separate Helicopter Regiment, near Belarus. These units still operate Mi-35M attack helicopters and each one has been augmented by at least one squadron of newly delivered Ka-52 or Mi-28N attack helicopters. The 15th Army Aviation Brigade operates all three types: one squadron of Ka-52s; one of Mi-28Ns/Mi-35Ms; and one detachment of heavy lift Mi-26 helicopters. According to satellite imagery assessment, almost 40% of the missile batteries of the air army's air defence division in north western Russia are now equipped with the S-400 surface-to-air missile system.

The Southern Military District's 4th Air and Air Defence Army has a different mix of aircraft and units because of the very distinct characteristics of its operating environment. Each of its main combat units has received new or upgraded aircraft and helicopters over the past 15 years. New Sukhoi Su-30SM and Su-35 fighters have been delivered and upgraded Su-27SM3 have been fielded in the 4th Army's air-superiority units. A full regiment of 40 Sukhoi Su-34 strike aircraft has been fielded to support its other Su-24 regiment, giving the 4th Army a significant precision-attack capability.

The 4th Army is unique because it has two regiments of Su-25s to support the district's ground forces. A significant transformation programme has been rolled out across the 4th Army's helicopter force with new Mil Mi-28, Mi-35M and Kamov Ka-52 attack helicopters replacing the old Mi-24P airframes. Older variants of the workhorse Mi-8/17 have also been replaced with new machines. One of the 4th Army's helicopter regiments was also expanded into a full army aviation brigade in 2015. The surveillance capability of the 4th Army was enhanced in 2019 by the establishment of a Forpost tactical UAV system at Mozdok airbase in North Ossetia.

The occupation of Crimea in 2014 prompted the establishment of two new RuAF regiments on the peninsula, one with Su-27 fighters and the other with a mix of Su-24s and Su-25s for attack duties. An RuAF helicopter regiment has been set up in Crimea with Mi-28N, Mi-8 and Ka-52 helicopters. The Naval Aviation assault regiment in Crimea has also been augmented by a dozen Su-30SM fighters and Russian Navy pilots have been involved in some of the most notable close encounters with US ships and planes over the Black Sea.

The Central Military District, based in the Urals and the west of Siberia, has fewer day-to-day operational tasks so its 14th Air and Air Defence Army is the smallest of the five air armies. It has two fighter regiments with MiG-31BMs and a regiment with a mix of Su-24s and new Su-34s. To support army units, the 14th Army has an aviation brigade with Mi-24s, Mi-8s and Mi-26s and a helicopter regiment with Mi-24s and Mi-8s. These are some of the last units to operate the vintage Mi-24P variant. Smaller aviation groups, with Su-25s and helicopters, are deployed to support the Russian military contingents in central Asian republics of Kyrgyzstan and Tajikistan.

Russia's Far East Military District is supported by the 11th Air and Air Defence Army and has three regiments of fighters with a mix of MiG-31s, Su-35Ss and Su-30SMs. It has a regiment each of Su-24 and Su-34 strike aircraft, as well as a regiment of Su-25s for ground attack. The air army has one aviation brigade with Ka-52s, Mi-8s and Mi-26s, as well as two helicopter regiments with Ka-52s, Mi-24Ps and Mi-8s.

The 45th Air and Air Defence Army supported the Northern Fleet Joint Strategic Command but all its fixed-wing aircraft and helicopters are provided by the fleet's Naval Aviation branch. It air defence missile units are provided by the RuAF. A similar joint air command operates in the Kaliningrad enclave, mixing RuAF and Naval Aviation jets, helicopters, air defence missiles, unmanned aerial vehicles and anti-ship missiles.

Russia's strategic air power is delivered by the RuAF's Long Range Aviation branch, via its force of 150 heavy bombers and 20 air-refuelling tankers. The modern LRA is a shadow of the Soviet bomber force - both navy and air force - that boasted more that 500 aircraft in the 1980s.

The LRA is now grouped in two operational divisions, one in European Russia and one in the Far East, administered from the LRA's headquarters in Moscow. Operational missions - both nuclear and conventional - are controlled directly from the Russian National Defence Command Centre in Moscow. This hi-tech command post was opened in December 2014 to direct all active Russian military operations. President Vladimir Putin has been filmed by Russian media practicing weapon-release authorisation procedures from this command centre during annual exercises by Russian strategic nuclear forces, including overseeing the test firing of ballistic missiles from submarines and air-launched cruise missiles from LRA bombers.

Open-source analysis of Russian media indicates that day-to-day administrative control of the LRA is devolved to two divisions, the 22nd Guards Donbass Heavy Bomber Division at Engels airbase near Saratov and the 326th Guards Sevastopol-Berlin Heavy Bomber Division at Ukrainka-Seryshevo airbase in the Amur region. The two divisions are not balanced forces, with the bulk of the LRA aircraft based at the 22nd Division's three main operating bases. Engels airbase is the main base for the Tupolev Tu-160 White Swan, or Blackjack as they were known to NATO, supersonic jet bombers, as well as a contingent of Tupolev Tu-95. The division's other two main bases operate Tupolev Tu-22M3s, which code-named Backfires by NATO. In the Far East, Ukrainka is the main Tu-95 base and the 326th Division's Tu-22M3s are based at Beleya airbase, in the Irkutsk region.

The LRA is responsible for its own training and logistic infrastructure, which is spread across several sites in European Russia. Aircrew training on large multi-engine aircraft is carried out at initially at Tambov and then type-conversion is undertaken at Ryazan. This later base is also home to the Il-78 fleet, which can also be tasked to support tactical aviation units. The small size of the RuAF aerial refuelling force significantly limits its power-projection capabilities.

Both the Tu-160 and Tu-95 are modified to employ nuclear and conventionally armed air launched cruise missiles (ALCM), with the main in-service conventional weapons being the MKB Raduga Kh-55 and its stealthy variant, the Kh-101.

From analysis of satellite imagery it is possible to build up a picture of how the LRA's inventory has evolved since Russia made its last declaration of nuclear configured bombers in the 2009 START treaty extension process, when it declared 16 active Tu-160s and 55 Tu-55s. The Tu-22M3s were not included because they lacked ALCM capability and air-to-air refuelling to give them an inter-continental range.

Although satellite imagery can only ever be a snap shot because aircraft might be airborne or deployed away from their home base during satellite passes overhead, it is, however, possible to use imagery taken over a number of years to spot trends in deployment and average-out numbers of air frames. It is also important to assess where aircraft are positioned on airbases to gain an understanding of whether they are in active use on flight ramps or parked up in storage. On several bases these storage ramps are very obvious, showing dozens of bombers crammed together in various states of repair.

Imagery analysis suggests that between 2014 and 2019 the LRA tried to keep around 10 Tu-160s in day-to-day use. The Tu-95 fleet has declined somewhat from the 2009 START declaration and the LRA keeps around 40 aircraft in active service. The most numerous LRA bomber is the Tu-22M3 with 59 remaining in use. More than 40 surplus Tu-22M3 airframes remain on LRA airfields. The tanker fleet has remained stable at some 18 Il-78s.

One striking feature of LRA bases is their lack of large maintenance hangars. This means that the LRA is heavily dependent on the Russian aerospace industry to provide major non-flight-line repair, maintenance and overhaul of its bombers. LRA aircraft can be observed at the main aviation plants involved in support activity. Tu-160s and Tu-22Ms are supported at the Kazan Aircraft Production Association (KAPO) in Tatarstan, where many of the aircraft were originally built in the Soviet era.

The Tu-95 fleet is supported by the Beriev Aviation Scientific Technical Complex in Taganrog and at the JSC Aviakor Aviation Plant (formerly Kuibyshev Aviation Plant No 18) in Samara. The later plant was where the first Tu-95s were built and the Taganrog site was home to production of the Tu-142 maritime patrol variant of the Tu-95 bomber.

Still images from inside these facilities, and overhead satellite imagery, allow assessments to be made of the throughput of airframes in the assembly halls. Between 2014 and 2019 a steady flow of airframes into and out of these sites was observed in overhead imagery, confirming local media reports of new contracts to repair and upgrade the LRA's aircraft.

A key player in the LRA industrial support network is the Raduga company, which designs and manufactures its Kh-55 and Kh-101 cruise missiles. However, there is little open-source imagery or information available about the manufacture and industrial support for long-range cruise missile development.

The home bases of the LRA do not appear to have benefited from major investment in infrastructure since 2015, other than the renewal of the aircraft ramp at Engels airbase and a single new hangar being built at Ryazan.

As well as its home or main operating bases, the LRA makes extensive use of forward operating locations (FOLs) close to Russia's borders and northern coast during exercises and operations, particularly for missions by its Tu-22M3s which lack air-to-air refuelling capability. Bombers are surged to FOLs for short periods, supported by a couple of transport aircraft carrying ground personnel and logistic equipment. They then return to their home base after the exercises. The FOL network was originally established during the Cold War but it fell into disuse during the 1990s. Since 2010 a number of the FOLs along Russia's northern coast have been reactivated for crew training as well as strategic positioning for the Arctic.

Mozdok airbase in North Ossetia has received major investment to enhance its ability to support LRA and other RuAF operations in the Middle East. It was home to detachments of between eight and 12 Tu-22M3s during the Syria conflict between 2015 and 2017. During this period satellite imagery showed that a new runway was built at the airfield and extensive renovations took place on other infrastructure around the base.

The strategic reach and diplomatic impact of Russian heavy bombers has obvious attractions for President Putin. The LRA is a neat fit into this agenda and it has benefited from sustained, if modest, investment in upgrades to its aircraft, infrastructure, precision-guided weapons and training since 2015. Scores of Tu-95s and Tu-22M3s are to receive upgrades and overhauls by 2030 and 12 brand new Tu-160M2s are to be built. If these plans are seen through then by 2030 they will see Tu-95 numbers remain broadly the same. The Tu-22M3 fleet could shrink, but the Tu-160 force will nearly double in size. Russia has long toyed with the idea of building a brand new futuristic bomber, dubbed the PAK-DA or the Prospective Aviation Complex for Long-Range Aviation but this project keeps being delayed on cost grounds so is unlikely to enter service before 2030 at the earliest. In the mean time, the legacy LRA fleets will have to soldier on.

The RuAF's other strategic force is its Military Transport Aviation branch, which plays a key role in sustaining the country's armed forces and projecting power around the world. This is built around 100 or so Ilyushin Il-76 medium transport/multirole airlifters and a dozen giant Antonov An-124 strategic transports.

The Il-76s are operated by transport regiments based at Migalovo, Pskov, Seshcha, Orenburg, Taganrog and Ussuriysk, close to the main garrisons of the Airborne Forces divisions. These units regularly practice dropping battalions of paratroopers and their equipment during strategic power projection exercises. These are impressive events that attract a lot of media attention, particularly when they involve the simultaneous dropping of dozens of BMD armoured vehicles. With only around 100 aircraft in its inventory it is debatable that the RuAF would ever be able to muster the 50-plus aircraft required to deliver a full airborne regiment and all its vehicles and equipment during a single drop.

The An-124s are operated out of Seshcha and Ussuriysk and are also hired out to commercial operators when not needed by the RuAF.

Both the Il-76s and An-124s played prominent roles in the deployment to Syria in 2015, moving cargo and personnel to establish and sustain the Russian air group in the Middle Eastern country. The An-124 units were called into action to move field bridges to help the Syrian army cross the Euphrates in 2017 and then took additional S-300 missile launchers to the country in 2018.

The Russian military's UAV fleet has seen a dramatic expansion over the past decade. In the first decade of the 21st Century, the Russian armed forces only operated a handful of Soviet-era systems that were generally based on the designs used for aerial targets. These were notoriously unreliable and lacked modern digital data-links to download imagery in real-time. As a result of the poor performance of the Russian military in the 2008 Georgia conflict, the Moscow government ordered a major effort to field a new generation of UAVs.

The most high-profile result of this drive was an agreement with Israel to allow the local assembly of the Searcher 2 tactical UAV. The first couple examples were provided direct from Israel Aerospace Industries (IAI), along with several mini-UAVs, for test and evaluation by Russian experts. The Ural Civil Aviation Plant (known as UZGA) in Ekaterinburg was then contracted to assemble around 30 air vehicles for use by the Russian armed forces.

The locally produced Searcher 2, which is designated the Forpost, took the skies in Russia in 2012. The Forposts are sometimes referred to as the Outposts in Russian reports, which is a reference to border guard post in frontier regions. UZGA has subsequently embarked on the manufacturing of a version known Forpost M or R, which is made from Russian-sourced components and will be fitted with optical and radar sensors as well as precision-guided munitions. A production contract for 30 air vehicles and 10 ground-control stations was signed in late 2019, according to Russian media reports, with deliveries starting in late 2020 or early 2021. The intention is to eventually buy a total of 84 of the upgraded air vehicles and 28 improved ground stations.

In 2011 the Russian Ministry of Defence launched several development contracts with local companies to field domestic UAVs. The results have been mixed. The St Petersburg-based Special Technology Centre has had considerable success with its Orlan 10, which has become the de-facto standard mini-UAV of the Russian military. Several types of mini-UAVs have been fielded by the Russian military over the past decade but many of the older systems have fallen out of favour after the Orlan-10 proved itself the most reliable and easy to use.

At the higher end of the spectrum, the Krondstadt Group was contracted to develop the Orion medium-altitude long-endurance (MALE) armed UAV and the Simonov Design Bureau began working on a high-altitude long-endurance (HALE) Altair UAV as part of the Altius programme. Russia's leading military aircraft manufacturer, the Sukhoi Design Bureau, is working on an unmanned combat aerial vehicle (UCAV) with low-observable or stealth features, known as the Sukhoi S-70 Okhotnik or Hunter. At the Army 2020 exhibit in August 2020 the Krondstadt Group showed off a full size mock up of a rival UCAV product, dubbed the Grom or Thunder, which appeared to be a rival to the Okhotnik. Russia has big ambitions to field domestically produced MALE, HALE and UCAV systems but progress appears to be slow with none of these systems entering serial production yet.

Russia's UAV capability is considerable but is very much focused on the tactical level, providing support to frontline ground units via mini-UAV systems. These have proliferated across the Russian Ground, Airborne and Coastal Forces to provide tactical intelligence to ground commanders, as well as targeting support to tube artillery and rocket units. Russian artillery and rocket units devastated Ukrainian forces on several occasions between July 2014 and February 2015. UAVs played an important role in these engagements, with Russian forces displaying considerable expertise in using their UAVs to identify targets and adjusting artillery and rocket fire onto them for maximum effect. In a number of cases, whole Ukrainian battalions were devastated in these engagements.

The bigger Forpost UAV has been used extensively in the Donbass region and Syria for a wide variety of tasks, including supporting operational-strategic level air and air launched cruise missile strikes. Forpost operations in Syria showed a level of sophistication above that displayed in the Donbass conflict with the UAVs operating across the length and breadth of the Middle Eastern country to identify targets for strikes by strategic weapon systems, operating from bases in Russia or being fired from warships off the Syrian coast. This created, in effect, a kill chain to conduct precision-guided strikes. Only a handful of nations have demonstrated they have this capability, including the USA, Israel and the UK.

Subsequently training exercises have taken place involving Forpost units of the Baltic and Northern Fleet that have seen complex scenarios combining naval gun fire support, air-ground operations and sea-launched Kalibr cruise missile strikes.

Overall, Russia's UAV capability is not as advanced as its US or Israeli counterparts. The Russian military, however, has shown itself able to rapidly absorb new UAV systems and generate useful battlefield capabilities. This experience has given Moscow's armed forces the ability to act as an "intelligent customer" and understand how to effectively contract new systems. The standing up of new UAV test and evaluation facilities is an interesting sign that the Russian military and defence industry is keen to develop a deeper understanding of how unmanned systems work and how to transform them into effective battlefield capabilities.

Does Russia's airpower give Moscow a war-winning advantage against any of its near neighbours or the European members of NATO? The Russian operation in Syria has given Russian airmen priceless experience in modern air combat in a complex and confusing operational environment but this has not translated into a wholesale transformation of the RuAF into an air arm focused on expeditionary or theatre-wide offensive operations.

Out of Russia's five air armies only one, the 4th Army in southern Russia, has numerical supremacy over its near neighbours. The 45th Army on the Kola peninsula and Arctic region faces strong Norwegian and Finnish forces, while in the Baltic region, the 6th Army, has less than 200 jets to challenge Swedish, Polish, German and Danish air forces which have some 300 fighters, according data published by their respective ministries of defence. If the Russian Naval Aviation contingent in Kaliningrad is factored in, with its 50 or so jets, this would be more than balanced by the regular deployment of British, American and other NATO jets to the Baltic States and Poland.

The 4th Army, with its 300 tactical jets and 250 combat helicopters, dwarfs the air forces of Ukraine and Georgia so could be expected to achieve air supremacy over their small air arms.

Reinforcements to the air units in western Russia could come from the 14th Army in the Urals and western Siberia but its 90-odd combat aircraft and 50 helicopters do not constitute an overwhelming reserve of air power. Most of its units have older variants of aircraft. Out in the Far East, the 11th Air Army has a strong defensive force but even with the presence of LRA aircraft it would be no match for the Japanese, US and South Korean air forces in an open war.

A major inhibiting factor in the projection of Russian airpower beyond its immediate neighbours is the small size of the RuAF's air-to-air refuelling tanker force. It has less than 20 Il-78 tankers in service so there is limited prospect of them supporting a sustained air campaign by tactical fighters far from their home bases, similar to those conducted by US-led air forces over the Balkans in the 1990s or Iraq and Afghanistan in the 21st Century. With most Russian tactical jets having operational ranges of less than 1000 kilometres, this limits their ability to operate far from Russia's borders in significant numbers. This means the availability of secure bases is a major limiting factor in Russian air operations and would prevent Moscow's tactical jets ranging over central and western Europe in time of war.

The LRA offers Russian leaders the prospect of launching precision missile strikes against strategic targets across Europe but with the 50 Tu-95s and Tu-160s available retaining their nuclear strike roles, it would seem that only a small fraction of these bombers could be employed in conventional strike roles. It is also unclear how many air-launched cruise missiles with conventional warheads are available. Even at the height of the Syrian campaign, LRA bombers seldom launched more than a couple of missiles at a time.

When placed in a defensive context, Russian airpower has to be looked at in a different way. The effectiveness of Russia's anti A2/AD umbrellas is transformed by the concentration of some of the RuAF's best combat aircraft on the Kola Peninsula, in Kaliningrad and Crimea. This is intended to create a deterrent effect and make Western powers cautious about intervening in what Russia perceives as its spheres of influence in the Black Sea, Crimea, Caucasus and Kaliningrad. When the RuAF's fighters are combined with advanced anti-aircraft missiles, anti-ship missiles and unmanned aerial vehicles, the Russian military aims in time of war or crisis to keep the Western armed forces at arm's length from the country's strategic regions. In the Black Sea regions, this means that Russian air and missile forces could potentially isolate Ukraine and Georgia from outside assistance in times of crisis. By creating "red lines" in the sky with its air power Moscow would be daring the US and NATO to contemplate all-out war with Russia if they tried to penetrate the A2/AD umbrella to provide military assistance to Kiev and Tbilisi during a major crisis. The deterrent effect of this type of operation would be considerably enhanced by the use of 1,500-kilometre- range air launched and ship-launched cruise missiles to threaten NATO air units and naval forces in the Black Sea region, forcing them to withdraw to safer zones in Greek, Italian, Turkish airspace or the waters of the Mediterranean.

For President Putin, who has invested considerable sums in modernising Russian airpower over the past two decades, the deterrent effect of its anti missile domes is what he was after. Airpower is a vital ingredient in ensuring that Russia can stop foreign powers interfering in its backyard.

Chapter 22
Russia's Defence Industrial Complex

A visit by Russia's President to a major defence factory follows a very ritualistic process. Vladimir Putin arrives at a nearby airport on his Presidential Ilyushin Il-96-300PU and is greeted by a phalanx of television crews, who follow his every move. Once on site, Putin loves to be filmed peering into half-built aircraft, ships and tanks while discussing the advanced technology they incorporate. Happy workers and managers are then relieved to hear the President tell them he has just placed an order for more hardware that is to be built in their factory.

These whirlwind visits are now a staple of Putin's diary and show he fully understands the political impact of defence spending on his popularity. Pork-barrel politics is just as important in Russia as anywhere else in the world. Closer examination of these announcements often reveals that they are not new and only repeat previously announced plans. However, some Western observers fall for the Putin spin and this just adds to the impression that he has embarked on a Soviet-era style military build-up.

These visits tells us a lot about the state of Russia's defence modernisation effort. Putin has interests in talking up Russian technological prowess and enjoys boasting to the media about new weapons that he claims are superior to those of Russia's Western rivals. Maintaining military parity with the United States and NATO is an intrinsic part of Putin's drive to project Russia as a global power deserving of respect on the world stage.

Whenever he details new weapon developments to domestic audiences, Putin carefully caveats his comments with reassurances that defence spending will not rise at the expense of domestic priorities. The day after his re-election in March 2018, Putin announced that Russian defence spending would actually fall during the coming two years, although he emphasised that this would not result in a decline in the country's military power.(1) It is not clear by how much the budget actually fell because the Russian President did not give any specific figures but he clearly felt it would be good politics to talk about declining defence spending. The Russian leader appears to want global respect but suspects that the Russian people are not willing to suffer a reduction in their living standards to pay for it. Lessons learned from the demise of the Soviet Union in 1980s, as a result of the Cold War arms race with the US, appear to have been taken on board by Russia's current leaders.

Later in 2018 the Stockholm International Peace Research Institute provided more context about these trends when it reported that "Russian military spending kept increasing until 2017, when it fell for the first time since 1998." It added that in 2017, "Russian military spending was $66.3 billion, a real-terms decrease of 20% compared with 2016. The fall in spending in 2017 brought the military burden down to 4.3% of gross domestic product, from 5.5% in 2016. (2)

These peaks and troughs in Russian defence spending correspond with the rise and fall of global oil and gas prices which underpin a significant element of Russian state spending. At the nadir of Boris Yeltsin's presidency in November 1998, oil was selling at $28 a barrel. By June 2008 oil prices had peaked at $164 and they stayed over $100 a barrel until August 2014.This corresponded with the boom years of Putin's defence modernisation period. Oil prices crashed to $36 a barrel in January 2016 and only stabilised to around $50 a barrel a year later, hence the need to rein-in defence spending. (3) The crash of oil prices in the first half of 2020 due to the Covid 19 pandemic led to comments from the Kremlin about economies in state spending but as oil prices surged again in 2021 talk of defence cuts disappeared.

The relationship between the oil price and Russian defence spending is a big change from the days of the Soviet Union when its economy was almost totally isolated from the global financial system. Russian defence spending is conducted in Rubles and the country does not import any significant amounts of equipment or components that require payment in foreign currency but this does not protect the Russian defence budget from turbulance in the financial merkets.

Russia today is highly dependent on foreign investment to develop its economy, particularly to fund the exploitation of new oil and gas reserves. Foreign currency is crucial to boosting living standards by funding the importing of foreign cars, food, computers and smart phones. This money will only continue flowing if the Kremlin can repay its debts in hard currency and the international money markets have proved very good at telling Moscow that they will not put up with uncontrolled state expenditure. (4) In the old Soviet days, this was just not a consideration and is why the Kremlin has not been able to embark upon a Soviet-style splurge of spending on the military. To keep its foreign creditors happy, increases in domestic spending - including on defence - have to be kept at levels on a par with Western countries. So when Western sanctions were imposed in 2014 after the Crimea crisis and the oil price started to nose dive later in that year, the Kremlin embarked on a round of budget cuts, including cuts in defence spending. Two ships destined for the Black Sea Fleet were sold to India for cash and aircraft deliveries slowed down or cancelled. (5)

Against this background, Russia's ambition to modernise its armed forces must be considered in the context of a tight fiscal position and demands from the Kremlin to be seen as more active on the world stage - a situation that Western counterparts of Russia's military are very familiar with.

The Russian government allocates funding to its armed forces through a process known as the State Armaments Programme (GPV). The GPV 2020, which covered the 2011-17 period, set in motion a strategic shift away from land forces to naval and air forces, with 26% of total funding going to the navy. This has since been succeeded by the GPV 2027, which covers 2018–27 and continues the priorities of the previous GPV. (6)

These documents were meant to bring to an end to two decades of stop-start funding of defence modernisation that more often than not resulted in major equipment programmes progressing at a glacial pace. For example, the development of Borei-class ballistic missile-firing and Yasen-class nuclear attack submarines took nearly 20 years to get off the drawing board and into the water. Each branch of the Russian armed forces has projects underway to recapitalise major items of equipment by upgrading existing systems and developing new ones.

The most high-profile programme for the Russian Aerospace Forces (RuAF) is the effort to produce the Sukhoi Su-57 fifth-generation combat aircraft, which has moved into the manufacturing and delivery phase. The new jet incorporates low-observable features, advanced weapons, and sensors. In May 2019, President Putin finally confirmed plans to buy 76 of the new jets over a ten year period. Meanwhile, images emerged in 2019 of Sukhoi's Okhotnik unmanned combat aerial vehicle (UCAV) under test, demonstrating the RuAF's continuing interest in fielding new air combat capabilities.

Ongoing deliveries of Su-35S, Su-30SM and Su-34 multirole combat aircraft helped the RuAF to replace its early-series Su-27 fighters and veteran Su-24 strike aircraft respectively but orders slowed at by 2020.

The anti-aircraft branch of the RuAF is receiving Almaz-Antey S-400-series long-range surface-to-air missiles to replace its S-300-series weapons, and new Pantsyr S-1 air-defence systems from KB Mashinostroyeniya to build a layered air defence network. Almaz-Antey S-350 Vityaz and S-500 Prometey surface-to-air missiles, which are envisaged to build on the capabilities of the S-300 and S-400 systems, are now moving into full-scale production.

Meanwhile, the long-term modernisation plans of the Russian Ground Forces are based on the Armata family of armoured fighting vehicles, which are being developed by the Uralvagonzavod Research and Production Corporation. Based on the Armata, the T-14, Russia's first truly new tank design since the T-72, has attracted attention for being the first tank without a manned turret. The family of vehicles also includes the T-15 heavy infantry fighting vehicle variant, as well as combat engineering, armoured tank support combat vehicle, self-propelled artillery, air-defence, and chemical and nuclear defence variants. Production of Kamaz Typhoon mine-protected vehicles, Gaz Tigr armoured utility vehicles, and Kalashnikov Uran-9 unmanned mine-clearance vehicles is continuing. Meanwhile, deliveries of the Special Technological Centre of Saint Petersburg Urlan-10 and Izhmash Granat-4 short-range tactical unmanned aerial vehicles are under way. These vehicles and systems, along with about 100 other capabilities, have been deployed in combat in Syria since 2015.

However, it seems that the Russian Navy has been the main beneficiary of the GPV process, particularly its submarine forces. The most recent GPV committed to the Yasen and Borei submarine programmes for the next 10 years, with six more Yasen-M nuclear attack submarines set to be completed by 2023 and six more Borei-class boats by 2027.

Meanwhile, conventional diesel-electric submarines (SSKs) production will continue at Admiralty shipyard in St Petersburg. Six Improved Kilo/Project

636.3 and 12 St Petersburg/Lada-class are being built for the Pacific and Baltic Fleets. Overhaul and modernisation of older Akula-, Victor-, Sierra-, and Oscar II-class nuclear attack submarines were also funded under the GPV.

However, this concentration on submarine development has negatively affected the navy's ambition to recapitalise its major surface vessels for blue water operations. Plans to build a new aircraft carrier to replace the veteran Admiral Kuznetsov have been put on the back burner, although funding has been found to enable the vessel to be overhauled. There is also no commitment to build more than the five Admiral Gorshkov-class frigates that are currently under contract. Meanwhile,one more Admiral Grigorovich-class frigates is also on order and about 30 Buyan-M-, Steregushchy-, and Karakurt-class corvettes are under construction or on order.

To bolster the navy's coastal defences, deliveries of NPO Mashinostroyeniya K-300P Bastion-P coastal defence systems with P-800 Oniks anti-ship and land-attack cruise missiles are continuing, along with those of the Bal-E coastal missile system, equipped with Zvezda Kh-35/Kh-35E anti-ship missiles.

Although Moscow is making efforts to field new equipment, these efforts are unlikely to result in the complete re-equipping of the force structure of the Russian armed forces during the next decade. As a result, all three services will continue to field a mix of new and legacy equipment until at least 2030. Much of Russia's legacy hardware dates from the 1980s and 1990s, although some of it has been upgraded and overhauled to extend its service life. However, the ability to keep this equipment – such as Su-24 strike bombers, T-72 main battle tanks, or Akula-class submarines – in fighting shape for another 10 years is questionable.

Inevitably, this could result in much of the Russian armed forces' inventory becoming increasingly obsolete compared with near-peer opponents. This looming crisis appears to be recognised by Russia's senior military leaders who have developed plans to mitigate the challenge.

A major impediment to Putin's ambitions to bring Russia's new military hardware into service during the next decade is the state of the country's defence manufacturing base. The demise of the Soviet Union hit the country's defence industry hard with factory closures, downsizing and privatisations.

This was an uneven process with some enterprises managing to stay afloat through export orders while many others had to lay off staff, sell facilities and close down assembly lines. As a result, critical research-and-development skills were lost, particularly those needed to transition new designs into serial production.

Russia's privately owned defence industries have mixed relations with their main customer and the past decade has seen several disputes break out in the Moscow media, particularly over about money. The United Shipbuilding Corporation, which owns most of Russia's naval yards, got into a major dispute with the navy over payments for submarine refits. (7) A major project to build new unmanned aerial vehicles was plagued by problems, leading to the Ministry of Defence stripping the prime contractor of the work. (8)

Despite this, Russia's fighter-aircraft industry and its associated supply chain has remained relatively intact and continued to build and upgrade Su-30/35/34 series aircraft during the past 20 years. Armoured fighting vehicle production has also continued and, in the naval domain, there has been some progress with building a new class of small warships, including fielding Kalibr cruise missiles on Buyan-M corvettes.

The biggest challenges for Russia are in the submarine-building and nuclear industries. For example, the first Borei-class submarine was laid down in 1996 but it was 13 years before the Yuriy Dolgorukiy was commissioned and even after it entered service its RSM-56 Bulava submarine-launched ballistic missiles were not fully cleared for submerged firing until 2019. The Yasen class suffered similar delays, with the first boat of the class delayed for 20 years until it was commissioned in 2013. To ensure fewer delays in producing the next five boats of each class, the shipyard has launched recruitment and training campaigns to up-skill its workforce.

Russia's new-generation equipment is much more sophisticated than its old Soviet-era platforms and comes with a much higher price tag. For some platforms, such as the Su-57 fighter and the Armata tank, the cost is reported to be almost double that of Soviet-era equivalents. Therefore, plans to field large numbers of these systems by 2020 have had to be scaled back. Despite first flying in 2010, it was only in May 2019 that the Russian MoD got the final go-ahead for the first batch production standard Su-57s. The funding of the Su-57 also seems to have drained money from other combat aircraft programmes with orders for new combat aircraft starting to dry up. By mid 2020, only contracts for 50 Su-35s and 20 Su-34Ms were still being worked on, suggesting that ambitions to replace all older Su-27s and Su-24s by the end of the decade will not be realised. (9)

Similar delay has hit the flagship T-14 Armata programme. The Russian military had planned to buy 2,300 Armata vehicles during the 2015 - 2020 timeframe but this effort has not been activated. Some senior Russian government officials have claimed there was no need to invest in new tanks when existing upgraded T-72s and T-90s were still on a par with Western vehicles. It was not until 2018 that the first batch of 32 T-15 tanks and 100 T-14 infantry fighting vehicles was formally ordered for delivery by 2021 to enable field trials to begin. There is considerable scepticism that these vehicles will be delivered on time. (10)

In January 2019 the Russian media made much of the arrival of 30 T-34 tanks dating from the Second World War in Moscow. The classic tanks had been donated by the Laotian government and the Russian military hoped to use them in parades and historical movies. It did not pass without comment that this was the largest shipment of tanks the Russian army planned to take delivery of in that year, which highlighted the central dilemma of Russia's defence modernisation efforts: Moscow can no longer afford to build overwhelming force and is conserving its resources to invest in next-generation weapon systems that are considered peer competitors with comparable Western systems.

Russia's defence modernisation effort is clearly a work in progress. To date the Russian armed forces have taken delivery of new precision-guided munitions, mine-protected vehicles, helicopters, soldier systems, unmanned aerial vehicles, mine-detection equipment, and small warships, all of which has been used to considerable effect in Syria and the Donbass region. The wider modernisation effort to recapitalise combat aircraft, armoured fighting vehicles, warships and submarines has not yet delivered the new equipment in the required quantities to create overwhelming numerical superiority over NATO forces. It does not look like this will happen in the near-to-medium term, if ever.

In a major turnaround from the days of the Soviet Union, when mass was at the heart of the Red Army's war-fighting strategy, the new Russian armed forces are aiming to field smaller quantities of high-quality equipment and combat units. Russian military leaders are also keen to explore innovative concepts of operation, organisational structures and tactical procedures to get more bang from their Ruble. The Russian government appears to be unwilling to embark upon an old-style arms race to out-produce the US and NATO in terms of numbers. The East-West rivalry is now being played out in terms of who can produce the more effective technology in the most cost-effective way and then quickly get it into service.

Chapter 23
Russia's Wonder Weapons

When the Russian President strode onto a stage at Moscow's Manezh Exhibition Centre on 1st March 2018 he had a spring in his step. Vladimir Putin then delivered one his bravura performances, describing with the aid of some very glitzy audio-visual aids the devastating capabilities of Russia's newest weaponry. He boasted about revolutionary nuclear armed underwater drones, laser weapons and hypersonic missiles. "Nobody has anything like this", he declared. This new weaponry would render NATO defences "completely useless", he claimed "Russia still has the greatest nuclear potential in the world, but nobody listened to us." (1)

This was not a dry old-style Soviet Politburo debate but an exercise in 21st Century political messaging. President Putin was clearly aiming to send a message to Washington as a series of international arms control agreements were approaching their expiry dates and moves were being made to start their renegotiation. Putin was also facing re-election a few days later. He appeared to be trying to reassure his population that Russia remained a nuclear superpower and that its weaponry was way ahead of that being fielded by its rivals.

While the Western news media lapped up the "doomsday" weaponry announced by the Russian President, they gave less coverage a few days later when Putin took to the airwaves to announce cuts in defence spending over the next two years. The leader of modern Russia was trying to show that he had learned the lessons of the final years of the Soviet Union when uncontrolled military spending had crippled the country's economy. (2)

Since President Putin's March 2018 speech, the progress on fielding these "wonder weapons" has been mixed, with some systems entering frontline service and others remaining under test. The status of these systems is still shrouded in secrecy but it is possible from a variety of sources to build up a picture of Russia's moves to bolster its nuclear arsenal. Russia's military is obviously trying to hide many of the technical secrets of its future strategic weapon systems, Moscow also wants their existence to be known to their adversaries to ensure they reap maximum political impact.

Putin is very keen to gain political benefit from the huge investment the Russian state is making in new weaponry. Western observers tend to concentrate on the Russian President's theatrical flourishes during dramatic public-relations events, but the strategic rationale for modernisation of the country's strategic nuclear systems has a long history and predates Putin taking up residence in the Kremlin in 2000. Much of Russia's nuclear arsenal dates from the Soviet era and it inevitably needs to be replaced as it reaches the end of its operational lifespan, so the progress of these programmes are by their very nature measured in decades.

During President Boris Yeltsin's time in office in the 1990s he repeatedly criticised US plans to install anti-ballistic missile (ABM) systems in Europe and the

Middle East. Washington said these defences were needed to protect US forces and allies from ballistic missiles fired from so-called "rogue" states in Iran, Iraq and Libya. These ABM initiatives were seen by Moscow as undermining the effectiveness of its strategic nuclear delivery systems based in European parts of Russia.

Putin shared his predecessor's concerns and after repeated overtures to the Americans to withdraw their ABM systems, the Russian President became determined to ensure that his country's nuclear deterrent would remain effective. During the first decade of the 21st Century, the Russian Ministry of Defence approved the acceleration of several research projects. These came to fruition a decade or so later. Soon some of these systems started to be spotted on commercial satellite imagery or were revealed by the Russian military. The confirmation of a number of these projects was reserved for President Putin's March 2018 event for maximum political impact.

Russia's land-based nuclear-armed intercontinental ballistic missiles (ICBMs) are one of the most easy-to-monitor elements of Moscow's strategic arsenal. They are based in just under 20 silo-fields or in garrisons for mobile launchers, so new weapons can be tracked by satellite surveillance relatively easily. Live tests of Russian ballistic missiles result in the weapons entering outerspace and impacting on a limited number of test ranges so the performance of missiles can be monitored extensively by US or other intelligence agencies.

It has therefore been possible to track the progress of the RS-28 Sarmat ICBM since it entered formal development in 2009. The first active tests took place at the Plesetsk Cosmodrome in December 2017 and in his March 2018 event President Putin showed off video footage of one of the weapons being test fired. Over the past decade various Russian military sources have predicted the missile's entry-to-service date but these targets have all been missed. In late 2019, President Putin was reported as saying in a military briefing that the 35,000-kilometre-range missile would complete its testing in 2021 and eventually replace all of Russia's existing silo-based ICBMs by 2027. Russian media reports have suggested the missiles will have their own active defensive systems to allow them to engage and kill ABM interceptors heading towards them. There have been no reports from Russian sources, or via US or other intelligence agencies, as to whether or not this revolutionary counter-measures system has actually been tested and found to work.

The other project that aims to enhance the land-based ICBM force is the Avengard re-entry vehicle, or hypersonic glide vehicle. Beyond a computer generated video clip shown by President Putin there have been few images released of the Avengard. In the video it is shown being released from a launch rocket and then manoeuvring to avoid the engagement zones of ABM batteries before delivering its nuclear payloads to targets. This video suggested the Avengard was constructed around a delta-wing configuration.

In December 2019, the Russian Ministry of Defence announced that the Avengard had been installed in RS-18B/UR-100N UTTKh ICBMs of the missile division based around Dombarovsky. It has been suggested that the Avengard is to be installed on other ICBMs but as yet no details of production or procurement plans have been revealed by official Russian sources.

A third new weapon system unveiled by Putin in March 2018 has since been confirmed as being in service with the Russian Strategic Missile Forces. In 2012 the Russian Ministry of Defence announced a competition to develop a laser weapon, which was then dubbed the Corrector. The system revealed in 2018 was initially known as the Complex 14TS034 and is now called the Peresvet. It has been identified in satellite imagery deployed at five locations to provide point defence to mobile ground launched ICBMs and missile silo fields. Imagery and video released by the Russian military shows the system is carried on low-loaders and supported by communications vans during deployments to field operating sites. These vehicles are in turn housed in purpose-built hangars with distinctive road layouts close to ICBM fields.

During the March 2018 briefing the laser was described as a "point defence" system that was designed to protect key targets from aircraft, missile or drone attack, indicating that the system is aimed at preventing a surprise conventional air attack neutralising Russian ICBMs.

Some of the most innovative weapon concepts unveiled by President Putin involve cruise and hypersonic missiles to be launched from aircraft, ships or land sites. These weapons offer the prospect of confounding conventional air defence radars and weapons because of their high speeds. By operating at several times the speed of sound hypersonic missiles potentially reduce the reaction time of defence systems, making it difficult to effectively employ conventional counter-measures or missile defence systems. This has prompted the promotion of artificial intelligence-based solutions as the only way to counter hypersonic weapons by taking the human element out of the defensive decision making chain.

The most mature Russian hypersonic weapon is the Kh-47M2 Kinzhad air launched hypersonic anti-ship missile, which despite being only unveiled in the March 2018 briefing, had been under development for many years before then. This weapon is an air-launched version of the 9M723 Iskander tactical ballistic missile, developed by the Kolomna Rocket Design Bureau, for carriage by a modified Mikoyan MiG-31K fighter aircraft. When Putin announced the existence of the weapon, he said it was already in service with the Russian Aerospace Force (RuAF) at the Akhtubinsk test centre on the Volga.

Since then the Russian military has announced that test firings have taken place from aircraft operating from Olenya airbase on the Kola Peninsula. Three MiG-31 units in the Northern Fleet, Central and Pacific military districts are to receive the missiles by 2026, says the Russian Ministry of Defence. Russian military sources say the weapon will also eventually be integrated onto the Tupolev Tu-22M3 long-range bombers. The MiG-31K-launched missiles are said by Russian sources to have a range of 2,000 kilometres and the Tu-22M3-launched missile is reported to have a range of 3,000 kilometre. It is unclear, however, if these distances are the operational range of the missile itself or the missile/aircraft combination.

The most intriguing weapon President Putin unveiled was the 9M370 Burevestnik nuclear-powered cruise missile. He claimed the missile has unlimited range, allowing it to fly around all known air defences to reach its target from unexpected directions. Some tests of the weapon have clearly taken place and three launch sites have been detected in satellite imagery of Novaya Zemlya island in the Arctic, at Nyonoksa in the Archangel region, and at the Kapustin Yar test range on the Volga.

A Russian Ministry of Defence video has shown what appears to be a prototype in flight and a missile check-out facility inside a factory. From this imagery its looks similar in shape to the Anglo-French MBDA Storm Shadow air-launched cruise missile but appeared to be twice its length and mass. It is also considerably bigger that the current Russian air launched cruise missiles - the Kh-55 or Kh-101 - so the Russian Long Range Aviation's current bombers, the Tupolev Tu-95 or Tu-160, would need to be substantially modified to carry the new weapon.

There is considerable uncertainty over how much progress has been made to field the Burevestnik and master its revolutionary propulsion technology. It is strongly suspected that an accident during a test of the weapon at the State Central Navy Testing Range at Nyonoksa, near to the port city of Severodvinsk, in August 2019 caused a radiation scare and the deaths of five technicians. There is no clarity from Russian officials or US intelligence sources on when the Burevestnik is due to enter operational service.

President Putin has placed great emphasis on the revolutionary potential of a nuclear-armed and nuclear-powered underwater unmanned vehicle to negate the effect of US ABM systems. With its claimed range of 6,000 nautical miles, the Poseidon is intended to navigate itself across the Atlantic or Pacific to attack US coastal cities or naval bases and then destroy them with a megaton-yield nuclear weapon.First indications of the existence of the Poseidon - or as it was originally titled, the Status 6 - emerged in 2015 when an artist's impression was "accidently on purpose" revealed on a Russian television news show. Since then the Russian Ministry of Defence has released video imagery of trials of the weapon involving the nuclear-powered submarine, the B-90 Sarov.

The Poseidon is so big that it requires a unique launch system to replace conventional torpedo tubes. To launch the weapon the Russian Navy is building at least two specially designed submarines to carry it. The first, a modified Project 09852-class submarine, the Belgorod, was launched from the Sevmash shipyard in Severodvinsk in April 2019.

Satellite imagery of the submarine in the shipyard confirms it has a specifically modified bow to accommodate the Poseidon weapon. Russian media reports predicted she would enter service in late 2020 and that eventually four new Poseidon-firing submarines will be required, with two each serving in the Northern and Pacific Fleets respectively.

The next Poseidon carrier, the Project 09851-class submarine the Khabarovsk, was expected to the floated out of the Sevmash yard late in 2020 and be made operational in 2022, according to Russian media reports. This appears to have slipped. Little is known about the configuration of the Khabarovsk as no photographs of her inside the Sevmash yard's submarine assembly hall have appeared in the public domain. Timeline for her construction suggests she is based on the design of the Borei class ballistic missile-firing submarine but with her missile compartment replaced by docking bays for mini-submarines.

Satellite imagery from the Sevmash yard over the past decade has picked up the loading of suspected Poseidon weapons on board the Sarov and an ice-breaking ship modified as a trials vessel. This latter activity has led to speculation that a version of the Poseidon, dubbed the Skif, could be developed that would be positioned on the seabed for remote activation.

The configuration of the Belgorod suggests she is the first of a new family of multi-role submarines that can be modified to operate a range of underwater unmanned vehicles, such as the Poesidon, as well as acting as a mothership for manned mini-submarines. This is an inherently flexible concept that would allow future generations of unmanned systems to be incorporated at a later date. Several other navies are exploring these concepts but the Russians appear to have stolen a march and got ahead of the game in this area of underwater warfare.

The Russian military has demonstrated considerable interest in new strategic weapons over and above the projects listed by President Putin in March 2018. It revealed the first work on hypersonic weapons in 1995. This project eventually became the 3M22 Tsirkon or Zirkon anti-ship missile. This came from the NPO Mashinostroyeniya enterprise, which already produces a portfolio of anti-ship missiles for the Russian Navy.

The scramjet-powered Tsirkon was first reported undergoing tests as far back as 2012-13 and has something of a troubled history. Russian media reports suggest it has achieved speeds in excess of Mach 8 in tests but in January 2020, the head of the Russian Navy, Admiral Nikolai Yevmenov, said it was still suffering from what he called "childhood diseases". (3)

Due to the delays in the weapon successfully completing its test programme there was a stop-go process of fielding with plans initially being announced for it being installed on Kirov-class nuclear cruisers after 2020. The cruiser Admiral Nakhimov was originally billed as the first warship to field the weapon from vertical launch tubes.

This plan appears to have been dropped in favour of the Admiral Gorshkov-class frigates being the first ships to operate the new weapon. The lead ship of the class, the Admiral Gorshkov, made the first test firing of the Tsirkon from an operational warship in January 2020 when she launched a missile from the Barents Sea to successfully hit a ground target 500 kilometres away on a test range in the Northern Urals region. Further tests from the frigate are planned for later in 2020, suggesting that its teething troubles are in the process of being resolved and the weapon could be fielded across the fleet in the near to medium term.

President Putin has claimed the Tsirkon has a range of 1,000 kilometres and can also be used in the land-attack role to complement the existing 3M14 Kalibr cruise missiles currently used by Russian warships and submarines. In December 2019, he said a land-based version of the Tsirkon was being developed.

Russian land-based missile programmes have became a source of renewed tension with the United States since 2018 when Washington announced it would withdraw from the 1987 Intermediate Nuclear Force (INF) Treaty. The US claimed that Moscow had developed a land-based cruise missile with a range greater than 500 kilometres, in violation of the treaty.

Moscow denied that the evolution of the Iskander-M tactical ballistic missile system to launch a cruise missile was in breach of the INF Treaty because it says the new missile's range is less than 500 kilometres. The US formally withdrew from the INF in August 2019 and Putin subsequently declared that Russia would not be bound by its terms.

The row developed after US intelligence claimed it had detected the new missile being tested, but the Russians denied it had been. The weapon system in question is based on the Iskander-K launch vehicle that incorporates a common launch tube that can fire different types of cruise missiles. Externally, the Iskander-K is almost indistinguishable from the regular Iskander-M launch vehicle and can only be identified once its distinctive missile launch tube is elevated into its firing position.

Two cruise missiles have been linked to the Iskander-K launch vehicle system. The 9M728, which is also known as R-500, is believed to be modified air-launched Kh-101/102 or ship/submarine-launched 3M14 Kalibr cruise missile. This is complemented by the 9M729 weapon, which the US says was in breach of the INF. The two weapons are often confused in media reports and there is little information from Russian sources on the origins of the 9M728 and 9M729 missiles.

Few confirmed images of either weapon have been published by American or Russia sources, although Russia did show off an Iskander-K launch vehicle and a 9M729 canister - but not an actual missile - at a media event at Kubinka military base outside Moscow in January 2019. With little independent information to judge either side's claims it is difficult to determine who is right. Washington's NATO allies subsequently backed the US position, saying they were convinced by the secret evidence presented to them by the US.

In the wake of the demise of the INF Treaty, Putin has made a number of speeches declaring that Russia would match any US moves to field new land-based cruises missiles, and he mentioned potential new cruise missile developments. The US has also said it was going to field a new land-based missile system. The row of the INF Treaty appears to have sparked a rhetorical arms race but there is little hard information available about the next moves by either the US or Russia.

Three years on from President Putin's unveiling of his package of advanced strategic weapons it is possible to make assessments of their progress. The Kh-47M2 Kinzhal hypersonic anti-ship missile and the Peresvet laser appear to have entered service. Russia has a distinct lead in the development of hypersonic missile technology and early in 2020 test fired its 3M22 Tsirkon or Zircon hypersonic missile from the frigate Admiral Gorshkov. The development of this weapon appears to be advanced but it did not feature on the March 2018 briefing. The Sarmat ICBM and Avengard are also at an advanced stage of their development and fielding. More questions remain over the status of the Poseidon and Burevestnik nuclear-powered weapon systems. They incorporate revolutionary technologies and Russian scientists and engineers would appear to be taking time to master them.

Despite hype surrounding President Putin's March 2018 event, the uneven progress in the development of Russia's "wonder weapons" suggests they are long-term projects that will take many years to come to fruition, in any significant numbers. The current balance of nuclear terror between Russia and the US is not going to disappear anytime soon.

In June 2020 Russia and the United States started negotiations in Vienna over the extension of the Strategic Arms Limitation Treaty (START) for another five years. Days after taking office in January 2021 US President Joe Biden agreed to five year extension to START to buy his administration time to work out its long term relationship with Moscow.

Both the US and Russia face huge costs to modernise their strategic weapons arsenals during 2020s so concessions would benefit both sides, potentially saving large amounts of money that could be spent on conventional forces or non-military projects. However, the Biden administration is pre-occupied with domestic issues, including recovering from the COVID-19 pandemic, so coming up with a successor to START is not a first order priority in Washington.

Moscow's portfolio of "wonder weapons" potentially gives it more cards than Washington to play in the futue START replacemnt negotiations. This has led to speculation that Moscow's nuclear modernisation is part of a gambit to prompt Washington to make concessions. Moscow could agree to halt or slow the fielding of these new weapons in return for US concessions on missile defence, total warhead inventories or delivery platform numbers. This would also provide the Russians with political cover to cancel potentially expensive projects without having to admit the technology does not work as it was imagined.

Conclusion
What has Putin got for his Money?

"Tim, Tim, you need to understand these guys in Moscow are not Soviets any more – they are Vikings". This was how veteran Russian military and political analyst Igor Sutyagin described the new rulers of his country to me. Igor is a force of nature who was one of the leading figures in an influential group of independent Russian journalists and academics who specialised in studying their country's military in the decade after the demise of the Soviet Union.

Igor and some of his colleagues were deemed to be too independent for the liking of some in Russia's intelligence and military establishments. In 1999 Igor found himself under arrest and spent 10 years in Russian prisons and labour camps for allegedly selling state secrets to a British risk-analysis company. He denied this, telling the court he was only involved the analysis of open-source information. To his great surprise in July 2010 he found himself on a plane, along with three other former prisoners heading to Vienna. On the airport tarmac in Austria, the four so-called Western spies were swapped for 10 Russians held in American jails. One of the Russians who shared the flight out Moscow with Igor was Sergei Skripal, who eight years later would be at the centre of the infamous Salisbury poisoning incident.

According to Igor, Russia's current government had long ago ditched any attachment to the old Soviet ideology of Communist global revolution. The current government in Moscow was only interested in money and political power. Igor's assessment was that President Putin was a modern day Viking raider whose foreign and domestic policy is predicated purely on the pursuit of financial and political advantage. Russia's defence policy since 2000 is just one facet of this phenomenon and the Kremlin's investment in military reform need to viewed in that context, he said.

So what has Vladimir Putin got for his money? The rebuilding of the Russian military was part of Putin's drive to restore the country's status as a great power. At the same time, by actually winning wars the Russian military showed it had vanquished the ghosts of Yeltsin-era incompetence. Restoring efficiency to the Russian military was part of wider drive by Putin to show that the country's government and state institutions were no longer a laughing stock.

The foray into Syria has transformed Russia's geopolitical position in the Middle East. President Putin is now a player in this strategic region. Gulf Arab leaders fete him at summits, Russian arms sales are booming across the region, once again the doors are open for Russian troops to train and advise their counter-parts in key countries. The coalition of countries intervening on the side of Field Marshal Haftar in Libya show how the world has changed, with Russia, Egypt, France and the United Arab Emirates lined up against Turkey and Qatar. At the heart of this intervention is a duel for the control of Libya's oil and gas reserves - a perfect modern-day Viking raid.

Defence spending plays an integral role in President Putin's domestic policies and his drive to build winning coalitions in presidential elections. Although he is regularly portrayed as an autocrat who pays little attention to public opinion, Putin is in reality a cunning politician who understands the need to use the power of the Russian state's treasury - which for much of the 21st Century has been buoyed by high oil and gas prices - to win and keep support from the wider population, local political leaders and key business leaders.

Some 900,000 military personnel, as well as their families, are dependent on the state for their wages and if these are paid on time, or even go up, then their hearts and minds will follow. There are also nearly two million workers in the defence industry who are dependent for their jobs on orders from the Russian Ministry of Defence, or export orders secured by President Putin's diplomacy. The Russian defence industry is now part privatised or run by state-owned pseudo-companies so the huge amounts of spent on Russian military equipment flows through the bank accounts of some of the richest men in the country. In the United States the awarding of defence contracts to win political favours is known as "pork barrel" politics and it is a well worn technique that is used many other countries. Russia is no different.

The final element of Vladimir Putin's winning formula has been the 2014 Crimea operation which tightly wrapped the Russian President in the country's flag. He tapped in to something deep in the Russia national psyche that viewed Crimea as a "natural" part of Mother Russia that had been ripped away in the chaotic demise of the Soviet Union. Just as Britons celebrated after the victory in 1982 Falklands war or Americans cheered their military's success in the 1983 Grenada crisis, Russians saw Crimea as a national endeavour that marked the end of an era of defeat and retreat. Such things cannot be bottled, manufactured and promoted by public-relations consultants.

The past two decades of military assertiveness have not been without cost to Russia. The Crimea and Donbass conflicts have resulted in US and European Union economic sanctions being imposed on Russia and key members of the Kremlin elite. The MH-17 airliner shoot-down in 2014 and the Salisbury poisoning in 2018 have added to the impression that Russia is a rogue nation. So far President Putin has just shrugged. Domestically, his foreign wars have cost him little. Casualties have been light and they have only involved professional soldiers and officers, not conscripts, so there has been no revolt of dead soldiers' mothers as during the Afghan and Chechen wars.

In terms of raw military power, what has President Putin's spending splurge bought? Despite the talk in the West of a new Cold War, the modern Russian armed forces have not benefited from a Soviet-era-type arms build-up. The size of the Russian armed forces has consistently shrunk over the past 30 years to around 900,000 regular personnel today from 5.4 million in 1990. The number of tanks, planes and warships in use with the Russian military have likewise dropped dramatically in the same period.

In place of a Soviet army manned by millions of conscript soldiers, President Putin and his generals have crafted a small professional military. They have replaced the steamroller with a stiletto. The implications of this are immense. The days of the Soviet high command planning to wage massive offensives across the length and breadth of Europe and the Middle East are history. In the new world, the European nations of NATO have more troops under arms than Russia, as well as more tanks, planes and ships. A successful Russian invasion of countries in the EU and NATO is a non-starter.

The idea that Russia's Northern Fleet of 11 major surface vessels, around 10 working submarines and one very unreliable aircraft carrier would be able to foray out into the Atlantic to cut Western Europe off from North America is not really credible.

Russian military strategy is now focused on ensuring the political and military domination of a few key regions on Russia's borders. The Arctic, Ukraine, Belarus, the Black Sea, the Caucasus and Central Asia are now the focus of Russian attention. Within these regions, Russian military power can be applied rapidly for strategic effect and its building of anti-missile domes is meant to ensure that no outside powers can interfere in any Kremlin moves against its near neighbours.

Within these regions, the places where Russian military forces are most likely to be drawn into conflict are Belarus, Ukraine, Georgia and the Arctic. In each theatre Russian forces have many advantages that would enable them to prevail should conflict break out.

Belarus is Russia's last major ally in Eastern Europe and any event that could result in the fall of the current pro-Russian government in Minsk is likely to be met with intervention from Moscow. There are strong pro-Russian elements across Belarusian society, government and military so it would be a receptive environment for a Donbass-style hybrid campaign of subversion and conventional action. The Russian public might also be receptive to the return of Belarus to the Motherland as long as it did not cost much in blood and treasure.

If any crisis with Ukraine should escalate into open conflict, Moscow has positioned strong forces on its borders. Four of the Russian Ground Forces' new divisions have been positioned within striking distance of the Ukrainian border, and they could be supported by the Black Sea Fleet's army corps in Crimea. These first-echelon forces could no doubt inflict a heavy defeat on the Ukrainian army in the border regions, but Ukraine is a country of 41 million people and is almost the same size as France. The 32,000 Russian troops in its four border divisions would need substantial reinforcements - possibly involving hundreds of thousands of troops, which Russian does not have - if any sort of long term occupation of Ukraine were to be undertaken.

Georgia is a better prospect for a major Russian intervention. The country's armed forces are heavily outnumbered and outgunned by the Southern Military District's air, land and sea power. However, a full-on and sustained occupation of the Caucasus country would require the movement of significant reinforcements from the Russian heartlands.

The Arctic is a different challenge for Russia's military and this would involve the projection of military forces across a large expanse of the wilderness region, with few bases or infra-structure to support operations of any significant size. Russian amphibious exercises in the region usually involve large company-sized groups of 200-300 Naval Infantry and one or two landing ships, which gives an indications of the Northern Fleet's ability to project power into the Arctic.

Russia has plenty of long-range firepower in the shape of naval Kalibr cruise missiles, air-launched Kh-55 or 101 cruise missiles, Bastion anti-ship missiles and long-range MiG-31 fighters, but it has few surface ships and land units capable of operating in the extreme climate of this region.

Russian interventions in the Middle East, the Eastern Mediterranean and Libya can be viewed as Viking raids aimed at securing economic advantage and political leverage. They have been undertaken with minimal force to reduce risks and costs.

How will this new world order evolve over the 2020s and what moves are the Russian military making in this power play? Current plans to procure military hardware do not give the impression that the Kremlin has any intention of moving beyond its current strategic horizon. The evidence from a variety of open sources, including commercial satellite imagery, seems to suggest that there is no secret Russian arms built-up or "missile gap", to use a Cold War analogy. Russia has staked its flag in the ground and challenged all comers to stay away from what it regards as its spheres of influence. It pushed back against what it saw as Western-inspired regime change in Kiev in 2014 and a bid to overthrow its long-term Syrian allies in 2015.

The ease with which the Russian Black Sea Fleet and Coast Guard contained the November 2018 attempt by the Ukrainian Navy to sail under the newly opened Kerch bridge into the Sea of Azov showed how foolhardy it would be to directly confront the new reality of Russian military power in its border regions.

The cold hard power of Russian military strength means that Western countries and their allies have few options but to resort to economic and diplomatic sanctions that have limited impact. This in turn reinforces the impression of Russian power amongst the leaders and populations of countries on Russia's borders that are not EU or NATO members. The psychology of this power imbalance means that its intimidatory effect is amplified many times over. Western reluctance to allow Georgia or Ukraine to become full members of NATO or the EU just demonstrates to their populations their exposure and vulnerability to Russian military power. In the battle for the hearts of minds of their populations, the apparent overwhelming supremacy of Russian military forces on their borders cannot be under-estimated. As the forlorn Ukrainian soldiers and sailors in Crimea found out, the West had little inclination to do anything or take any risks on their behalf. The vast majority of them believed they were sacrificial lambs in a lost cause, and jumped ship to the Russian side.

It was not clever cyber attacks that lost Crimea but the unwillingness of the

West to draw a line in the sand. Up to now, American the US and European governments have shown little inclination to do this anywhere east of the current borders of NATO, or in Syria and Libya. Unless this changes then the winning streak of the Russian military will continue.

Perhaps the most important thing Putin has been able to achieve has been the restoration of the Russian military's winning reputation. The Soviet General Staff was renowned during World War Two for its strategic and operational brilliance but this was lost with the demise of the Soviet Union. The "brain" of the Russian military seems to be back in business and this makes it a far more serious opponent than any of its individual weapon systems.

Sources

In researching this book I have not followed the traditional path when writing military history or military analysis. The nature of the modern Russian military means it is just not possible to gain access to documents, interview important participants or visit the scenes of its recent combat operations.

Often the only eye that can be opened on the Russian military is through non-traditional sources - social-media feeds from a variety of entities, as well as analysis of news media and commercial satellite imagery. The internet has made it possible to view modern Russian military campaigns to a degree that has not been possible in earlier conflicts, except by use of highly classified intelligence capabilities.

This is also the era of real-time monitoring of aircraft and ship movements which opens up new perspectives for military analysis that has just not been available before.

Aircraft movements can tracked from their ADS-B transponder data, via:
https://www.flightradar24.com/

Ship movements can similarly be tracked through AIS transponder data, via:
https://www.vesselfinder.com/

The movement of ships through the Bosphorus is also monitored by a network of ship spotters based in the Turkish city of Istanbul. A lot of their work is posted on:

https://turkishnavy.net/foreign-warship-on-bosphorus/foreign-warship-on-bosphorus-in-2020/

The site also archive ship sightings back to 2013. The are also a number of Twitter feeds where the ship spotters report naval activity, with the most informative being: @YorukIsik and @Saturn5

A key part of monitoring the Russian armed forces is accessing commercial satellite imagery that is now available to allow a level of ground truth geolocating still or video imagery to confirm its veracity. I have made extensive use of the following sites:

http://wikimapia.org/country/Syria/

https://www.terraserver.com/

https://www.google.co.uk/intl/en_uk/earth/

There are several online communities and Twitter sites devoted to geolocating locations and tracking Russian military activity. These include:

@obretix

@galandecZP

@halmiso1

@Capt_Navy

@GDarkconrad

@RALee85

@askai707

@CovertShores

There are a number of online investigative organisations that monitor the Russian armed forces. The most famous is https://www.bellingcat.com which is run by Elliott Higgins. The Ukrainian-based https://informnapalm.org and https://censor.net.ua/ specialise in investigations into the Russian military and the war in Crimea, Donbass and Syria.

Since 1991 several independent Russian think tanks and publications dedicated researching the country's armed forces and defence industry have emerged. The Russian Strategic Nuclear Forces group has website, http://russianforces.org/, which is well respected. The Russian Defence Policy website, https://russiandefpolicy.com/, is a very useful resource of information about senior Russian military officers and units. The Centre for Analysis of Strategies and Technologies has live blog, https://bmpd.livejournal.com/3935520.html, that is often first to post photographs of new Russian equipment and military events.

Since 2014 I have been monitoring the development of the Russian armed forces and their operations through a variety of means, creating a series of Powerpoint briefings incorporating multiple sources of information. These extensive briefings are reproduced on my website and can be accessed via: http:www.timripley.co.uk. Each chapter has its own Powerpoint briefings which combine still imagery from social-media posts and screen grabs from video clips posted online by individuals or news media organisations. It builds up into a comprehensive source of information about the main branches of the Russian armed forces and their recent operations.

References

The core references for each chapter is presented in Powerpoints briefings that are posted on my website, as mentioned above. In several chapters I have referenced a number of specific secondary sources, such as news and government websites as well as social-media posts, as follows:

Little Green Men

1. https://www.bbc.co.uk/news/world-europe-26532154
2. https://www.facebook.com/vladislav.seleznev.94/posts/411202715683124?stream_ref=10
3. https://varlamov.ru/1017094.html

Sources and Methods – Hiding in Plain Sight

1. *Unravelling a Cold War Mystery, The ALFA SSN: Challenging Paradigms, Finding New Truths, 1969–79*, Gerhardt Thamm, CIA, 2008
2. https://www.internetlivestats.com/internet-users/russia/
3. *Hidden in Plain Sight: CNA and the Soviet Navy*, N. Bradford Dismukes, Centre of Naval Analysis, February 2018

1. Operation Crimea Spring

1. https://www.youtube.com/watch?v=DUH-A3IF3h0, 1 March 2014 and http://www.youtube.com/watch?feature=player_detailpage&v=tcpXwuzPvZg, 27 Feb 2014
2. Crimea Way Back Home is available on https://vimeo.com/123319119
3. *All the Kremlin's Men: Inside the Court of Vladimir Putin*, Mikhail Zygar, Public Affairs, 2016, p.269
4. *All the Kremlin's Men: Inside the Court of Vladimir Putin*, Mikhail Zygar, Public Affairs, 2016, p.277
5. *All the Kremlin's Men: Inside the Court of Vladimir Putin*, Mikhail Zygar, Public Affairs, 2016,

p.277
6. https://www.kyivpost.com/article/content/euromaidan/two-die-in-rallies-outside-crimean-parliament-says-ex-head-of-mejlis-337708.html
7. *All the Kremlin's Men: Inside the Court of Vladimir Putin,* Mikhail Zygar, Public Affairs, 2016, p.277
8. https://www.bbc.co.uk/news/world-europe-38056242, https://www.gazeta.ru/army/2016/11/22/10356719.shtml#page1
9. https://informnapalm.org/ua/orsk-2020/
10. https://dpsu.gov.ua/en/news/the-chronology-of-irregular-actions-on-the-part-of-russian-federation-in-the-autonomous-republic-of-crimea/
11. https://en.interfax.com.ua/news/general/193305.html
12. http://www.youtube.com/watch?v=4Lj4cvvDY-o
13. https://informnapalm.org/en/list-1097-how-the-russian-18th-brigade-occupied-crimea/
14. https://customer.janes.com/DefenceWeekly/Display/jdw54910-jdw-2014
15. http://itar-tass.com/mezhdunarodnaya-panorama/1015853
16. https://www.bbc.co.uk/news/world-europe-38056242, https://www.gazeta.ru/army/2016/11/22/10356719.shtml#page1
17. https://customer.janes.com/Janes/Display/jdw54934-jdw-2014
18. https://customer.janes.com/Janes/Display/jdw55025-jdw-2014
19. jhttps://customer.janes.com/Janes/Display/jdw55025-jdw-2014
20. https://www.youtube.com/watch?feature=player_detailpage&v=8EYMEIvA6Kg&feature=player_embedded
21. https://customer.janes.com/Janes/Display/jdw55115-jdw-2014

2 Putin and his Generals

1. https://www.themoscowtimes.com/2019/12/09/russia-plans-to-set-up-arctic-air-defense-dome-with-s-400-missiles-a68530

3 Hybrid Warfare – Dial Moscow for Subversion

1. https://www.reuters.com/article/us-ukraine-crisis-russia-military/putin-puts-troops-in-western-russia-on-alert-in-drill-idUSBREA1P0RW20140226
2. *All the Kremlin's Men: Inside the Court of Vladimir Putin,* Mikhail Zygar, Public Affairs, 2016, p.276
3. https://time.com/11952/putin-ukraine-crimea-russia/
4. https://informnapalm.org/3001-vozvrashhenye-28-j-otdelnoj-motostrelkovoj-brygady-yz-ekaterynburga-v-rostovskuyu-oblast-v-sostav-gruppyrovky-syl-vtorzhenyya, https://informnapalm.org/en/base-camp-of-the-belgorod-group-of-russian-invasion-forces/, https://informnapalm.org/3600-sostav-svodnogo-podrazdelenyya-35-j-msbr-syl-vtorzhenyya/
5. Interview with UK intelligence operative, 7th March 2014
6. *All the Kremlin's Men: Inside the Court of Vladimir Putin*, Mikhail Zygar, Public Affairs, 2016, p.284
7. https://www.bellingcat.com/news/uk-and-europe/2016/09/30/revelations-confirmations-mh17-jit-press-conference/
8. https://www.rferl.org/a/ukraine-luhansk-standoff-police/25324437.html
9. https://www.youtube.com/watch?feature=player_detailpage&v=ceynuwnNeSA
10. https://www.youtube.com/watch?v=qmxBjsU2rig&feature=player_detailpage
11. https://customer.janes.com/DefenceWeekly/Display/jdw55127-jdw-2014
12. http://en.kremlin.ru/events/president/news/20796
13. https://www.kyivpost.com/article/content/ukraine-politics/sbu-nabs-russian-two-ukrainians-suspected-of-working-for-russian-intelligence-bodies-344900.html, https://www.unian.info/society/sbu-nabs-russian-spy-who-gathered-intel-on-ukrainian-missile-systems-10986950.html
14. SSU Has Established Identity of Leader of Russian Subversive Group Terrorizing Civilian Population in Sloviansk, SBU webpost 18 April 2014 https://www.youtube.com/watch?feature=player_embedded&v=APQaE_gaUeI
15. https://www.youtube.com/watch?feature=player_detailpage&v=DinMf_7dQK4
16. https://customer.janes.com/DefenceWeekly/Display/jdw55127-jdw-2014
17. https://www.kyivpost.com/article/content/war-against-ukraine/shootout-near-sloviansk-leaves-at-least-man-killed-several-wounded-343296.html
18. https://www.youtube.com/watch?feature=player_detailpage&v=DinMf_7dQK4
19. All the Kremlin's Men: Inside the Court of Vladimir Putin, Mikhail Zygar, Public Affairs, 2016, p.285-6

20. https://web.archive.org/web/20140408213918/http://en.itar-tass.com/world/726779
21. http://www.youtube.com/watch?v=ztXHNYCtM8k&feature=player_embedded
22. https://web.archive.org/web/20140422214843/http://euromaidanpr.com/2014/04/13/counter-terrorism-operation-announced-in-sloviansk/
23. http://www.youtube.com/watch?v=DhWJTNhhaUU&feature=player_embedded, http://www.youtube.com/watch?v=PeHy6e73dd4&feature=player_detailpage, http://www.youtube.com/watch?feature=player_embedded&v=jJk6bNcClk4
24. http://www.youtube.com/watch?feature=player_detailpage&v=dwhErv6Wujc
25. https://www.telegraph.co.uk/news/worldnews/europe/ukraine/10767005/Ukraine-launches-anti-terrorist-operation-in-the-east.html
26. http://www.youtube.com/watch?v=Gc2Idf-_-So&feature=player_embedded
27. http://www.youtube.com/watch?feature=player_embedded&v=VdgQCZ3UxR4
28. https://www.worldbulletin.net/europe/rebels-down-ukraine-helicopters-putin-denounces-city-assault-updated-h135261.html, http://www.youtube.com/watch?v=eTu5dpmvOAo&feature=player_embedded
29. https://www.reddit.com/r/MilitaryPorn/comments/24t1f8/a_mi24_attack_helicopter_that_w
30. http://www.youtube.com/watch?v=TwRqMnIKOKc&feature=player_embedded
31. https://www.bellingcat.com/news/uk-and-europe/2019/07/17/jit-indictments-and-reactions-analyzing-new-evidence-linking-separatists-and-russian-officials-to-mh17/
32. https://customer.janes.com/DefenceWeekly/Display/jdw55492-jdw-2014
33. https://customer.janes.com/DefenceWeekly/Display/jdw55492-jdw-2014
34. https://www.youtube.com/watch?v=hIiQ7Yh719w&feature=youtu.be
35. Reuters photograph 10 April 2014
36. https://www.bellingcat.com/news/uk-and-europe/2019/07/17/jit-indictments-and-reactions-analyzing-new-evidence-linking-separatists-and-russian-officials-to-mh17/
37. https://www.bellingcat.com/news/uk-and-europe/2019/07/17/jit-indictments-and-reactions-analyzing-new-evidence-linking-separatists-and-russian-officials-to-mh17/
38. https://www.bellingcat.com/news/uk-and-europe/2016/03/04/8110/
39. https://www.bellingcat.com/news/uk-and-europe/2016/03/04/8110/
40. https://www.bellingcat.com/news/uk-and-europe/2019/07/17/jit-indictments-and-reactions-analyzing-new-evidence-linking-separatists-and-russian-officials-to-mh17/
41. https://www.bellingcat.com/app/uploads/2019/06/a-birdie-is-flying-towards-you.pdf, p.5

4 The Russian Army Rolls

1. *All the Kremlin's Men: Inside the Court of Vladimir Putin,* Mikhail Zygar, Public Affairs, 2016, p.288
2. A*ll the Kremlin's Men: Inside the Court of Vladimir Putin,* Mikhail Zygar, Public Affairs, 2016, p.290
3. https://informnapalm.org/en/general-armored-car/, http://www.trud.ru/article/10-06-2013/1294976_komandarm_gurulev_stal_figurantom_ugolovnogo_dela.html, https://tass.ru/armiya-i-opk/3548771
4. https://www.bellingcat.com/news/uk-and-europe/2019/07/17/jit-indictments-and-reactions-analyzing-new-evidence-linking-separatists-and-russian-officials-to-mh17/
5. https://www.bellingcat.com/news/uk-and-europe/2019/07/17/jit-indictments-and-reactions-analyzing-new-evidence-linking-separatists-and-russian-officials-to-mh17/
6. https://www.bellingcat.com/news/uk-and-europe/2019/07/17/jit-indictments-and-reactions-analyzing-new-evidence-linking-separatists-and-russian-officials-to-mh17/
7. https://www.bellingcat.com/news/uk-and-europe/2016/03/04/8110/
8. https://www.interpretermag.com/russia-this-week-lurid-anti-ukraine-propaganda-broadcast-on-state-tv/

5 Frozen War - Battle of Debaltsevo

1. All the Kremlin's Men: Inside the Court of Vladimir Putin, Mikhail Zygar, Public Affairs, 2016, p.290
2. https://www.bellingcat.com/news/uk-and-europe/2019/07/17/jit-indictments-and-reactions-analyzing-new-evidence-linking-separatists-and-russian-officials-to-mh17/
3. https://novayagazeta.ru/articles/2015/03/02/63264-171-my-vse-znali-na-chto-idem-i-chto-mozhet-byt-187, https://informnapalm.org/en/5th-tank-brigade-russian-army-battle-debaltseve/

7 The Syria Express

1. https://www.nytimes.com/2015/08/13/world/middleeast/us-says-iranian-military-figures-visit-to-russia-violates-un-ban.html

2. *Every Day is Extra,* John Kerry, Simon & Schuster, 2018, p.548

Background to the early phases of the Russian intervention in Syria are described in the following articles:

https://thesaker.is/the-commander-of-the-russian-military-grouping-in-syria-gives-first-interview/

http://www.reuters.com/article/us-mideast-crisis-syria-soleimani-in¬sigh-idUSKCN0S-02BV20151006

https://www.nytimes.com/2015/09/28/world/middleeast/iraq-agrees-to-share-intelligence-on-isis-with-russia-syria-and-iran.html?_r=0

http://www.newsweek.com/man-who-stares-boats-449088

http://www.newsweek.com/russian-votes-syria-hint-size-military-deployment-501515

http://www.euronews.com/2015/09/29/russian-navy-pours-south-through-bosphorus

https://theintercept.com/2016/01/28/israeli-drone-feeds-hacked-by-british-and-american-intelligence/

https://informnapalm.org/en/russia-began-a-concealed-ground-operation-in-syria/

8 Air War Russian Style

The experiences of Russia pilots and military personnel in Russia are recounted in the following articles:

https://bmpd.livejournal.com/2495624.html

http://sensei-yoda.blogspot.co.uk/2016/11/35.html

http://otvaga2004.ru/voyny/wars-mid-east/syria/avianavodchik-desantnik-v-sirii/

http://otvaga2004.ru/voyny/wars-mid-east/syria/oni-vooruzhayut-nashi-su-24m-v-sirii/

http://otvaga2004.ru/boyevoe-primenenie/boyevoye-primeneniye04/sokrushayushhij-alligator-v-sirii/

http://otvaga2004.ru/voyny/wars-mid-east/syria/avianavodchik-desantnik-v-sirii/

http://otvaga2004.ru/voyny/wars-mid-east/syria/sirii-rossijskie-nochnye-oxotniki/-

10 Mediterranean Squadron

1. https://russiandefpolicy.com/2010/11/28/master-and-commanders/

11 A2AD and Douma Crisis

1. https://www.youtube.com/watch?v=m8AetEXh80s, http://eng.mil.ru/en/news_page/country/more.htm?id=12171300@egNews

2. https://dod.defense.gov/News/Transcripts/Transcript-View/Article/1493749/department-of-defense-press-briefing-by-pentagon-chief-spokesperson-dana-w-whit/

3. https://www.reuters.com/article/us-mideast-crisis-syria-russia-diplomat/russian-envoy-to-lebanon-any-u-s-missiles-fired-at-syria-will-be-shot-down-idUSKBN1HI0PU

12 Russia in Libya

1. https://www.fpri.org/article/2019/10/diplomacy-and-dividends-who-really-controls-the-wagner-group/, https://informnapalm.org/en/tag/wagner-pmc/

13 Battle of Idlib – Drone Wars with Turkey

1. https://web.archive.org/web/20200229213920/https://www.msn.com/en-us/news/world/dozens-of-turkish-soldiers-killed-in-strike-in-idlib-in-syria/ar-BB10uvmc?li=BBnb7Kz

2. https://www.gov.uk/government/speeches/defence-secretary-ben-wallace-gives-a-speech-at-the-air-and-space-power-conference

17. Russia's Warriors

. 1 http://old.redstar.ru/2008/07/30_07/2_01.html

2. https://www.newsru.com/arch/russia/22apr2004/colonel.html

3. https://informnapalm.org/en/corrupt-russian-general-gurulev-exposed-by-soldiers-of-russian-army-136th-brigade/

4. https://www.globalsecurity.org/military/world/russia/personnel.htm

5. https://russiandefpolicy.com/2010/11/28/master-and-commanders/

6. https://novayagazeta.ru/articles/2015/03/02/63264-171-my-vse-znali-na-chto-idem-i-chto-mozhet-byt-187, https://informnapalm.org/en/5th-tank-brigade-russian-army-battle-debaltseve/

7. https://www.ruaviation.com/news/2016/7/12/5968/, https://sputniknews.com/middleeast/201607241043553860-russian-pilots-killed-syria/

8. Commander and 40 paratroopers: a drunk colonel of the airborne forces called for armed assistance to the conflict in a cafe, Komsomolskaya Pravda, 5 Nov 2018

9. Sergei Shoigu briefing 27 March 2017, reported. https://www.vedomosti.ru/politics/articles/2020/03/22/825872-novaya-diviziya and @RALee85

10. https://www.youtube.com/watch?v=Dtq7cTBzsqk

18. Russia's Land Power

1. *Russia's New Ground Forces: Capabilities, Limitations and Implications for International Security,* by Igor Sutyagin and Justin Bronk, RUSI, 2017, p.135-7
2. https://chacr.org.uk/wp-content/uploads/2019/11/20161208-Ares-and-Athena-06.pdf, p.6

19. Russia's Surface Fleet

1. *Jane's Fighting Ships 1983-84*, Captain John Moore RN, Jane's Publishing Company, 1983, p.485-486
2. *The Fleet That Had to Die.* Richard Alexander Hough, Ballantine Paperbacks, 1960

20. Submarines of the Northern Fleet

1. https://www.youtube.com/watch?v=__wiB_hVApY
2. https://www.gov.uk/government/speeches/rusi-sea-power-conference-speech
3. https://www.telegraph.co.uk/news/2020/08/21/defence-review-prioritise-protecting-under-sea-cables-russian/
4. https://rusi.org/sites/default/files/20171214-rusi-cds_annual_lecture-acm_peach.pdf
5. https://www.ft.com/content/40236a0a-e711-11e7-97e2-916d4fbac0da
6. Interview with author
7. *Jane's Fighting Ships 1983-84,* Captain John Moore RN, Jane's Publishing Company, 1983, p.485-486
8. https://eng.mil.ru/en/structure/forces/navy/structure/submarine_forces.htm
9. Interview with author
10. Jane's Fighting Ships 1983-84, Captain John Moore RN, Jane's Publishing Company, 1983, p.485-486

21. Russia Air Power

1. https://assets.publishing.service.gov.uk/government/uploads/system/uploads/attachment_data/file/905460/20200708-RAF-Quick-Reaction-Alert-launches-January-june-2020-7300.pdf, https://assets.publishing.service.gov.uk/government/uploads/system/uploads/attachment_data/file/865073/Information_regarding_the_list_of_all_QRA_responses_from_RAF_Lossiemouth_during_2019___2019_13302.pdf
2. https://aif.ru/dontknows/infographics/vozdushno-kosmicheskie_sily_rossiyskoy_federacii_infografika

22. Russia's Defence Industrial Complex

1. https://tass.com/defense/994572
2. https://www.ft.com/content/092f8cc6-4dce-11e8-8a8e-22951a2d8493
3. https://www.macrotrends.net/1369/crude-oil-price-history-chart
4. https://www.chathamhouse.org/sites/default/files/CHHJ7799-Russia-Economics-RP-WEB-FINAL.pdf
5. Flash Point Russia. Russia's Airpower: Capabilities and Structure, Piotr Butowski, Harpia Publishing, 2019, p.127-134 , https://www.navyrecognition.com/index.php/news/defence-news/2017/november-2017-navy-naval-forces-defense-industry-technology-maritime-security-global-news/5729-yantar-shipyard-launched-two-project-11356-frigates-in-kaliningrad.html, https://tass.com/defense/1031650
6. https://reader.chathamhouse.org/russia-s-new-state-armament-programme-implications-russian-armed-forces-and-military
7. https://www.maritime-executive.com/article/russia-sues-its-own-shipyard-over-naval-repairs8. https://www.business-gazeta.ru/article/398202 , https://eng.mil.ru/en/news_page/country/more.htm?id=12274342@egNews
9. aircraft orders
10. https://russiandefpolicy.com/2020/02/20/tanks-in-gpv-2027/

23. Putin's Wonder Weapons

1. https://www.thedrive.com/the-war-zone/18906/heres-the-six-super-weapons-putin-unveiled-during-fiery-address
2. https://tass.com/defense/994572
3 https://radiosputnik.ria.ru/20200121/1563671078.html

Bibliography

The following books were referenced during the writing of Little Green Men.

The Deadly Trade: The Complete History of Submarine Warfare from Archimedes to the Present, Ian Ballantyne, Weidenfeld & Nicholson, 2018

The Soviet War Machine, Ray Bonds, Salamander Books, 1980

The Middle East Military Balance 1999-2000, Shlomo Brom, Belfer Centre Studies in International Security, 2003

Flash Point Russia. Russia's Airpower: Capabilities and Structure, Piotr Butowski, Harpia Publishing, 2019

The Threat: Inside the Soviet Military Machine, Andrew Cockburn, Hutchinson, 1983

Hidden in Plain Sight: CNA and the Soviet Navy, N. Bradford Dismukes, Centre of Naval Analysis, February 2018

100 Years of the Trade: Royal Navy Submarines, Past, Present and Future, Edited by Martin Edmonds, CDISS, 2001

Armies of Russia's War in Ukraine, Mark Galeotti, Osprey, 2019

Sukhoi Su-25 Frogfoot: Close Air Support Aircraft, Yefim Gordon and Alan Dawes, Airlife, 2004

Sukhoi Su-24 Fencer: Soviet Swing-Wing Bomber, Yefim Gordon and Keith Dexter, Aerofax 2005

Flankers: The New Generation, Yefim Gordon, Midland, 2001

Ilyushin/Beriev A-50: The 'Soviet Sentry',Yefim Gordon, Casemate, 2015

Mikoyan Mig-29 Fulcrum: Multi-Role Fighter, Yefim Gordon, Airlife, 1999

Soviet/*Russian Aircraft Weapons: Since World War Two,* Yefim Gordon, Midland, 2004

Soviet/Russian Unmanned Aerial Vehicles, Yefim Gordon, Midland, 2005

Tupolev Tu-95 and Tu-142, Yefim Gordon, Crecy, 2017

Ilyushin Il-76: Russia's Versatile Jet Freighter, Yefim Gordon and Dmitriy Kommissarov, Aerofax, 2006

Mil Mi-8 / Mi-17 Rotary-Wing Workhorse and Warhorse, Yefim Gordon and Dmitriy Komissarov, Midland, 2003

Mil Mi-24 Hind: Attack Helicopter, Yefim Gordon and Dmitriy Komissarov, Airlife, 2002

Soviet / Russian AWACS Aircraft, Yefim Gordon and Dmitriy Komissarov, Midland, 2005

Sukhoi Su-24: Famous Russian Aircraft, Yefim Gordon and Dmitriy Komissarov, Crecy, 2015

The Silent Deep: The Royal Navy Submarine Service since 1945, Peter Hennessy and James Jinks, Penguin Random House, 2015

Every Day is Extra, John Kerry, Simon & Schuster, 2018

Antonov's Turboprop Twins: An-24/An-26/An-30/An-32, Dmitriy Komissarov and Yefim Gordon, Midland, 2003

OKB Ilyushin: A History of the Design Bureau and Its Aircraft, Sergey Komis-

sarov and Yefim Gordon, Midland, 2004
Russian Tactical Aviation: Since 2001, Dmitriy Komissarov and Yefim Gordon, Hikoki, 2017209
Tupolev Tu-160: Soviet Strike Force Spearhead, Dmitriy Komissarov and Yefim Gordon, Schiffer Military History, 2016
The Syrian Jihad: The Evolution of an Insurgency, Charles Lister, Oxford University Press, 2017
Su-25 'Frogfoot' Units In Combat, by Alexander Mladenov, Rolando Ugolini and Gareth Hector, Osprey 2015
Jane's Fighting Ships 1983-84, Captain John Moore RN, Jane's Publishing Company, 1983
Operation Aleppo, Tim Ripley, Herrick-Telic Publications, 2018
Russia's New Ground Forces: Capabilities, Limitations and Implications for International Security, by Igor Sutyagin and Justin Bronk, RUSI, 2017
War in Afghanistan, Mark Urban, MacMillan, 1988
Unravelling a Cold War Mystery, The ALFA SSN: Challenging Paradigms, Finding New Truths, 1969–79, Gerhardt Thamm, CIA, 2008
Soviet Air Defence Missiles, Steven Zaloga, Jane's 1985
Soviet Military Power: Prospects for Change 1989, US Department of Defence, 1989
All the Kremlin's Men: Inside the Court of Vladimir Putin, Mikhail Zygar, Public Affairs, 2016

Glossary

AWACS	Airborne Warning and Control System (US)
ALCM	Air Launched Cruise Missiles
A2AD	Anti-Access, Area Denial
AAA	Anti-Aircraft Artillery
ASW	Anti Submarine Warfare
AGI	Auxiliary Intelligence-Gathering ship (Russia)
CENTCOM	Central Command (US)
CIA	Central Intelligence Agency (US)
CMD	Central Military District (Russia)
DNR	Donetsk People's Republic
ELINT	Electronic Intelligence
EMD	Eastern Military District (Russia)
EW	Electronic Warfare
EU	European Union
FSB	Federal Security Service (Russia)
FIR	Flight Information Region
GPV	State Armaments Programme (Russia)
GRU	Main Directorate of the General Staff (Russia)
GUGI	Main Directorate of Deep Sea Research (Russia)
GCHQ	Government Communications Headquarters (UK)
JSOC	Joint Special Operations Command (US)
JSC	Joint Strategic Command (Russia)
JSC	Joint Stock Company (Russia)
HALE	High Altitude, Long Endurance UAV
HTS	Hay'at Tahrir al Sham (Syria)
IADS	Integrated Air Defence System
IAI	Israel Aerospace Industries
ICBM	Intercontinental Ballistic Missile
ICRC	International Committee for the Red Cross
INF	Intermediate Nuclear Force Treaty
ISIS	Islamic State
KAPO	Kazan Aircraft Production Association (Russia)
KGB	Committee for State Security (USSR)
KLZ	Kobani Landing Zone
LNR	Luhansk People's Republic
LRA	Long Range Aviation (Russia)
MALE	Medium Altitude, Long Endurance UAV
MANPAD	manportable surface to air missile
MP	Military Police
MLRS	Multiple Launch Rocket System
NATO	North Atlantic Treaty Organisations
NOTAM	Notice to Airmen

NSA	National Security Agency (US)
OPSEC	Operational Security
OSCE	Organisation for Security and Co-operation in Europe
QRA	Quick Reaction Alert
RAF	Royal Air Force (UK)
RuAF	Russian Aerospace Force
SyADF	Syrian Air Defence Force
SAA	Syrian Arab Army
SAM	Surface-to-Air Missile (SAM)
SANA	Syrian State News Agency
SAS	Special Air Service (UK)
SBU	Security Service of Ukraine
SIGINT	Signals Intelligence
SDF	Syrian Democratic Forces
SMD	Southern Military District
SOAR	Special Operations Aviation Regiment (US)
SOJTF-OIR	Special Operation Joint Task Force - Operation Inherent Resolve
SSAN	Nuclear Powered Auxiliary Submarines
SSBN	Nuclear Powered Ballistic Missile Firing Submarine
SSGN	Cruise Missile Firing Nuclear Powered Submarines
SSK	Conventionally Powered Attack Submarine
SSN	Nuclear Powered attack Submarine
START	Strategic Arms Reduction Treaty
TAI	Turkish Aerospace Industries
TASS	Russian State News Agency
UAV	Unmanned Aerial Vehicle
UCAV	Unmanned Combat Aerial Vehicle
UN	United Nations
USSR	Union of Soviet Socialist Republics
USAF	United States Air Force
USMC	United States Marine Corps
UUS	Unmanned Underwater Systems
UZGA	Ural Civil Aviation Plant
VDV	Airborne Forces (Russia)
VK	Russian social media network
WMD	Western Military District (Russia)
YPG	People's Protection Units (Kurdish)

Index

People

Non-Russian

President Bashar al Assad (Syrian) 67, 69, 92, 100, 138
Brigadier General Bradford Gering (US) 136
President Recep Tayyip Erdoğan (Turkey) 112, 116, 121, 126
Defence Secretary Sir Michael Fallon (UK) 167
Secretary of State John Kerry (US) 72, 73
Field Marshall Khalifa Haftar (Libya) 133, 134, 135, 222
Colonel Suheil al Hassan (Syrian) 93
Special Envoy for Syria, James Jeffrey (US) 120
Rear Admiral Andrew Lennon (NATO) 180
Vice Admiral Andrew Lewis (US) 180
Angela Merkel (German) 44, 63
President Barack Obama (US) 20, 73
Air Chief Marshal Sir Stu Peach (UK) 180
First Sea Lord Admiral Tony Radakin (UK) 180
General Sir Patrick Sanders (UK) 111
Major General Qassem Soleimani (Iranian) 67, 72, 149
President Donald Trump (US) 110, 112, 113, 115, 118
Defence Secretary Gavin Williamson (UK) 180

Russian

Lieutenant General Valery Asapov 148
Head of the Republic of Crimea Sergey Aksyonov 16, 20
Rear Admiral Oleg Belaventsev 16
Privare Dorzhi Batomunkuev 62, 63, 152
Colonel General Alexander Dvornikov 71, 73, 90, 91, 93, 144, 149
General Valery Gerasimov 27, 127, 148
Major General Andrey Gurulev 45, 150
Lieutenant General Sergei Kuralenko 94
Lieutenant General Alexander Lapin 145
Lieutenant General Alexander Lentsov 59, 61, 63
Foreign Minister Sergei Lavrov 72, 73, 133
President Dmitriy Medvedev 99, 151
Vice Admiral Aleksandr Moiseyev 145, 168
Yevgeny Prigozhin, CEO Wagner Group 135
President Vladimir Putin 4, 7, 12, 14, 15, 20, 24, 25, 26, 27, 28, 29, 30, 31, 32, 33, 35, 39, 40, 41, 43, 44, 50, 54, 55, 63, 67, 70, 71, 73, 75, 78, 79, 81, 82, 84, 87, 100, 103, 116, 126, 127, 135, 138, 140, 142, 143, 144, 145, 149, 150, 152, 156, 157, 172, 178, 179, 180, 185, 195, 202, 204, 208, 209, 211, 215, 216, 217, 218, 219, 220, 22, 223, 226
Rear Admiral Arkady Yurevich Romanov 188
Lieutenant General Sergei Rudskoy 105
Colonel Vladimir Seliverstov 153
Defence Minister Anatoliy Serdyukov 26, 148, 157, 159

Colonel General Andrey Serdyukov 149
Defence Minister Sergey Shoigu 15, 16, 26, 27, 127, 148
Sergei Skripal 183, 222
Vladislav Surkov 15, 39, 40, 42, 58, 65
Colonel General Sergei Surovikin 127, 150
Admiral Aleksandr Vitko 17, 19, 21, 149, 172, 173, 174
Major General Anatoly Volchkov 147
Ambassador Alexander Zasypkin 108
Lieutenant General Alexander Zhuravlev 90, 91, 96, 144, 163
Media Organsiations and Journalists
AFP French News Agency 35, 121
Bellingcat investigative website 42, 183, 228
Flightfinder Radar 70
Inform Napalm investigative website 154, 183
Jane's Information Group 3, 6, 10, 22
Russia Today (RT) 34, 118, 140, 141
Sputnik 34
Ivan Sidorenko 83
John Suchet 140
Igor Sutyagin 6, 222
VK social network 30, 44, 141, 153. 182
Yörük Işık 68
Mikhail Zygar 32, 44
Locations - Syria
Abu Kamal 75, 85, 87
Bassel al Assad International Airport 69
Dumayr airbase 107
Hmeinyan airbase 69, 70, 71, 72, 75, 76, 80, 83, 84, 85, 89, 90, 93, 94, 101, 103, 133, 125, 136, 137, 138
Kobani Landing Zone 114, 115, 118
Kweires airbase 117
Qamishli airport 117, 118
T-4 airbase 85, 108
Locations -Libya
al Jufra Airbase 133, 135, 136
Al Khadim airbase 135
Russian Airbases and Missile Test Centre
Akhtubinsk 217
Balbek 18, 21
Baltimor 76
Belaya 85, 87
Engels 81, 202, 204
Gvardeyskoye 13, 16, 18, 21
Kapustin Yar 218

Korenovsk 153
Kubinka 220
Migalovo 205
Mozdok 79, 81, 85, 86, 87, 201, 204
Novaya Zemlya 218
Nyonoksa 218
Primorsko 46, 49, 77
Pskov 13, 16, 163m 205
Olenya/Olenegorsk 85, 87
Orenburg 205
Ryazan 203, 204
Seshcha 205
Sheykovka 85, 87
Shogol, near Chelyabinsk 77
Taganrog 46, 50, 171, 203, 205
Ukrainka-Seryshevo 202
Ussuriysk 205
Yeysk 22
Intelligence and Other Organisation
Central Intelligence Agency (CIA) (US) 9, 10, 12, 113, 115
Centre for Naval Analysis (US) 12
Main Directorate of Deep Sea Research (GUGI) (Russia) 145, 187
Main Directorate of the General Staff (GRU) (Russia) 14, 16, 18, 19, 35, 36, 42, 65, 66, 145, 158, 159
GCHQ (UK) 72
FSB (Russia) 18, 35, 36
KGB (USSR) 24
International Committee for the Red Cross (ICRC) 95
Organisation for Security and Co-operation in Europe (OSCE) 45, 58, 59, 63
Special Air Service (SAS) (UK) 114
Syrian Democratic Forces (SDF) 96, 112, 113, 115, 116, 117, 118
SBU (Ukraine) 21, 34, 35, 36, 42, 44, 47
Wagner Group (Russia) 18, 61, 62, 134, 135, 136, 139
People's Protection Units(YPG) (Kurdish) 96
Russian Federation Armed Forces Units
Russian Centre for Reconciliation of Opposing Sides in the Syrian Arab Republic 93, 97
National Defence Command Centre 79, 82, 91, 143, 145, 158, 194, 202
Airborne Forces
76th Guards Air Assault Division 13, 17, 18, 29, 51
31st Guards Air Assault Brigade 53
51st Guards Airborne Regiment 54
108th Guards Air Assault Regiment 19
137th Guards Airborne Regiment 53
234rd Guards Air Assault Regiment 51, 52

247th Guards Air Assault Regiment 53, 54
331st Guards Airborne Regiment 53, 153
GRU Spetsnaz
2nd Spetsnaz Brigade 53
Ground Forces
1st Guards Tank Army 159
6th Army 159
8th Guards Army 159
20th Guards Army 159
49th Army 164
58th Army 45, 46, 164
5th Guards Tank Brigade 61, 62, 63
6th Tank Brigade 54
8th Motor Rifle Brigade 53, 54
15th Motor Rifle Brigade 52
17th Motor Rifle Brigade 48, 51, 53
18th Motor Rifle Brigade 19, 41, 52, 53
21st Motor Rifle Brigade 53
35th Guards Motor Rifle Brigade 51
36th Guards Motor Rifle Brigade 50, 52
74th Motor Rifle Brigade 52, 55
136th Guards Motor Rifle Brigade 50, 52
138th Guards Motor Rifle Brigade 61
120th Artillery Brigade 70
291st Artillery Brigade 48, 50
943rd Rocket Artillery Regiment 19
1140th Guards Artillery Regiment 51
Military Police Battalions 95, 97, 112, 116, 117, 118, 119, 138, 161
69th Logistic Brigade 52
7th Military Base 48
Russia Aerospace Forces
4th Air and Air Defence Army 46, 201
6th Air and Air Defence Army 130, 201
11th Air and Air Defence Army 202, 207
14th Air and Air Defence Army 202
45th Air and Air Defence Army 202
22nd Guards Donbass Heavy Bomber Division 202
326th Guards Sevastopol-Berlin Heavy Bomber Division 202, 203
40th Composite Aviation Regiment 85
47th Independent Composite Aviation Regiment 76
52nd Guards Heavy Bomber Regiment 85
55th Helicopter Regiment 18, 153
155th Army Aviation Brigade 201
159th Fighter Regiment 201

200th Guards Heavy Bomber Regiment 48, 52
334th Berlin Red Banner Military Transport Aviation Regiment 13, 77
440th Helicopter Regiment 201
790th Fighter Regiment 201
960th Assault Aviation Regiment 77
Russia Navy
Naval Units
Kola Mixed Force Flotilla 168, 188
7th Submarine Division 131, 188
11th Submarine Division 188
24th Submarine Division 188
29th Submarine Division 187, 192
31st Submarine Division 187
121st Brigade of Landing Ships 168
159th Independent Battalion of Reconnaissance Ships 168
161st Brigade of Submarines 188, 189, 192
Russian Navy Coastal Forces
Kamchatka Flotilla Coast Forces/North Eastern Group of Troops and Forces 145
61st Naval Infantry Brigade 168
80th Independent (Arctic) Motor Rifle Brigade 168
200th Separate Motor Rifle Brigade 52, 55, 61, 168
382nd Separate Naval Infantry Battalion 17
810th Naval Infantry Brigade 17, 18, 69, 94, 172
11th Independent Coastal Missile 173
15th Coastal Missile Brigade 173
Russian Navy Warships
Admiral Gorshkov (Gorshkov-class frigate) 168, 212, 219, 221
Admiral Grigorovich (Admiral Grigorovich-class frigate) 20, 101, 103, 107, 173, 178, 212
Admiral Kuznetsov (Kuznetsov class aircraft carrier) 91, 101, 106, 133, 138, 166, 167, 169, 179, 212
Admiral Nakhimov (Kirov-class cruiser) 168, 219
Moskova (Slava class-cruiser) 18, 82
Marshal Ustinov (Slava-class cruiser) 168
Nikolai Filchenkov (Landing Ship) 110
Pyotr Velikiy (Kirov class nuclear powered battlecruiser) 101, 168
PD-50 (floating dock) 169, 190
Submarines
B-90 Sarov (mothership submarine) 218
Belgorod (mothership submarine) 218, 219
Dmitriy Donskoy (Typhoon-class nuclear submarine) 185
Kazan (Yasen-M-class nuclear attack submarine) 9
Khabarovsk (mothership submarine) 219
Kursk (Oscar II-class nuclear submarine) 25, 156, 166, 185, 186
Harpsichord-2R-PM (unmanned underwater vehicle) 187

K-3 Leninsky Komsomol (first Soviet nuclear submarine) 190
Losharik (mini-submarine) 187, 196
Nelma (mini-submarine) 187
St Petersburg (Lada-class conventional submarine) 168, 189, 211
Rostov on Don (Improved Kilo-class conventional submarine) 100
Aerospace and Defence Companies
Almaz-Antey 105, 211
Beriev Aviation Scientific Technical Complex 203
GAZ 71, 90, 96, 116, 211
Israel Aerospace Industries (IAI) 84, 85, 169, 205
Izhmash 211
Kalashnikov 211
Kamaz 17, 41, 51, 96, 124, 211
Kazan Aircraft Production Association (KAPO) 203
KB Mashinostroyeniya 105, 211
Kolomna Rocket Design Bureau 212
KDP 105
Krondstadt Group 206
JSC Aviakor Aviation Plant (formerly Kuibyshev Aviation Plant No 18) 203
NPO Mashinostroyeniya 101, 212, 219
Oboronlogistika 100
OPK Oboronprom 84
Special Technology Centre 206
Sukhoi Design Bureau 206
Ural Civil Aviation Plant (known as UZGA) 84, 205
Uralvagonzavod Research and Production Corporation 211
Zvezda 105, 212
Shipyads
Admiralty 177, 191, 211
Amur 178
Feodosiya 178
Joint Stock Company Ship repairing Centre Zvezdochka 183, 190
More 178
Pella 177
Rosneft 182, 190
Sredne-Nevsky 177
Severnaya Verf 177
Sevmash 9, 182, 183, 186, 190, 191, 218, 219
United Shipbuilding Corporation 182, 190, 212
Yantar 178
Zelenodolsk 178
Equipment
Russian Tanks and Vehicles
BTR-80 and 82 troop carrier 18, 19, 21, 22, 42, 47, 50, 52, 55, 69, 102, 160

BMP infantry fighting vehicle 40, 48, 55, 61, 63, 120, 160
BMD airborne troop carrier 30, 37, 38, 51, 53, 128, 159, 160, 205
Iveco Lynx 90
T-14 Armata tank 160, 211, 213
T-34 tank 213
T-64 tank 42, 47, 50, 62, 213
T-72 tank 21, 50, 51, 53, 54, 61, 63, 116, 128, 152, 160, 211, 212, 213
T-80 tank 61, 160, 213
T-90 tank 50, 51, 52, 69, 160, 213
Tigr vehicle 71, 90, 96. 116, 160, 211
Typhoon mine protected vehicle 96, 160, 211
Russian Artillery and Rocket systems
TOS-1A thermobaric rocket system 70
BM--21 rocket system 41, 47, 48, 61, 70, 116, 121,
BM-27 Uragan rocket system 48, 61, 121
BM-30 Smerch rocket system 48, 55, 61, 78, 128
MSTA-S 152mm self-propelled artillery 160
2A56 MSTA-B 152mm artillery 48, 70, 124
2S1 122mm self propelled artillery42, 48, 50, 160
Russian Air Force (RuAF) Aircraft
A-50 radar aircraft 22, 105, 107
An-26 transport aircraft 21, 41, 49, 135, 169, 205
An-124 transport aircraft 69, 70, 205
Forpost tactical drone 46, 48, 53, 60, 83, 84, 85, 123, 126, 169, 170, 174, 193, 201, 205, 206
Il-20M reconnaisance aircraft 110, 130
Il-76 transport aircraft 13, 16, 18, 29, 41, 69, 70, 86, 117, 118, 135, 136, 137, 201, 205
Il-78 tanker 69, 70, 85, 86, 101, 203, 207
Ka-52 attack helicopter 200, 201, 202
Mi-8/17 transport helicopter 18, 37, 38, 41, 45, 70, 112, 117, 118, 153, 169, 174, 200, 201, 202
Mi-24/25 attack helicopter 18, 37, 38, 39, 41, 46, 52, 70, 75, 86, 153, 174, 200, 201, 202
Mi-26 heavy lift helicopter 200, 201, 202
Mi-28 attack helicopter 200, 201
Mi-35 attack helicopter 112, 117, 118, 201
MiG-31 fighter aircraft 168, 200, 201, 202, 217, 225
MiG-29 fighter aircraft 133, 135, 136, 137
Orlan-10 mini drone 60, 123, 124, 126, 134, 206
S-70 Okhotnik-B UCAV 206
Su-24M strike jet 69, 77, 106, 122, 123, 133, 135, 136, 168, 172, 173, 174
Su-25SM ground aircraft 41, 42, 49, 69, 77, 81, 85, 200, 201, 202
Su-30SM fighter aircraft 46, 49, 69, 75, 76, 101, 105, 174, 200, 201, 202, 211
Su-34 strike jet 70, 76, 80, 83, 86, 132, 200, 201, 202, 211, 213
Su-35S fighter aircraft 76, 77, 201, 202, 211, 213
Su-57 fighter aircraft 211, 213
Tu-22M3 bomber 75, 78, 79, 81, 82, 83, 85, 86, 87, 198, 203, 204, 217

Tu-95 bomber 78, 79, 81, 82, 86, 170, 197, 202, 203, 204, 207, 218
Tu-160 bomber 25, 78, 79, 81, 82, 102, 130, 170, 202, 203, 204, 207, 218
Tu-134 transport aircraft 136, 169
Tu-154 transport aircraft 133, 135, 136
Tu-214R reconnaissance aircraft 124
Thunder UCAV 206

Russian Naval Aviation Aircraft

Beriev Be-12 amphibian 21
Ka-27PS&PL/KA-29TB/Ka-31 naval helicopters 21, 168, 174, 175
Il-38 maritime patrol aircraft 103, 105, 107, 168, 175
MiG-29KR fighter jet 168
Mi-14 maritime helicopter 21
Su-33 fighter jet 101, 168
Tu-142 maritime patrol aircraft 101, 142, 175, 198, 203

Coalition Aircraft & Weapons

Anka UAV (Turkish) 125
AH-64D Apache attack helicopter (US) 112, 114, 115
B-52 bomber 79, 198
C-130 Hercules (US & UK) 92, 114, 115, 137
F-16 Fighting Falcon (US, Danish, Israel, Jordan, Portugal, Turkey) 108, 112
MQ-9 Reaper armed drone (US & UK) 113
Tomahawk Land Attack Missile (US) 79, 109, 186
Typhoon fighter (UK) 113, 197
V-22 Osprey tilt rotor (US) 114
Kale-Baykar Bayraktar TB2 UAV (Turkish) 125

Civiilain Aircraft

Airbus A321 airliner (Metrojet) 81
Boeing 777 airliner (Malaysia Airlines Flight MH17) 42, 43, 47, 49, 183

Russian Missiles and Weapons

Avengard re-entry vehicle, or hypersonic glide vehicle 216, 217, 221
Bal anti-ship missiles 105, 173, 174, 212
Bastion-P anti-ship missile 101, 103, 105, 168, 174, 175, 212
Burevestnik nuclear-powered weapon systems 218, 221
Complex 14TS034 and is now called the Peresvet 217, 221
Iskander tactical ballistic missile 105, 106, 174, 217, 220
3M14 Kalibr ship and submarine launched cruise missile 26, 79, 87, 91, 100, 101, 103, 105, 107, 129, 168, 170, 173, 178, 186, 191, 193, 194, 206, 213, 220, 225
Kh-47M2 Kinzhad air launched hypersonic anti-ship missile 217, 221
Kh-55 air launched cruise missile 218, 225
Kh-101 air launched cruise missile 81, 86, 170, 203, 204, 218, 220
Poseidon/Status 6 underwater nuclear weapon 190, 191, 218, 219, 221
P-800 Onik missiles 173, 212
RS-18B/UR-100N UTTKh intercontinental ballistic missile 216
RS-28 Sarmat intercontinental ballistic missile 216, 221

RSM-56 Bulava submarine-launched ballistic missiles 185, 213
3M22 Tsirkon or Zirkon anti-ship missile 219
Russian Air Defence Systems
Buk tactical surface to air missile (SA-17) 43, 49, 106, 109, 110, 125
Kvadrat/Kub surface to air missile (SA-6) 109
Pantsir S1 anti-aircraft system (SA-22) 22, 49, 105, 106, 107, 109, 117, 125, 135
Osa surface to air missile (SA-8) 109
9K35 Strela-10 manportable surface to air missile (SA-13) 41, 49, 109
S-200 surface to air missile (SA-5) 109
S-300 surface to air missile (SA-10) 21, 22, 105, 110, 200, 205, 211
S-400 surface to air missile (SA-21) 105, 106, 107, 131, 170, 174, 200, 201, 211
Ukrainian Government Leaders
Interior Minister Arsen Avakov 37
Rear Admiral Denis Berezovsky 21
President, Petro Poroshenko 40, 63
Ukrainian Government Forces
25th Airborne Brigade 37, 38
72nd Motorised Brigade 48
79th Air Assault Brigade 47
National Guard Donbas Battalion 40
Omega Spetsnaz battalion 38
SBU's Alpha Group 38
Donbass rebel leaders and pro-Russian Oligarchs
Rinat Akhmetov 39
Igor Bezler 36
Alexander Borodai 40, 42
Yevgeniy Lykhozhon 36
Konstantin Malofeev 44, 50
Volodymyr Sivkovych 36
Igor Strelkov, AKA Igor Girkin 36, 39, 40, 45, 47, 49, 58
Donbass rebel Units
Vostok or 'East' Battalion 40, 41
1st Corps of the DNR 59
2nd Corps of LNR 59

Printed in Great Britain
by Amazon

84033536R00140